AF656581

CASTE AND BUDDHIST PHILOSOPHY

Continuity of Some Buddhist Arguments against the Realist Interpretation of Social Denominations

BUDDHIST TRADITION SERIES

VOLUME 60

General Editor
ERNST STEINKELLNER

Joint General Editor
ALEXANDER VON ROSPATT

Founder Editor
LATE ALEX WAYMAN

Editorial Advisory Board
KATSUMI MIMAKI

LOKESH CHANDRA

MICHAEL HAHN

CASTE AND BUDDHIST PHILOSOPHY

Continuity of Some Buddhist Arguments against the Realist Interpretation of Social Denominations

VINCENT ELTSCHINGER

Tr. from French to English by
RAYNALD PRÉVÈREAU
in collaboration with the author

MOTILAL BANARSIDASS
PUBLISHING HOUSE • DELHI
Email: naraina@mlbd.in • Website: www.mlbd.in
@mlbdofficial
+91 89 2999 9000

Reprint: Delhi, ***2024***
First Edition: Delhi, 2012
First Published in French: 2000
by Arbeiskreis fur Tibetische und Buddhistiche Studien, Vienna as
Wiener Studien zur Tibetologie und Buddismuskunde, No. 47

Copyright © VINCENT ELTSCHINGER
All Rights Reserved.

No part of this book may be reprinted or
reproduced or utilised in any form or by any electronic,
mechanical, or other means, now known or hereafter invented,
including, but not limited to, photocopying and recording,
or in any information storage or retrieval system,
without permission in writing from the
authors and publishers.

ISBN: 978-93-5903-215-3 (Hardcover)
ISBN: 978-93-5903-198-9 (Paperback)

Printed & Published by
Rajendra P Jain *for*
Motilal Banarsidass Publishing House
A-44, Naraina Industrial Area, Phase I,
New Delhi–110 028 (INDIA)
Email: naraina@mlbd.in Website: www.mlbd.in
Tel.: (+91-11)4751 1592
Delhi Showroom:
4637/20, F-2, Hari Sadan, First Floor, Ansari Road, Daryaganj
Delhi–110 002 (Opp. Fire Station) ***Tel.***: (+91-11)4559 7999
Bengaluru Showroom:
1st Floor, 1/2 Rathnavilas Road, Basvanagudi, Next to Pai Vista
Convention Hall, South End Circle Bengaluru - 560004 (India)

Contents

Editors' foreword

The rigorous denial by the Buddha and his followers of the Brahmanic idea of castes as a natural fact is a well-known detail in the long history of the study of India's social structures and their ideological background. From early canonical texts to later philosophical literature, this denial is regularly attested. The early Buddhist positions and refutations have been extensively documented, beginning with the seminal study by Richard Fick (German: Kiel 1897, English: Varanasi 1972). However, with the exception of P. L. Barua, who presents early arguments against caste as a fact of nature, the study of these positions has focussed on the social and historical data they may provide. Until now, the later systematic and post-systematic developments in Buddhist philosophical traditions have not been taken into consideration. It is these that are the focus of this volume.

The author offers a detailed analysis of the arguments against the Brahmanic "naturalization of caste," as propounded by Dharmakīrti (ca. 600 CE) and his successors up to Prajñākaragupta (ca. 800 CE), and in the process pays close attention to their historical context as exemplified by the writings of Āryadeva, Vasubandhu, Dharmapāla, and Candrakīrti. The first section provides a survey of the canonical material in relevant Pāli Suttas and subsequent Avadāna and Jātaka literature. This introduces the reader to the sources for the arguments concerning caste, both against caste as a natural fact and for caste as an outcome of social conventions. Arguing from biological and genealogical standpoints, and pointing to the instability of brahmanity as a social category, these early materials reject that "brahmanity" is a natural given. While it is evident that one objective of these early sources was to proselytize, the attempts to systematize the Buddha's teachings in the different scholastic Abhidharmas were in the main intent on doctrinal clarifications within the various Buddhist groups. The question whether castes are a natural given rather than a social construct was only of marginal interest. In the sixth and seventh centuries, however, with Dharmapāla and Dharmakīrti and his contemporary Candrakīrti, Buddhist scholasticism increasingly confronted non-Buddhist traditions. As a result Buddhist polemics against the innateness of caste were provided with a more rigorous philosophical foundation. Dharmakīrti in particular "was the first to move the polemic to the level of epistemology and ontology" (p. 59). This transformed the traditional reasoning into strict arguments formed in terms of the standards Dharmakīrti had shaped in his ontology, epistemology and logic.

The main part of the book presents the final stage in the evolution of polemics against the "naturalization" of caste in the sense of "any attempt to include caste among the things that do not depend or proceed exclusively from human thought and arbitrary conventions, i.e., to consider caste as agreeing with nature' and not merely with people's social and linguistic habits" (p. xix). This section focuses on the arguments of Dharmakīrti. These are set into the context of pre- and post-Dharmakīrtian Buddhist voices, including Vasubandhu, Āryadeva, Candrakīrti, Dharmapāla, Dharmakīrti's commentators Śākyabuddhi, Karṇakagomin and Prajñākaragupta, as well as Śāntarakṣita and Kamalaśīla. Representing the Brahmanic opposition, the Mīmāṃsaka Kumārila was in all likelihood Dharmakīrti's main opponent for his arguments concerning the perceptibility of distinct classes. Internally, Dharmakīrti's arguments are found in the context of his explanations concerning nominalistic ontology and linguistic theory. This is because he does not separate the problem of caste from that of universals in general.

Throughout the volume, these steps are carefully attested with clear translations and textual documentation. Wrapping up the results of his study, the author's conclusions draw a succinct picture of the Buddhist position on caste, gained through the broader understanding of the historical and social facts and changes that took place during the periods these documents were created. Moreover, in considering the validity of his study for present-day India, the author ventures the opinion that "the vast majority of points raised in the Buddhist argumentations remain a burning question, even today" (p. 175).

Ernst Steinkellner
Austrian Academy of Sciences
Vienna

Alexander von Rospatt
University of California
Berkeley

Preface to the English translation

The French original of this book was published in 2000 as I was still a doctoral student at the University of Lausanne. Since then, I have never turned back to the issue of the Buddhist treatment of the caste-classes, and, to the best of my knowledge, no substantial study has been dedicated to this topic in the meantime. While revising Raynald Prévèreau's excellent translation, I became increasingly aware of the many defects of the original study. Among the most congenial and hence irredeemable ones, let me mention a lack of sociohistorical contextualization, the teleological nature of the presentation, and my disregard for issues of canonicity and canonization. Since then, my reading of scholars like R.M. Davidson, A. Sanderson and G. Schopen, to name but a few, has convinced me that such a purely "internalist" way of dealing with textual sources should belong to the past. Fortunately, this English translation has provided me with the opportunity to improve my reading of certain passages, to add a few source materials and to update bibliographical references. Moreover, following a recent study by H. Krasser (2011), I am now inclined to ascribe earlier dates to Dharmakīrti (a junior contemporary of Dharmapāla and a senior contemporary of Bhāviveka, some time during the sixth century). I have tried my best in order to accommodate my argument with this new chronology. Most sincere thanks are due to Alexander von Rospatt and Ernst Steinkellner (as ever!) for their readiness to publish this monograph in the Buddhist Tradition Series, and to the Elisabet de Boer Fund for financing its English translation. Finally, Raynald Prévèreau deserves my heartfelt gratitude for all he has been doing, from the first version of his translation to the tiresome incorporation of my final corrections.

Vienna

August 7, 2009

Preface to the French original

This book is an enlarged version of two lectures given at the University of Lausanne in March and April 1998. Originally, I intended to discuss in just one lecture the arguments of Dharmakīrti and his direct commentators against what I call the Brahmanic "naturalization" of caste. But it soon became evident that the arguments I wished to investigate were based on earlier canonical argumentative strategies that had been modified to face the tradition's new challenges. Those canonical strategies in fact came in such bewildering numbers that they required an attempt to identify the ones that had inspired the philosophers' polemic, from Āryadeva to Prajñākaragupta. Two lectures therefore ended up being given. In the first lecture, I investigated the materials dispersed in the non-philosophical Buddhist literature, while in the second I studied the modalities of their perpetuation and restatement by the philosophers. The division of this book in two chapters of unequal length reflects that double concern. While the text presented below has been largely expanded and heavily annotated, my original intent remains unchanged.

The first chapter, which is half the size of the second, may be read as an introduction to the remaining part of the book. It offers a schematic and typological picture of the canonical antecedents to the polemic on caste. But *I only take up the material likely to facilitate, or even condition, the understanding of the arguments proposed by the philosophers.* In that respect, J. W. de Jong's (1988) brief summary of primary sources, offered in "Buddhism and the Equality of the Four Castes," turned out to be very valuable to the task of identifying and selecting that material. From the Pali sources, I chose to focus on the *Vāseṭṭha Sutta*, the *Assalāyana Sutta*, the *Ambaṭṭha Sutta* and the *Aggañña Sutta*. I also make occasional references to the *Soṇadaṇḍa Sutta*, the *Madhura Sutta* and the *Dhammapada*, as well as to the *Lokapaññatti* and *Mahāvastu* which both show minor variants and developments of the *Aggañña Sutta*, and precede Vasubandhu and Candrakīrti. But the first chapter is mostly based on the important *Śārdūlakarṇāvadāna* and *Vajrasūcī*, two polemical texts extensively quoted in the later *Kalpadrumāvadānamālā*. I also use the verses of the *Bhūridattajātaka* edited and translated by Alsdorf (1977), the *Karmavibhaṅga* and *Karmavibhaṅgopadeśa* edited by Lévi (1932), as well as Kumāralāta's *Kalpanāmaṇḍitikā*. Since I do not read Chinese, I read the *Kalpanāmaṇḍitikā* in Huber's (1908) French translation of what was then known as Aśvaghosa's *Sūtrālaṅkāra*, for the Sanskrit fragments collated and edited by Lüders (1926) are too scarce to produce a translation from the original Indian version. Let it be noted, lastly, that no attempt is made in that chapter to determine those texts' chronological order or dates since I have nothing to add to what de Jong (1988) has already written on the issue.

The second chapter investigates Buddhist arguments as they (re-)appear in various philosophers' works. I consider more or less successively the arguments found in Āryadeva's *Catuḥśataka*, Vasubandhu's *Abhidharmakośa(bhāṣya)*, Dharmapāla's *Guǎng bǎi lùn shì lùn* (廣百論釋論) on *Catuḥśataka* XII, Candrakīrti's *Catuḥśatakavṛtti/ṭīkā* on *Catuḥśataka* IV and XII, Dharmakīrti's *Pramāṇavārttika(svavṛtti)* with the two commentaries of Śākyabuddhi and Karṇakagomin, Śāntarakṣita's *Tattvasaṅgraha*, Kamalaśīla's *Tattvasaṅgrahapañjikā*, and finally Prajñākaragupta's *Pramāṇavārttikālaṅkāra* on *Pramāṇavārttika* II, III and IV. I have read the Chinese of Dharmapāla in Tillemans' (1990) translation, as well as part of Saṅghabhadra's in Cox's (1995). And I read Āryadeva, Candrakīrti and Śākyabuddhi in Tibetan—along with the Sanskrit fragments of *Catuḥśataka* and *Catuḥṣatakavṛtti* edited by Suzuki (1994), as well as Karṇakagomin's *Pramāṇavārttikasvavṛttiṭīkā*. But I read the other texts in their original Sanskrit version, along with the Tibetan translations preserved in the Peking edition of the Tibetan Canon. In addition to those Buddhist texts, the second chapter also deals at length with the position developed by Kumārila, the most eminent anti-Buddhist philosopher, in his *Ślokavārttika* and *Tantravārttika*. As we shall see, the Buddhist argumentation is impoverished when it becomes more philosophical and is appended to the ontological debate on classes and universals. Perhaps more accurately, it is given a new focus. I develop a hypothesis in that chapter that could account for that reorientation. My hypothesis is inspired from the work of Halbfass, especially his remarkable *Zur Theorie der Kastenordnung in der indischen Philosophie* (1976), which addresses the Brahmanic realist thematizations of caste (Mīmāṃsā, Nyāya, Vaiśeṣika).

The secondary literature on the specifically Buddhist treatment of caste is rather skimp. One century has passed since Fick's pioneering *Social Organization in North-East India in Buddha's Time*, which still goes unsurpassed for its systematic approach but only marginally addresses the very numerous Buddhist arguments put forward against the Brahmanic naturalization of social divisions. The book was written from a historical perspective and based mainly on materials from the *Jātaka*. Since then, several studies have contributed to our knowledge of social differentiation in early Buddhist literature, especially those of Mehta (1939), Law (1980) and, to some extent, Sharma (1958). And nothing new is to be expected here in this regard. But with the notable exception of Law (1937), Malalasekera and Jayatilleke (1958), Malalasekera (1971), Masson (1975), Krishan (1986) and Masefield (1986), who do discuss some Buddhist *arguments*, most of today's secondary literature is still only concerned with the *social* and *historical* data found in Buddhist sources. To this day, Barua (1959) has given the most complete account of Buddhist arguments against the naturalization of caste, and his account is limited to arguments from the Pali Canon. This book thus intends to correct important lacuna in the history of Buddhist social and philosophical ideas by studying some of the arguments developed by Buddhist philosophers.

This study does not attempt, however, to cover *all* Buddhist arguments against the naturalization of caste. Its primary focus is rather the arguments developed by the philosophers, especially those of Dharmakīrti and his successors, i.e., those of the school of Buddhist logicians and epistemologists that flourished in India as early as the sixth century CE. One further reason for not covering *all* Buddhist arguments is that it is rather difficult to draw a clear distinction between arguments *stricto sensu* and other types of discourse, since narrative or etymological descriptions can easily pass for factual arguments.

Instead of listing all Buddhist arguments against the naturalization of caste, this book primarily attempts to shed light on the *continuity* of the Buddhist argumentation from the *Suttanipāta* to Prajñākaragupta, i.e., over a period of more than a millennium. I attempt to show how the arguments advanced by the philosophers fall in line with the tradition; in other words, I bring out their typically Buddhist character. And that is why I do not attempt to be exhaustive in my discussion of the canonical arguments. The *Assalāyana Sutta*, for example, contains many important "ethnographic" and eschatological arguments that will not be discussed in this book.[1] The same is true of many arguments found in the *Vajrasūcī* and repeated or further developed in the *Kalpadrumāvadānamālā*. I instead focus on the arguments that directly contribute to our understanding and to the proper contextualization of those developed by the later tradition. The principle adopted for their selection is therefore *retrospective*, in spite of the difficulties occasioned by that method from a historical point of view.

This book also does not pretend to develop the central Buddhist theme of the "true Brahmin" (and its corollary theme, the "degeneration of Brahmins"),[2] where the term "Brahmin" (*brāhmaṇa*) has a normative value and is used to refer to moral and spiritual accomplishment instead of birth and social status. Since Buddhist philosophers paid no attention to that theme, I only indirectly address the issue in the conclusions. This goes also for the very delicate (and sometimes perhaps contradictory) question of the connection between social status and kar-

1 Many of those arguments are discussed in Barua (1959), some also in Malalasekera (1971) and Masson (1975).

2 See Masson (1975, 97ff.) and Masefield (1985, 150ff.).

mic retribution. The subject is almost never discussed in polemical sources, but I do say a few words on the matter in the conclusions.

Buddhism has not created a social reform in India, despite various elements in its literature that could have served such purpose. Nonetheless, at least in the texts here investigated, Buddhism has developed an original *explanation* of caste, several *arguments* against its naturalization, as well as an unfailing soteriological *abolitionism*. My conclusions serve to organize those three aspects of the Buddhist argumentation and offer a comparative picture of its methods, targets and objectives. They also provide an occasion to briefly discuss the themes of the "true Brahmin" and retribution of actions.

At this point, some remarks are in order on the Sanskrit terms *jāti* and *varṇa*, for which it is nearly impossible to adopt fixed translations. Those terms are almost never defined in Buddhist texts and are often used interchangeably, without much consistency.[3] The term *varṇa* generally refers, with some exceptions, to the classical fourfold partition of society into the classes of Brahmins, *kṣatriyas*, *vaiśyas* and *śūdras*. As Dumont has said: "The feature which most contrasts with the caste system is perhaps the stress laid on function rather than birth."[4] As for the term *jāti*, apart from ontological contexts its translation is often a real puzzle since it may alternatively denote birth, caste or class (in the sense of "natural kind"). While in Brahmanic contexts the notion of caste prolongs and regularly presupposes the notion of birth, the opposite is not systematically true in other contexts, especially for the Buddhists who criticize the very idea that caste, or status, is acquired at birth. The two concepts must therefore be distinguished, even if the same Sanskrit word *jāti* is used in both cases. One further difficulty lies in the fact that

3 See de Jong (1988, 423–424 and notes).

4 Dumont (1972, 109[96]). Note that whenever two page references are given, the first refers to the English translation and the second, in square brakets, refers to the original publication.

even today, the notion of "caste" is not easy to define. And it is hard to determine to what extent the institution was operative in ancient times.[5] It should be noted, finally, that Tibetans used the word *rigs* to render alternatively *jāti* and *varṇa*, but also *kula* (which can in fact have the same meaning as *varṇa*), or even *gotra* (also often translated by the Tib. *rus*). When the Sanskrit is lacking, the Tibetan term *rigs* remains ambiguous. Trying to define caste is accordingly quite a challenge.

Keeping those considerations in mind, I regularly use the word "caste" to indicate *any given* social division that, in so far as it is naturalized, is the target of Buddhist critique. In fact, in the exclusively argumentative context of the literature here investigated, there is little interest in knowing the name, nature and number of the pseudo-entities being questioned. Only their naturalization is criticized, and the argumentation will not change whether there are two castes or a thousand. I normally restrict my use of the word "class" (1) to ontological contexts (close to "universal," or even to "genus" or "kind" here translating the Skt. *jāti*) and (2) to refer to the fourfold classification into Brahmins, *kṣatriyas*, *vaiśyas* and *śūdras* (here translating the Skt. *varṇa*). In more general or theoretical contexts, however, I do not hesitate to speak in terms of social statuses, social or statutory denominations, and social or statutory divisions instead of castes. In those cases, I no longer distinguish the

5 See Fick (1972). See also the suggestive comments in Dumont (1972, 103–118[90–108], §§31–34). "We have said that the classical texts described in terms of varna what must surely have been at the time a caste system in embryo. The word *jāti* does occur, but it is generally confused with *varṇa* (except in Yajñavalkya II, 69, 206) and, according to Kane, the emphasis is birth rather than function. ... Although from a very early epoch the Buddhist texts confirm the actual existence of despised castes and inferior occupations, the normative Hindu texts mostly present the groups they name as if they were products of crossing between varnas. This is the very detailed theory according to which the "mixing of varnas" gave birth to mixed categories, inferior and more or less hierarchized. It is generally admitted that this theory was used to refer real *jāti* to the varnas." Dumont (1972, 110[98]).

normative and historically arbitrary entities of the fourfold classification from caste as such, which according to Bouglé is characterized by hereditary specialization, hierarchical organization and mutual repulsion.[6] Those terms then refer without distinction to Brahmins, *śūdras*, *kaivartas* (fishermen), *caṇḍālas* or *carmakāras* (curriers), for example.

I must finally explain the recurring concept of "naturalization." By "naturalization" I mean any attempt to include caste among the things that do not depend or proceed exclusively from human thought and arbitrary conventions, i.e., to consider caste as agreeing with "nature" and not merely with people's social and linguistic habits. In some contexts, I give an ideological connotation to naturalization, when the theory pretending to reflect the real order of things in fact serves a given group's vested interests. In what follows, any reference to biological facts, genealogy (including the notion of innate status), cosmogony or anthropogony, as well as gnoseology (for example, the theory of sensory perception), is regarded as a form of naturalization to the extent that it seeks to establish castes as so many real classes or universals. Included in my understanding of naturalization is therefore what a Buddhist, i.e., a nominalist, would describe as the reification of an entity of pure designation (*prajñaptisat*).

It must be noted, moreover, that the naturalization practised, deliberately or not, by the Brahmin described in our sources is designed to situate caste in the total order of things (cosmic, social, political, ritualistic and eschatological). That is to say, it makes caste and its preservation a reality and an obligation prescribed by dharma. In that context, Halbfass' remarks are illuminating: "From the beginning, the concept of the four classes—first that of the Brahmin, serving as a model—establishes a strong relation between the cosmic and social dimensions, between ethical norm and biological fact. It corresponds to a world-view in which the key concepts bring together the norma-

---

6 See Bouglé (1993, 11–26).

tive and the factual, the ethical and the physical dimensions. Within that world view, this [combination] is fundamentally not a problem, and fits well with the doctrines of retribution of actions (*karman*) and the cycle of existence (*saṃsāra*) once those doctrines are developed."[7] The intention behind the Buddhist arguments is precisely to criticize such a naturalization, that is to say, as Halbfass once again brilliantly summarizes, to criticize the juxtaposition of descriptive and normative elements: "The Buddhist critique falls in that context. Its ethical valorisation of the concepts of caste is in no way a radical and revolutionary reinterpretation, but refers to aspects long understood to fall within the semantic scope of those concepts by emphasizing the ethical as essential and true in contrast to the other elements. Only then does the interaction and occasional concurrence of the ethical/normative and the factual/hereditary become a problem. Bringing them together results in a strong contrast between the relevant and the irrelevant. In the end, the very point of making a distinction of caste is brought into question, and the traditional criteria are radically criticized."[8] This book focuses on one aspect of the Buddhist treatment of that problem.

Finally, it is my pleasant duty to express my gratitude to Maya Burger and Cristina Scherrer-Schaub, as well as to John Dunne, Jacques May, François Obrist, Motoi Ono, Yves Ramseier, Tom Tillemans and Toru Tomabechi, all of whom have been helpful in answering my numerous requests while working on this project. Didier Monay encouraged me to be clearer. Claude Verdon improved my understanding of some biological data. Pierre-Antoine Schorderet knows the extent of my intellectual debt towards him. Johannes Bronkhorst and Jan Willem de Jong (†) have taken the time to read the manuscript in its entirety, allowing me to correct numerous errors and improve certain readings: I wish to take this occasion to thank them warmly. I also wish to express my gratitude to Ernst Steinkellner for ac-

7 English translation of Halbfass (1976, 279[7]).

8 English translation of Halbfass (1976, 280[8]).

cepting to read my manuscript and proposing its publication in the series *Wiener Studien zur Tibetologie und Buddhismuskunde*. Tom Tillemans, administrator of the Elisabeth de Boer Fund, deserves my gratitude for offering the financial support necessary for the publication of this book.

Villars-sur-Glâne
February 26, 1999

Vienna
December 14, 2006

Chapter 1

Canonical antecedents

1.1 Outline of a Buddhist explanation

1.1.1 This first chapter is to be read as a long introduction to the problems discussed in chapter two. Accordingly, I only address the themes from the non-philosophical canonical literature on caste that were later used and developed by the philosophers. The typology of non-philosophical arguments that I propose therefore does no attempt to integrate all of the available material. Nor do I systematically discuss the numerous argumentative variations, although the heavy annotation attests that at least some of them, as well as linguistic variants, have been addressed. In the body of the text, I keep to a presentation of each argument's general idea, while all additional details or discussion of divergent views appear in the notes.

Before looking at the arguments as such, let me draw a brief outline of the Buddhist position on the issue of caste. I will come back to it in the general conclusions.

1.1.2 One characteristic feature of Buddhist thought is the distinction it draws between the real and the nominal and, consequently, its condemnation of hypostases and reifications. Rooted in a non-substantialist anthropology, the tendency to deny ontological ground to classes and universals went beyond discussion on the *ātman* and came to influence the way in which Buddhists approached every question. The debate on castes and classes made no exception. In the final analysis, castes and classes are treated as factitious hypostases. The status of the Brahmin, *kṣatriya*, *vaiśya* and *śūdra* are thus nothing but words that lack a substantial basis. They instead refer, through social conventions, to entities of designation. For reasons that I will discuss below, statutory distinctions were respectively described in the *Vāseṭṭha Sutta* (VāS), the *Śārdūlakarṇāvadāna* (ŚKA) and the *Kalpadrumāvadānamālā* (KDAM) as designations or denominations (*samaññā*), nominal designations (*sañjñā*) or mere nominal designations (*sañjñāmātra*).[1] With Dharmakīrti, a

[1] In VāS, Sn. 611: *paccattaṃ sasarīresu manussesv-etaṃ na vijjati / vokārañ ca manussesu samaññāya pavuccati //*. ŚKA M43.10–11/ CN637.13–14: *sañjñā kṛteyaṃ lokasya brāhmaṇāḥ kṣatriyās tathā / vaiśyāś caiva tathā śūdrāḥ sañjñeyaṃ samprakīrtitā //*. Compare with KDAM, p. LV, verse 159: *sañjñāmātreṇa kalpyante brāhmaṇāḥ kṣatriyās tathā / vaiśyāḥ śūdrās tathānye 'pi sañjñāmātre hi kīrtitāḥ //*. See also the "refrain" of Triśaṅku to the Brahmin Puṣkarasārin in ŚKA: *tasmāt te brāhmaṇa bravīmi sañjñāmātrakam idaṃ lokasya yad uta brāhmaṇa iti vā kṣatriya iti vā vaiśya iti vā śūdra iti vā / ekam idaṃ sarvam idam ekam /*. The word *sañjñā*, as is often the case, is here nearly synonymous with *nāman* (name). But *sañjñā* (ideation) is one of those terms that is very rich in meaning in Buddhist scholasticism. The ideation aggregate (*sañjñāskandha*), for example, which is continuously defined as the prehension of characteristics (*nimittodgrahaṇa*), plays a predominant role in the Buddhist analysis of reification and hypostasis. Far from simply apprehending (*upalabdhi, grahaṇamātra*) entities, it grasps a perceptual data (e.g., blue) as belonging to a certain class (e.g., the colour blue). Ideation is in fact strictly correlated with verbalization and language (both of which require unique and stable referents), and thus plays a very important role in the falsification of reality, in so far as "*sañjñā* creates *prajñaptisat* entities" (Williams 1980, 17). Its process of identification based on signs governs the construction of classes. Consequently, ideation plays a major role in the superimposition of factitious entities on the data of experience. Claiming, therefore, that castes or caste distinctions are merely nominal designations clearly suggests that their referents are factitious hypostases. On that aspect of ideation, see Williams (1980, 14–16) and Johansson (1979, 92–95).

Except for some Sarvāstivādin positions (see section 2.1.1.1, p. 59, below), and contrary to nearly all Brahmanic philosophers, Buddhists do not accept the reality of classes and universals. In most of the arguments that will be presented in this study, however, their reality is provisionally accepted along the model of biological species. The Buddhist strategy therefore consists in showing the fallacious or deviant

contrast was then made between the distinction based on name and usage (*nāmavyavahārabheda*), and the distinction based on intrinsic nature (*svabhāvabheda*).[2] And his commentators Śākyabuddhi and Karṇakagomin spoke of conventions (*samaya, saṅketa*) and distinctions based on nominal designation (*sañjñābheda*).[3] Since they are imperceptible, Prajñākaragupta concluded that classes are nothing but conventions.[4] For the Buddhists, therefore, class distinctions are merely social conventions. A nominal designation does not create, nor does it express, the essence of the thing to which it is referring. If this were the case, says the ŚKA, among a man's four sons named respectively Nandaka, Jīvaka, Aśoka and Śatāyus, Nandaka would rejoice, Jīvaka would live, Aśoka would not be sad and Śatāyus would live hundred years.[5]

The texts and arguments that I shall discuss all agree: the social denominations associated with specific individuals do not imply, nor do they suppose, for example, that those individuals possess a physical or mental property shared by all Brahmins and no non-Brahmin; a property that would justify our speaking of "classes" as we do of "species" in biology. A simile from the ŚKA and the KDAM illustrates very well the Buddhist conventionalist position: "Indeed, just as sand does not become food [simply] because a child says [so] when young children playing

---

(*vyabhicārin*) character of the evidences or criteria (*liṅga, nimitta, viśeṣaṇa*) advanced by the opponents to include some human individuals in a given class, i.e., in a caste. In demonstrating the extent to which those criteria are fallacious, Buddhists attempt to neutralize the identification of those entities of designation and expose their inanity.

2 See section 2.3.2, p. 107, below.

3 See section 2.3.2, p. 107, below.

4 See section 2.4.3, p. 127, below.

5 ŚKA M29.11–30.2/CN629.23–28: *tad yathāpi nāma brāhmaṇa kasyacit puruṣasya catvāraḥ putrā bhaveyuḥ / sa teṣāṃ nāmāni kuryān nandaka iti vā jīvaka iti vāśoka iti vā śatāyur iti vā / iṣṭāś ca te punar bhor etasya puruṣasya putrā bhaveyuḥ / tatra yo nandakaḥ sa nandet / yo jīvakaḥ sa jīvet / yo 'śokaḥ sa na śocet / yaḥ śatāyuḥ sa varṣaśataṃ jīvet /*. See also Law (1937, 14).

on a main road build sand pies and give them names [by saying]: 'This one is milk, this one is butter, this one is meat and this one is curd,' so it is with the four classes as you, the Brahmin, describe them."[6] In other words, denominations of status do not signal any real group of properties in the individuals to which they apply as a whole. Making the assertion that a man is a Brahmin, i.e., including that man in a class such as brahmanity, is to make an assertion that rests only on a convention, and not on criteria or signs that can be observed to recur in all Brahmin individuals. Outside that convention, there is no ground for a distribution of men into real classes of which they would be the proper instances. In the end, those classes are merely reifications and superimpositions.

1.1.3 In its analysis of social differentiation, Buddhist philosophy has developed, as it did in its description of human existence or its theory of knowledge, an explanation that is aetiological, processual and functional. The explanation is *aetiological* in so far as it identifies certain events to be the cause of the current social divisions. It is *processual* in that it considers the issue in terms of a gradual differentiation into human groups. Finally, it is *functional* or occupational in so far as contingent activities, occupations and means of subsistence are considered to be the only differentiating characteristics of those groups. The archetype of that explicative schema is found in the *Aggañña Sutta* (AgS),[7] a foundational text to which we can trace the parallel

---

6 ŚKA M24.1–5/CN626.13–17: *yathā hi dārakā*[1] *bālāḥ krīḍamānā mahāpathe / pāṃśupuñjāni sampiṇḍya svayaṃ nāmāni kurvate // idaṃ kṣīram idaṃ dadhīdaṃ māṃsam idaṃ ghṛtam*[2] */ na ca bālasya vacanāt pāṃśavo 'nnaṃ*[3] *bhavanti hi // varṇās tathaiva catvāro yathā brāhmaṇa bhāṣase*[4] */*. Compare with KDAM, p. LIV, verses 152–154ab: 1: *bālakā*; 2: *idaṃ māṃsam idaṃ ghṛtam idaṃ dadhi*; 3: *'nnā*; 4: *subhūta iti kalpitāḥ*. See also Law (1937, 14).

7 On the AgS and its interpretation, see Gombrich (1992), Collins (1993), Gethin (1997) and Schmithausen (2005). Ascribing to Buddhists a processual and narrative explanation of social differentiation is to be confronted with the debated problem of determining the intention of

the AgS and, consequently, of the texts that were derived from it. Gombrich (1992) holds that the AgS is essentially satirical; that it is a parody, notably, of some Vedic cosmogonies and of the Brahmanic science of etymologies (*nirukti*). According to Gombrich (1992, 161), the Buddha (i.e., the author of the AgS, whoever this may be) never intended here to present an aetiology of the universe and the society of castes. On that interpretation, then, it becomes nearly impossible to credit the mythical narrative of the AgS with any explicative pretension. And consequently, its narrative and processual aspects could be omitted from the Buddhist position and explanation of social differentiation.

Let it first be noted that, whatever the intention of the AgS may have been, the LP, the MVastu, the ŚKA, the AKBh and the CŚV at least partially perpetuated its content, and that with the possible exception of the ŚKA, they all proposed a very literal reading of its teachings, especially in cosmological matters. From my perspective, the original intention of the principle developed in the AgS is therefore not as important as the continuity of its themes and, especially, the literality of their later comprehensions. For that reason, I believe it is legitimate to speak in processual terms.

Let it be noted also that in their satirical critique, the AgS and its derivatives conclude with a *positive* teaching. For nowhere in the passages in which I am interested, do those texts refer to birth as the principle of status acquisition. They moreover use, against the Brahmins, two explicative techniques of which the latter had become the champions, namely mythical narration and etymology. In so doing, they first demonstrate that an aetiological myth about a society that was *initially undifferentiated* cannot explain how social divisions may be part of the natural order of things. By never appealing to birth, those passages further teach that such an initial situation *supposes* that the different statuses proceed from a gradual differentiation according to people's aspirations, occupations and means of subsistence. As for the denominations themselves, they are, if I may say, the actual, yet encrypted, symbols of each step of the differentiation, and each refers to the reason for the appearance of a given group (new aspirations and/or occupations and/or means of subsistence). Etymology, as a *clavis hermeneutica*, then makes it possible to retrace that reason, which evidently has nothing to do with birth. To summarize, we may say that (1) the structure of the aetiological myth implies a processual explanation, not a genealogical explanation (this would be a mono-genesis!), and that (2) the etymologies refer to occupations, not to birth. In both cases,

passages of the ŚKA and the KDAM. That important schema is also developed in the *Lokapaññatti* (LP), the *Mahāvastu* (MVastu), the *Abhidharmakośabhāṣya* (AKBh) and the *Catuḥśatakavṛtti* (CŚV). Strangely enough, the *Vajrasūcī* (VSū) remains silent on the evolutionary, or processual, aspect of social divisions, although it agrees with its essentially occupational character.[8]

After having considered several mythical events pertaining to the world's origin, the AgS describes a primeval situation where no social and occupational differentiation prevails.[9] The aetiology of social divisions and their denominations then begins with a conflictual episode reminiscent of the "law of the fishes" (*matsyanyāya*, i.e., the state of nature) described in the *Mahābhārata* and the *Purāṇas*. It is brought to a conclusion and resolved by a contractual explanation[10] that is also reminiscent of the epic myths on the institution of kingship.[11] The AgS, ŚKA, LP, MVastu, AKBh and CŚV[12] thus see in the appearance of the *kṣatriya* and the establishment of kingship the first consensual

---

tools that were notoriously used by Brahmins, now serve to support conclusions that contradict the Brahmanic positions on caste.

8 VSū 225.9: *tasmād aniyataṃ brāhmaṇyam / kriyāviśeṣeṇa khalu caturvarṇavyavasthā kriyate /*. "That is why brahmanity is indeterminate. In fact, the differentiation (*vyavasthā*) into four castes originates from the particular activity [usually performed by its members]."

9 AgS, D.N. III 93 and 94–96: *teṣaṃ ñeva sattānaṃ anaññesaṃ sadisānaṃ ñeva no asadisānaṃ....* Note also ŚKA M32.3–5/CN631.1–4: *na khalv evaṃ brāhmaṇa prāthamakalpikāṇāṃ sattvānām etad abhavad yad uta brāhmaṇa iti vā kṣatriya iti vā vaiśya iti vā śūdra iti vā / ekam idaṃ sarvam idam ekam /*.

10 See, however, Collins (1993, 187–189), "Appendix 2: Is there a 'social contract' in A[ggañña] S[utta]?" See also Lang (1992, 233–35).

11 On this, see the surveys of Dumont (1966, appendix C, 6–8; not included in the 1972 English translation) and Klimkeit (1981, 27–42).

12 In order not to encumber my presentation with too many narrative variants, I will essentially base my argument on the AgS and ŚKA. For references to the AKBh and CŚV, see section 2.1.1.2, p. 71, below. In the MVastu, the aetiology ends with the *kṣatriya,* the king (*rājan*) and the person who is elected or honoured by all (*mahāsammata*). See Senart (1882, I.621 note on 348.5).

step toward social differentiation. This all began, on those accounts, when a man unhappy with his plot of rice coveted and then took possession of another's. The event marked the appearance of theft and, consequently, of blame, lie and punishment. The community then held an assembly to confer on a man of distinguished qualities (notably his beauty) the use of punishment (literally, the sceptre; *daṇḍa*), in exchange for which he would receive a share of the harvest. Elected by all the people (*mahājanasammata*), the first king was Mahāsammata.[13] Lord of the fields (*khettānaṃ pati*), he was called "*khattiya*."[14] Gladdening others with his justice (*dhammena rañjeti*), he was called "*rājan*," the king.[15] In their account of the origin of social divisions, the AgS and ŚKA therefore introduce two intermingling types of explanation. The first one is narrative: it explains a series of events and, more broadly, a process. The second is etymological: it traces the origin of a given statutory denomina-

---

13 AgS, D.N. III 93: *mahājanasammato ti kho Vāseṭṭha mahāsammato, mahāsammato tv eva paṭhamaṃ akkharaṃ upanibbattaṃ*. See Collins (1993, 379–386), "Appendix 1: On the word *mahāsammata*." Neither the ŚKA nor the KDAM mention Mahāsammata.

14 AgS, D.N. III 93: *khettānaṃ patīti kho Vāseṭṭha khattiyo, khattiyo tv eva dutiyaṃ akkharaṃ upanibbattaṃ*. On the etymology of *khattiya*, see Schneider (1954, 576–578), where the Middle Indic form *khetta* is proposed for the Sanskrit *kṣatra*, and the Middle Indic *khettiya* is proposed for the Sanskrit *kṣatriya*, the latter having then been rendered in Pali by *khattiya*. See also Balbir (1991, 133–134). ŚKA M32.6–8/CN631.5–7: *tato 'nye sattvāḥ śālikṣetrāṇi kelāyanti gopāyanti vāpayanti vā / te 'mī kṣatriyā iti sañjñodapādi /*. KDAM, p. LVII, verse 174: *ye ca kṣetrāṇi rakṣantaḥ pālayanti sadā prajāḥ / sattvarakṣāvratācārāḥ kṣatriyās te nṛpā narāḥ //*. Compare with LP 212.6–213.3 and MVastu I 347.16–348.7.

15 AgS, D.N. III 93: *dhammena pare rañjetīti kho Vāseṭṭha rājā, rājā tv eva tatiyaṃ akkharaṃ upanibbattaṃ*. On that etymology, see Schneider (1954, 581–582) and Gombrich (1992, 174), with the Atharvedic reference. Collins' (1993, 371) references to the epics may be added to those of Schneider. ŚKA M33.12–13/CN632.4–5: *yo bhāṣyeṇa ca parṣadaṃ rañjayati dharmeṇa śīlavratasamācāreṇa samyak tasya rājeti sañjñā 'bhūt /*. KDAM, p. LVII, verse 175: *ye rañjayanti dharmārthe lokān nītiprayojakāḥ / rājānas te mahāvīrāḥ sarvadharmābhipālakāḥ //*.

tion's phonetic texture to the verb or verbal noun that initially designated someone's occupation, function or institution.[16]

That twofold approach is used also in the aetiology of other classes (*varṇa*). Despite some differences in their proposed etymologies, the AgS and ŚKA's descriptions of the situation that led to the "Brahmin" denomination are similar. According to the AgS, some men from the initial community were troubled by the unwholesome moral inclinations described above and chose to discard them (*bāhenti*). That is how they came to be called "Brahmins" (*brāhmaṇa*).[17] According to the ŚKA, those men were also troubled by the malice of possessions (*parigraha*)[18] and therefore left for the forest where, having built leaf-huts, they meditated without interruption except to go on alms in the nearby villages.[19] But the villagers were surprised to see such

---

[16] On that explicative method, see Balbir (1991, 123–125).

[17] AgS, D.N. III 93–94: *te pāpake akusale dhamme bāhesum. pāpake akusale dhamme bāhentīti kho Vāseṭṭha brāhmaṇā, brāhmaṇā tv eva paṭhamaṃ akkharaṃ upanibbattam.* On the etymological connection between *brāhmaṇa* and *bāhenti*, see Schneider (1954, 578), Balbir (1991, 132–133) and von Hinüber (1991, 186). Note also ŚrBh II 254.1–2: *bāhitā bhavanty anena pāpakā akuśalā dharmāḥ /*. The etymology can be explained if we take the Middle Indic **bāhaṇa* as equivalent to *brāhmaṇa*. See also, for example, DhP 388: *bāhitapāpo ti brāhmaṇo...* "Because he has discarded evil, he is called a Brahmin." That etymology is also found in the works of Śāntarakṣita and Kamalaśīla; TS 3589ab: *ye ca bāhitapāpatvād brāhmaṇāḥ pāramārthikāḥ /*. TSP 923.5: *bāhitapāpadharmatvād brāhmaṇā iti niruktiḥ /*. On the etymology of *brāhmaṇa* through *bāhitapāpa*, see MMVR 246.5–8 and 249.9–12.

[18] ŚKA M32.8–11/CN631.6–11: *athātra brāhmaṇa tadanyatamānāṃ sattvānām etad abhavat / parigraho rogaḥ parigraho gaṇḍaḥ parigrahaḥ śalyaḥ / yan nu vayaṃ svaparigraham apahāyāraṇyāyatanaṃ gatvā tṛṇakāṣṭhaśākhāpatraparṇapalāśakān upasaṃhṛtya tṛṇakuṭikāṃ vā parṇakuṭikāṃ vā kṛtvā praviśya dhyāyema iti /*. Note that the etymological explanation proposed by the LP (213.3–12) is based on *bāhenti* (AgS) and the theme of the malice of possessions (*parigraha*, ŚKA); see in particular LP 213.8–9: *atha kho te sattā pariggahaṃ pahāya pariggahe bāhitvā araññe paṇṇakuṭīsu ajjhāvasanti.*

[19] AgS, D.N. III 94: *te araññāyatane paṇṇakuṭiyo karitvā paṇṇakuṭīsu jhāyanti, vītaṅgārā vītadhūmā paṇṇamusalā sāyaṃ sāyamāsāya pāto pāta-*

men withdrawn (< *bahis*, lit. outwards, outside) from all human contact and thought that they were "out of mind" (MMW *bahirmanaska*).[20] Hence they called them "Brahmins."[21] In the AgS, however, villagers called those men "meditators" (*jhāyaka*) upon seeing that they meditate (*jhāyanti*) as soon as they have found enough food to subsist.[22]

But some of those men stopped meditating. They settled in villages to compile books[23] (*ganthe karontā acchenti*) or recite the verses of mantras[24] (*mantrapadān svādhyāyanti*). When the villagers saw them, they nodded: "These ones do not meditate" (AgS *na jhāyanti*; ŚKA **adhyāyaka*), and called them "reciters [of the Veda]"[25] (AgS *ajjhāyaka*;[26] ŚKA *adhyāpaka*).

---

rāsāya gāmanigamarājadhāniyo osaranti ghāsam esanā. ŚKA M32.12–15/CN631.11–15: *atha te sattvās taṃ svakaṃ parigraham apahāyāraṇyāyatanaṃ gatvā tṛṇakāṣṭhaśākhāpatraparṇapalāśakais tṛṇakuṭiṃ vā parṇakuṭikāṃ vā kṛtvā tatraiva praviśya dhyāyanti sma / te tatra sāyam āsanahetoḥ prāntavāṭikāṃ prātar aśanahetoś ca grāmaṃ piṇḍāya praviśanti sma /.*

20 The etymology with *bahir* and *manas* will occur also in the AKBh and CŚV. See section 2.1.1.2, p. 71, below.

21 ŚKA M32.16–19/CN631.15–20: *atha teṣāṃ grāmavāsināṃ sattvānām etad abhavat / duṣkarakārakā vata bhoḥ sattvā ye svakaṃ parigraham utsṛjya grāmanigamajanapadebhyo bahir nirgatās teṣāṃ bahirmanaskā brāhmaṇā iti sañjñodapādi / te ca punar grāmavāsinaḥ sattvās tān atīva satkurvanti sma / teṣāṃ ca dātavyaṃ manyante sma /.*

22 AgS, D.N. III 94: *te ghāsaṃ paṭilabhitvā punad eva araññāyatane paṇṇakuṭīsu jhāyanti. jhāyantīti kho pana Vāseṭṭha jhāyakā, jhāyakā tv eva dutiyaṃ akkharaṃ upanibbattaṃ.* Collins (1993, 346) translates: "'They meditate' (*jhāyanti*), monks, (is what) 'those who tend a (sacrificial) fire' (*jhāyakā*) (means): 'jhāyaka' was the second term (for the Brahmin class) to appear." On the translation of *jhāyaka*, see Collins (1993, 373).

23 According to the AgS. On that point, see Collins (1993, 373–374).

24 According to the ŚKA. Compare with LP 213.12–14.

25 AgS, D.N. III 94: *tesaṃ ñeva kho Vāseṭṭha sattānaṃ ekacce sattā araññāyatane paṇṇakuṭīsu taṃ jhānaṃ anabhisambhuṇamānā gāmasāmantaṃ nigamasāmantam osaritvā ganthe karontā acchenti. tam enaṃ manussā disvā evam āhaṃsu: "ime kho bho sattā araññāyatane paṇṇakuṭīsu taṃ jhānaṃ anabhisambhuṇamānā gāmasāmantaṃ nigama-*

Again according to the AgS and ŚKA, those who engaged in sexual intercourse (AgS) and diverse activities (AgS *vis(s)u(ta)-kammanta*; ŚKA *vividhakarmānta*) related to profit (ŚKA) were called "*vaiśyas*."[27] The KDAM also correlates the term "*vaiśya*" to "*vividha*," but adds that the *vaiśyas* cause creatures to enter (*veśayanti*) the dharma and are, in that respect, the most eminent among men.[28] But in order to survive, some of those men also engaged in cruel practices (*luddācāra*) and earned their living by means of vile work (AgS *khuddhācāra*; ŚKA *kṣudreṇa karmaṇā*). That is why they were called "*śūdras*."[29]

---

sāmantaṃ osaritvā ganthe karontā acchenti. na dān' ime jhāyanti." na dān' ime jhāyantīti kho Vāseṭṭha ajjhāyaka, ajjhāyakā tv eva tatiyaṃ akkharaṃ upanibbattaṃ. ŚKA M33.1–3/CN631.20–24: *atha teṣām eva sattvānām anyatame sattvās tāni dhyānāny asambhāvayanto grāmeṣv avatīrya mantrapadān svādhyāyanti sma / tāṃs te grāmavāsina āhur "na kevalam ime sattvā [adhyāyakā?] ime 'dhyāpakās" teṣām adhyāpakā iti loke sañjñodapādi / ayaṃ hetur ayaṃ pratyayo brāhmaṇānāṃ loke prādurbhāvāya /*. See also LP 213.14–17.

26 Where the Pali *a-jjhāyaka* (= Skt. *a-dhyāyaka*) plays on *ajjhāyaka* (= Skt. *adhy-āyaka*).

27 AgS, D.N. III 95: *tesaṃ ñeva kho Vāseṭṭha sattānaṃ ekacce sattā methunadhammaṃ samādāya vissutakammante payojesuṃ. "methunadhammaṃ samādāya vissutakammante payojentīti" kho Vāseṭṭha vessā, vessā tv eva akkharaṃ upanibbattaṃ.* On the etymology of *vessa*, see Schneider (1954, 578–580), who reads *vis(s)ukammante*, and derives the Pali *vis(s)u* from the Middle Indic *vissa* and *vis(s)u*. Against that interpretation, see Collins (1993, 373–374), who maintains *vissuta*. The Sanskrit *vividha*, which is semantically close to *vis(s)u*, is used in the corresponding passages of the ŚKA and the KDAM. ŚKA M33.4–6/CN631.25–27: *athānyatame sattvā vivekakālapratisaṃyuktān karmāntān vividhān arthapratisaṃyuktān kurvanti sma / teṣāṃ vaiśyā iti sañjñodapādi /*. See also LP 213.19–20.

28 KDAM, p. LVII, verse 176: *ye ca sattvahitādhāne vividhārthānukāriṇaḥ / veśayanti prajā dharme vaiśyās te hi narottamāḥ //*.

29 AgS, D.N. III 95: *tesaṃ ñeva kho Vāseṭṭha sattānaṃ ye te sattā avasesā te luddācārā ahesum. "luddācārā khuddhācārā ti" kho Vāseṭṭha suddā, suddā tv eva akkharaṃ upanibbattaṃ.* On the etymology of *sudda*, see Schneider (1954, 580–581). See also Collins (1993, 375–376). ŚKA M33.7–8/CN631.27–28: *athānyatame sattvāḥ kṣudreṇa karmaṇā jīva-*

Both the AgS and the ŚKA thus explain in a narrative form a process that is developing from the centre outwards. Both texts describe social segmentation as a result of the gradual appearance of functions and occupations within a group where no differentiation initially prevailed.

1.1.4 For the Buddhists, therefore, the only acceptable social categories are those that define a community in terms of its occupation, function and means of subsistence. Accordingly, statutory designations are legitimate only if the groups and individuals to whom they refer meet the occupational criterion.[30] For while determinations due to birth may be quite important, they do not in any way preclude anyone from changing his occupation and, therefore, from changing his denomination and status. In that sense, except in a soteriological context, Buddhists do not criticize the *empirical existence* of those denominations as much as the *criterion* that governs their application. In other words, Buddhists here question the *naturalization* of denominations that results from asserting that they are determined by birth, as in the Brahmanic theory. At any rate, the Buddhist and Brahmanic positions, as well as the debate that ensued, remain unintelligible outside a social context made of corporations and guilds,[31] or at least a context of prevailing heredity and fixity of the means of subsistence.

Around the time of the first codifications of dharma and the emergence of Buddhism, there seems to have been an acceleration of the differentiation process in Indian society (at least

---

kāṃ kalpayanti sma / teṣāṃ śūdrā iti sañjñodapādi /. The explanation provided in the KDAM, p. LVII, verse 177, is totally different: *vratācāra-vihīnā ye sattvarakṣārthacāriṇaḥ / manyante sevayā śuddhiṃ śūdrās te śreṣṭhinas tathā //*. "Likewise, the eminent craftsmen who, being excluded from religious observances and acting in order to take care of [other] beings, aspire to purity (*śuddhi*) by serving [others, those are called] *śūdras*."

30 Barua (1959, 145) and Law (1937, 11 and 12).

31 On corporations and guilds, see Fick's (1972, 283[183]) interesting comments.

around the Ganges basin) as a result of the progressive appearance of urban centres, which were themselves favoured by the emergence of an agrarian economy with (low) surplus.[32] On the Brahmanic side, the mixture of classes (*varṇasaṅkara*) theory,[33] which was normative and appealed to the heredity principle, was developed quite early in order to rationalize, naturalize and therefore *normalize* the phenomenon by restoring the four classes classification system. There are reasons to believe that the normative Brahmanic model was developed in an extra-urban context that was possibly hostile to the new urban culture. But the model's low explicative potential has long been known. Buddhism, on the other hand, appears to have sided early with the urban culture, and benefited from the new functions (commerce, public functions) and problems that it created. This is reflected, I believe, in the Buddhist explanation of statutory distinctions. More mobile and by far more economical in terms of its basic principles, the Buddhists' occupational position did not lead to the same absurdities as the Brahmanic theory. It could easily account narratively, as we have seen, and functionally, as we will see, for *both* the existence of class distinctions and their developing process.

As early as the VāS, the Buddha explained denominations in terms of functions and means of livelihood. For example, a person who subsists (*upajīvati, jīvati*) by keeping the cattle (*gorakkha*) is called a farmer (*kassaka*), not a Brahmin. One who earns a living by means of various crafts (*puthu sippena*) is called a craftsman (*sippika*), not a Brahmin. And one who subsists by trading (*vohāra*) is called a merchant (*vāṇija*), not a Brahmin.[34]

---

[32] See Gombrich (1988, 49–50) and Collins (1993, 303–312).

[33] The theory of the mixture of classes, or system of the mixed caste, was studied by Brinkhaus (1978); see also Kane (1974). According to Gombrich (1992, 170–171), the *Ariyavaṃsa Sutta* (A.N. II 28) may be a Buddhist satire/parody of the Brahmanic theory of the mixture of classes.

[34] VāS, Sn. 612: *yo hi koci manussesu gorakkhaṃ upajīvati, evaṃ Vāseṭṭha jānāhi, kassako so, na brāhmaṇo.* Sn. 613: ... *puthu sippena jīvati,* ... *sippiko so, na brāhmaṇo.* Sn. 614: *vohāraṃ upajīvati,* ... *vāṇijo so, na*

The same principle applies to the servant (*pessika* < *parapessa*), the thief (*cora* < *adinnaṃ upajīvati*), the warrior (*yodhājīva* < *issattha*), the sacrificer (*yājaka* < *porohicca*) and the king (*rājā* < *gāmaṃ raṭṭhañ ca*).[35] Many centuries later, the ŚKA,[36] and especially the KDAM's compiler,[37] will follow that model. The KDAM provides a long commented list of denominations. For example, the zealous men who make important business by storing riches are called merchants (*vaṇij*). Those who are versed in the science of stars, make calculations (*gaṇayanti*) day and night and know the end of eras (*yugānta*) are called astrologers (*gaṇaka*). Similarly, we call great negotiators (*sārthavāha*) the men who erect caravans (*sārtha*) and make jewels upon returning from the mines.[38] And we call doctors (*bhiṣaj*) those who know the elements and humours and prescribe medicines (*bhaiṣajya*) to heal people.[39] The very long enumeration goes from preceptors

---

brāhmaṇo. Brahmins, agriculturists and tradesmen in Fick (1972, 241[156] and 246[160]).

35 VāS, Sn. 615: *yo hi koci manussesu parapessena jīvati, evaṃ Vāseṭṭha jānāhi, pessiko so, na brāhmaṇo*. Sn. 616: ... *adinnaṃ upajīvati*, ... *coro eso, na brāhmaṇo*. Sn. 617: ... *issatthaṃ upajīvati*, ... *yodhājīvo, na brāhmaṇo*. Sn. 618: ... *porohiccena jīvati*, ... *yājako so, na brāhmaṇo*. Sn. 619: ... *gāmaṃ raṭṭhañ ca bhuñjati*, ... *rājā eso, na brāhmaṇo*. On that passage, see Fick (1972, 220–22[143–44]). The same Fick (1972, 9–10 note 1[7 note 1]) reproduces, based on Senart, a long list of occupations that forbid Brahmins to perform the ritual.

36 ŚKA M33.9–34.2/CN631.28–632.8: *bhūtapūrvaṃ brāhmaṇa anyatamaḥ sattvo vadhūm ādāya ratham āruhyānyatamasminn araṇyapradeśe gataḥ / tatra ca ratho bhagnaḥ / tasmān mātaṅga* [*mā tvaṃ gamaḥ*] *iti sañjñodapādi / kṣetraṃ karṣanti ye teṣāṃ karṣakā iti sañjñā pravṛttā / ... tato 'nye sattvā vāṇijyayā jīvikāṃ kalpayanti / teṣāṃ vaṇija iti sañjñodapādi / tataś cānye sattvāḥ pravrajanti sma / pravrajitvā parān jayanti kleśān jayantīti teṣāṃ pravrajitā iti loke sañjñodapādi /*.

37 See KDAM, pp. LV–LIX, verses 163–164.

38 On the great negotiator (*satthavāha*), see Fick (1972, 262[169] and 271–77[175–78]).

39 KDAM, pp. LVI–LVIII, respectively verse 179: *sādhayanti mahatkāryaṃ dhanādivastusaṅgrahaiḥ / vaṇikkarmābhisaṃyuktā vaṇijas te mahodyamāḥ //*. 182: *jyotirvidyāvido ye ca gaṇayanti divāniśam / yugāntakālavijñātā gaṇakās te 'pi mānavāḥ //*. 180: *ye ca sārthān samāhṛtya*

(*upādhyāya*) to ploughmen (*kṛṣika*), and from seers (*ṛṣi*) and craftsmen (*śilpin*) to those followers of the Śaiva sect who wear necklaces made of skulls (*kāpālika*). Even the disliked *caṇḍāla* denomination is explained: "We call *caṇḍāla*s those men who, bloodthirsty and showing no pity, harm beings and behave cruelly (*caṇḍavṛtti*)."[40]

Acknowledging as it does the social segmentation suggested by language, the (late) KDAM's schema also covers the complex constellation of confessional and sectarian denominations. Thus mentioned more or less successively are the groups of devotees to Śiva (*śaiva*) and his consort goddess Kālī (*māhāraudra*, *bhairavika*, *kālika*), to Viṣṇu (*vaiṣṇava*) and Brahma (*brāhmaṇa*), and the followers of the Buddha (*bauddha*) and the Jina (*jaina*).[41]

---

ratnākarasamāgatāḥ / sādhayanti ca ratnāni sārthavāhāś ca te narāḥ //. 183: *dhātudoṣāṇy abhijñāya lokānāṃ paricārakāḥ / bhaiṣajyaṃ ye dadanty eva bhiṣajas te hi vaidyakāḥ //*.

40 KDAM, p. LVIII, verse 186: *ye mānavāḥ krūrā nirdayāḥ sattvahiṃsakāḥ / caṇḍavṛttipracārāś ca caṇḍālā iti te smṛtāḥ //*. See also LP 214.2–12.

41 KDAM, pp. LVI–LIX, respectively verse 187: *ye bhajanti śivaṃ nityaṃ śivabhaktiparāyaṇāḥ / te śaivā manujā jñeyāḥ śivadharmānucārataḥ //*. 188: *ye bhajanti viṣṇuṃ nityaṃ viṣṇubhaktiparāyaṇāḥ / viṣṇudharmasamācārād vaiṣṇavās te 'pi mānavāḥ //*. 189: *brahmāṇaṃ ye bhajanty eva brahmabhaktiparāyaṇāḥ / brahmadharmasamācārād brāhmaṇās te 'pi mānavāḥ //*. 190: *ye bhajanti mahāraudraṃ bhairavabhaktimānasāḥ / māhāraudrāś ca te khyātā bhairavikāś ca mānavāḥ //*. 191: *ye ca maheśvarīṃ devīṃ bhajanti kuladharmiṇaḥ / maheśvarīvratādhārāḥ kālikās te 'pi mānavāḥ //*. 192: *ye bhajanti sadā buddhaṃ bauddhadharmaparāyaṇāḥ / te 'pi ca mānavā bauddhāḥ sambodhipadasādhinaḥ //*. 193: *ye bhajanti jinaṃ caiva jainadharmaparāyaṇāḥ / te 'pi ca manujā jainā jainadharmānucāraṇāt //*. In verse 172, the KDAM also mentions the Kāpālika, which is not presented as a sectarian movement (indicated in the KDAM by *ye bhajanti...*): *ye ca bhasmaviliptāṅgā hārābharaṇabhūṣitāḥ / kāpālikāś ca te vīrāḥ śmaśānavratacāriṇaḥ //*. "And the men who, their limbs smeared with ashes and wearing necklaces of skulls, practice their observances in funerary cremation areas, those [are called] Kāpālikas." Note also the interesting explanation of the class of ascetics (*samaṇa*/*śramaṇa*) found in the AgS, D.N. III 95–96;

Devotions to Śiva, Viṣṇu or the Buddha are therefore perceived as activities and practices denoted by language. From that perspective, one is a devotee to the great deity in the same way as one is a goldsmith or an astrologer.

1.1.5 To summarize those preliminary remarks, let us note that the contrast is total between the Brahmanic and Buddhist perspectives: each element of the Brahmanic explanation finds its antithesis in the Buddhist's.

It is first striking to discover how Buddhists opposed an "evolutionary" and dynamic answer to a "fixist"[42] and static conception of castes (and, therefore, of society). According to the *Puruṣasūkta* (*Ṛgveda* X 90) , the appearance of classes coincided with the very appearance of humanity, which is to say that human beings never shared an undifferentiated state. On the contrary, since they were born from different causes (i.e., the primeval being's different limbs), members of the four classes differ *by nature* from the very beginning, as they will always do independently of human decisions.[43] The AgS replies by tracing the origin of classes and castes to a succession of multiple events that occurred in the first cosmic period after a long period of

see the translation by Collins (1993, 347). For an account of sectarian denominations in terms of classes, see Lorenzen (1991, 46–48).

42 I borrow the notions of "fixism," "fixist" and "fixity" from the history of biology. I here mean by "fixism" the theory according to which biological species were created *once and for all*, at the beginning of time, *by an infinite being*. Brahmins in fact understand classes (*jāti/varṇa*) (1) under the model of biological species; (2) as resulting *in illo tempore* from the dismembering/sacrifice of a primeval being (Puruṣa, Prajāpati); (3) as established once and for all, as permanent. Brahmins, in that sense, believe in the fixity of castes. Let it be clear here that in calling the Buddhist perspective "evolutionary," I *never* mean to interpret the debate between Buddhists and Brahmins along the historical model of the debate that opposed, in the nineteenth century, the Moderns like Lamarck or Darwin (transformism and evolutionism) to the Ancients like Linnaeus or Cuvier (fixism and catastrophism).

43 For a systematic Buddhist critique of the Brahmanic arguments based on the *Puruṣasūkta*, see section 1.3.4, p. 42, below.

undifferentiation. Since they share the same gradual evolution, humans form a unique group and only begin to differ in their occupations and aspirations. Such a difference is therefore not due to nature, but to contingent decisions. The AgS tells of a process of differentiation from which any difference of nature is excluded, and where each group issues from the larger group that preceded it. Buddhist texts moreover suggest that the process of differentiation is still underway.

The seed of the remaining oppositions can also already be found in the competing aetiologies discussed so far. For to ground a naturalist explanation of statutory differences on the *Puruṣa-sūkta* rendition is equivalent to saying that all individuals instantiating one or any of the classes (*jāti/varṇa*) possess *real* common properties that members of other classes do not possess. Those properties, since they are inscribed in something like an "order of things," thus serve as criteria or discriminants for the classes that they specify (see below). A realist view of caste therefore follows from a naturalist explanation. The aim of the Buddhist arguments presented below will consist in showing that none of those discriminants or criteria is sufficient to establish the reality of the alleged classes. Without anticipating Dharmakīrti, early Buddhists will argue that statutory differences are not due to nature but are mere conventions. In other words, they will argue that castes have only nominal existence; that they exist only as designations. Finally, the naturalist Brahmin will hold to the position that status is innate, and will grant predominance to birth (whether biological and/or ritualistic, see below) among each class' defining criteria. The conventionalist Buddhist, on the other hand, will hold that status results from occupation and erect professional occupation and means of subsistence (which are at least virtually variable, despite a strong heredity) as the sole criteria for the application of lexical conventions. A given term will conventionally designate all individuals who earn a living through a given activity.

1.2 Biological arguments: animal and plant species[44]

In the VāS, we encounter, in the persona of the Brahmins Vāseṭṭha and Bhāradvāja, two conflicting strategies for the justification of brahmanity. For Vāseṭṭha, one becomes a Brahmin through one's actions (*kammanā*), whereas for Bhāradvāja, this condition is acquired at birth (*jātiyā*).[45] The Buddha's answer starts from the premise that if brahmanity were acquired at birth, the Brahmin individual would come to represent an autonomous species (*jāti*) differentiated from other species. He then tries to determine the conditions under which a given group of individuals may properly be called a "species." And finally, he shows that what is true of animals and plants is not true of human individuals. The Buddha will therefore expose, as it truly is (*yathātathaṃ*), the division of living beings into numerous species.[46] To do so, he first takes the example of grass and trees (*tiṇarukkhe*, Sn. 601), and then, according to their various modes of locomotion, he takes many examples from the animal world: insects (Sn. 602), quadrupeds (*catuppada*, Sn. 603), snakes (*pādūdara*, Sn. 606), fishes (*maccha*, Sn. 605) and birds (*pakkhin*, Sn. 606).[47] He argues that each species can itself be divided into

---

44 On some of those arguments, see Law (1937, 11–12), Barua (1959, 144–145), Malalasekera (1971, 691b–692a) and Masson (1975, 90).

45 The argument against action being a criterion of brahmanity goes as follows in the VāS: *yato kho bho sīlavā ca hoti vatasampanno ca, ettāvatā kho brāhmaṇo hotīti*. "When one possesses virtuous conduct and is endowed with (good) vows, to such an extent one becomes a Brahmin." Translation by Norman (1984, 103). As for the argument against birth being a criterion of brahmanity, it reads: *yato kho bho ubhato sujāto hoti mātito ca pitito ca saṃsuddhagahaṇiko yāva sattamā pitāmahayugā akkhitto anupakkuṭṭho jātivādena, ettāvatā brāhmaṇo hoti*. "When one is well born on both the father's and the mother's side, and is of pure descent for seven generations, uncriticized and irreproachable with reference to birth, to such extent one becomes a Brahmin." Translation by Norman (1984, 103).

46 VāS, Sn. 600: ... *jātivibhaṅgaṃ pāṇānaṃ, aññamaññā hi jātiyo.*

47 The insects in question here are beetles (*kīṭa*), moths (*pataṅga*), ants (*kuntha*) and termites (*kippīlikā*).

sub-species whose members share a *specific set of characteristics* (*liṅgaṃ jātimayaṃ*). But this is not the case for human beings (*manussa*, Sn. 607), who possess no characteristic on the basis of which, from an alleged class of individuals to another, they could be differentiated into species. No organic, physiological or anatomic characteristic distinguishes the Brahmin from the non-Brahmin.[48] The conclusion is therefore self-evident: "This (difference) is not found individually among men in respect of their own bodies, but among men difference is spoken of as a matter of designation."[49]

The biological argument reappears, in a more elaborate form, in the VSū, the ŚKA and the KDAM. Those texts, however, show signs of a slight evolution in their argumentation. For it seems that their authors sensed a problem with the notions of "configuration" (*saṃsthāna*), "specific form" (*ākṛti*) and "external physical aspect" (*ākāra*). Later philosophers will give full consideration to that problem by rephrasing it in terms of the perceptibility (*pratyakṣatā*) of classes/genus (*jāti*) and universals (*sāmānya*).[50]

---

48 VāS, Sn. 608–610: *na kesehi na sīsena na kaṇṇehi na akkhihi* (/) *na mukhena na nāsāya na oṭṭhehi bhamūhi vā* (//) *na gīvāya na aṃsehi na udarena na piṭṭhiyā* (/) *na soṇiyā na urasā na sambādhe na methune* (//) *na hatthehi na pādehi na aṅgulīhi nakhehi vā* (/) *na janghāhi na ūrūhi na vaṇṇena sarena vā* (/) *liṅgaṃ jātimayaṃ n'eva, yathā aññāsu jātisu* (//). See Norman's (1984, 104) translation. J.W. de Jong (1988, 428) has already noted that an approximate Sanskrit version of that passage is found in the ŚKA; it also appears, in a modified version, in the KDAM, p. LV, verses 155–157. ŚKA M24.7–12/CN626.18–23: *na keśena na karṇābhyāṃ*[1] *na śīrṣeṇa na cakṣuṣā / na mukhena na nāsayā na grīvayā na bāhunā // norasāpy atha*[2] *pārśvābhyāṃ*[3] *na pṛṣṭhenodareṇa ca*[4] */ norubhyām atha jaṅghābhyāṃ pāṇipādanakhena ca*[5] *// na svareṇa na varṇena na sarvāṃśair na maithunaiḥ / nānāviśeṣaḥ sarveṣu manuṣyeṣu hi vidyate*[6] //. Compare with the KDAM: 1: *karṇena*; 2: *norasā na ca*; 3: *pārśveṅa*; 4: *vā* (also in CN); 5: *pāṇipādanakhair na ca*; 6: *naikā viśeṣatā vāpi manuṣyeṣu na* (also in CN) *vidyate*.

49 VāS, Sn. 611: see note 1, p. 2, above for the Pali; translation by Norman (1984, 104).

50 See sections 2.4.1–3, pp. 116–137, below.

Along those lines, the VSū introduces an interesting element to the "classical" biological argumentation:[51] the form and con-

---

51 VSū 224.9–21: *iha hi gohastyaśvamṛgasiṃhavyāghrādīnāṃ padaviśeṣo dṛṣṭo goḥ padam idaṃ hastipadam idam aśvapadam idaṃ mṛgapadam idaṃ siṃhapadam idaṃ vyāghrapadam idam iti / na ca brāhmaṇādīnāṃ brāhmaṇapadam idaṃ kṣatriyapadam idaṃ vaiśyapadam idaṃ śūdrapadam idam iti / ataḥ padaviśeṣābhāvād api paśyāma ekavarṇo nāsti cāturvarṇyam iti // iha gomahiṣāśvakuñjarakharavānarachāgaiḍakādīnāṃ bhagaliṅgavarṇasaṃsthānamalamūtragandhadhvaniviśeṣo dṛṣṭo na tu brāhmaṇakṣatriyādīnām ato 'py aviśeṣād eka eva varṇa iti // api ca yathā haṃsapārāvataśukakokilaśikhaṇḍiprabhṛtīnāṃ rūpaparṇalomatuṇḍaviśeṣo dṛṣṭo na tathā brāhmaṇādīnām ato 'py aviśeṣād eka eva varṇa iti // yathā vaṭabakulapalāśāśokatamālanāgakesaraśirīṣacampakaprabhṛtīnāṃ vṛkṣāṇāṃ viśeṣo dṛśyate padato daṇḍataś ca patrataś ca puṣpataś ca tvagasthibījarasagandhataś ca na tathā brahmakṣatriyaviṭśūdrāṇām aṅgapratyaṅgaviśeṣo na ca tvaṅmāṃsaśoṇitāsthiśukramalavarṇasaṃsthānaviśeṣaṇaṃ nāpi prasavaviśeṣo dṛśyate tato 'py aviśeṣād eka eva varṇo bhavati //*. See Weber's (1860, 246) translation. The VSū's arguments are similar to those of the VāS. They state the example of quadruped mammals (cow, buffalo, horse, elephant, donkey, monkey, goat, ram) who differ from one another in terms of their male or female genitals (*bhagaliṅga*), their colour, their configuration, their feces, their urine, their smell and the sound that they produce. Birds (swan, turtle-dove, parrot, cuckoo, peacock) also differ from one another in terms of their form/colour (*rūpa*), wings, feathers and beak. And the author of the VSū continues his demonstration with the example of a variety of trees that are distinguished by their roots, trunk, leaves, flowers, bark, wood (*asthi*?, Weber "Holz"), seed, flavour and perfume. As for Brahmins and *śūdra*s, for example, contrary to those animal and vegetal classes, they do not differ neither in skin, flesh, blood, sperm, bones, feces, colour, configuration, nor generation. The conclusion, once again, is self-evident: "Therefore, since there is no difference [in this regard] either, there is only one class [of human beings]."

Let it be noted that after considering physical, physiological and anatomic characteristics, the VSū (224.22–23) considers some potential psychological and, even, "existential" discriminating factors: *api bho brāhmaṇa sukhaduḥkhajīvitabuddhivyāpāravyavahāramaraṇotpattibhayamaithunopacārasamatayā nāsty eva viśeṣo brāhmaṇādīnām /*. "Moreover, oh Brahmin, since their pleasure, pain, life, intelligence, occupation, practice, death, birth, fear and sexual union are identical,

stitution of the feet of superior mammals like cows, elephants or tigers are sufficiently distinct to enable us to *recognize* their owner from the footprint[52] left on the ground. But while it is possible to say "This is a tiger's foot," it is not possible to say "This is a Brahmin's foot," "This is a *kṣatriya*'s foot," etc. If Brahmins, *kṣatriyas*, *vaiśyas* and *śūdras* could be recognized from their footprints, we could indeed suppose that they belong to distinct classes. But the fact that it is impossible to do so means that they belong to one and the same class.

The ŚKA and the KDAM,[53] both of which include long developments on the properly biological problem, differ from the preceding texts only in that they make a more extensive use of the notions of external physical aspect, specific form and configuration.[54] According to the KDAM, individuals alleged to be Brahmins would be instances of a distinct class if their head, mouth/face (*mukha*), ears, nose, eyebrows, shape (*rūpa*), configuration, colour, external physical aspect, mode of birth (*yoni*), sustenance or origin (*sambhava*) differed. But those individuals who are alleged to belong to the Brahmin species do not differ from *kṣatriyas*, *vaiśyas*, *śūdras* or others, neither in their body, mouth, colour (*varṇa*), the sounds that they produce, their smell

---

Brahmins are not at all different [from non-Brahmins]." In one of its numerous intermediate conclusions, the ŚKA M29.9–10/CN626.21–23 also speaks of pleasure and pain: *sahāsthimāṃsāḥ sanakhāḥ sacarmaṇo duḥkhaṃ sukhaṃ mūtrapurīṣam ekam / pañcendriyair nāsti yato viśeṣaṇaṃ tasmān na vai varṇacatuṣka eṣaḥ //*. "[All humans] have bones and flesh, nails and skin; their pleasure, pain, urine and feces are one. Since there is [among them] no difference with respect to the five faculties [for example], there is no fourfold division into classes."

52 Like Weber, I tend to understand *pada* as the mark, footprint or trace left by the foot, rather than the foot itself. That interpretation is well attested in Pali as well as Classical Sanskrit.

53 ŚKA M25.11–27.11/CN627.11–628.22; KDAM, pp. LI–LII, verses 139–151.

54 The ŚKA refers four times to configuration (*saṃsthāna*) and once to the external physical aspect (*ākāra*). In the 13 verses from the KDAM, configuration is mentioned six times, specific form (*ākṛti*) twice and the external physical aspect four times.

or their six faculties. Nor do they differ in terms of the properties of their flesh or bones (*māṃsāsthiguṇa*), configuration, specific form or external physical aspect. Contrary to the multiple varieties of animals,[55] plants,[56] metals or minerals,[57] humans are

---

55 The ŚKA introduces the classical fourfold division of living beings based on their mode of birth (the four *yonis*, as in AKBh III 8cd–9): birth from an egg (*aṇḍaja*), from the womb (*jarāyuja*), from exudation (*saṃsvedaja*) and apparitional birth (*aupapāduka*). Animals (cow, horse, ass, bull, deer, bird, goat and ram) differ from one another in terms of their footprints (*pāda*), mouth (*mukha*), colour (*varṇa*), configuration, sustenance (*āhāra*) and mode of birth (*yonisambhava*). The KDAM successively mentions animals such as lions (*siṃhādijantu*, verse 139), birds such as the swan and the peacock (*haṃsamayūrādipakṣin*, verse 140), worms and beetles (*kṛmikīṭa*, verse 141).

56 The ŚKA offers an almost innumerable list of examples, divided into six categories. ŚKA M26.7–10/CN627.21–27: *phalavṛkṣa* (fruit-bearing trees; CN *phalguvṛkṣa*), M26.11–14/CN628.4–8: *sthalavṛkṣa* (trees growing on dry land), M26.15–18/CN627.27–628.3: *kṣīravṛkṣa* (trees secreting milky or resinous sap), M26.19–27/CN628.8–14: *phalabhaiṣajyavṛkṣa* (trees with medicinal fruits), M27.3–6/CN628.14–18: *sthalajapuṣpavṛkṣa* (flower-bearing trees growing on dry land), M27.7–9/CN628.18–22: *jalajapuṣpa* (aquatic flowers). Trees generally differ from one another in terms of their roots (*mūla*), body (*skandha*), bark (*tvagbhāga*), sap (*sāra*), leaves (*patra*), flowers (*puṣpa*), fruits (*phala*) and, where applicable, their clustered aspect (*gulma*). Flower-bearing trees growing on dry land and flowers growing in water differ in terms of their form (*rūpa*), colour (*varṇa*), smell (*gandha*) and configuration. The KDAM mentions the earth-eating tree (*bhūruhavṛkṣa*, verse 142), herbs such as *tṛṇa* and *auṣadha* (*tṛṇauṣadhādiśaspa*, verse 143), varieties of rice such as the *dhānya* rice (*dhānyādivrīhijāti*, verse 144), flowers such as *jasminum grandiflorum* (*jātikundapuṣpa*, verse 145), flowers growing in water such as the lotus (**jalajāni puṣpāṇi padmādīni*, verse 146), the fruits of trees such as the mango tree (*āmrādiphala*, verse 147).

57 The KDAM states the example of metals such as gold (*hemādidhātu*, verse 149a) and precious stones such as diamond (*vajrādiratna*, verse 150a).

of a unique variety, i.e., they constitute one single species or class.[58]

One ultimate and important biological argument must finally be mentioned. In the preceding arguments, the various animal and vegetal species were depicted as possessing distinctive characteristics and it was insisted that each species can be known through some signs or class discriminants. Now the Buddha gives to Assalāyana one further argument based on the possibility or impossibility of hybridization between different individuals.[59] In the course of the discussion, Assalāyana is first forced to admit that if a *kṣatriya* man (*khattiyakumāra*) and a Brahmin woman (*brāhmaṇakaññā*) (or a Brahmin man and a *kṣatriya* woman) conceive offsprings, those children will be similar to their mother and father, and will have both the status of the *kṣatriya* and Brahmin. The Buddha then asks what would happen with the offspring of a mare (*vaḷavā*) and a donkey (*gadra-*

---

58 Both texts offer numerous conclusions along those lines: ŚKA M23.10–11/CN626.9–11: *sapādajaṅghāḥ sanakhāḥ samāṃsāḥ sapārśvapṛṣṭhāś ca narā bhavanti / ekāṃśato nāsti yato viśeṣo varṇāś catvāra ito na santi //*. "Humans have foot and calves, nails, flesh, ribs and backs. Since there is no difference among them with respect to any limb, it is therefore not the case that there are four classes." ŚKA M24.15–16/CN626.24–26: *saśīrṣakāś cātha narā asthiyuktāḥ sacarmakāḥ sendriyasodarāś ca / ekāṃśato nāsti yato viśeṣo varṇā na yuktāś caturo 'bhidhātum //*. "But if [all] humans have one head, a skeletal structure, a skin, sense faculties and an abdomen, we are not justified in saying that there are four classes since there is no difference [between them] with respect to any limb." We find parallel conclusions in the KDAM, p. LV, verse 158: *tathā nāsti yathānyāsu jāter liṅgaṃ pṛthak pṛthak / sāmānyakāraṇaṃ manye kiṃcin na bhedalakṣaṇam //*. "Thus there are not, [among humans taken] each separately, any sign of a class as [is the case] with [all] other [classes; there is among them], it seems to me, no distinctive sign (*bhedalakṣaṇa*) [to act] as the cause of a universal [such as brahmanity]." Compare with ŚKA M24.13–14/CN626.23–24: *yathā hi jātiṣv anyāsu liṅgaṃ jāteḥ pṛthak pṛthak / sāmānyaṃ kāraṇaṃ tatra kiṃ vā jātiṣu manyase //*. In both cases, the important word *liṅga* (sign) of the VāS is reintroduced.

59 AsS, M.N. II 153–154.

bha). Would it be similar to both the male and female parents and would it have to be called both "mare" and "donkey"? Assalāyana admits that this case is different from that of human offsprings. For while the child is similar to both his mother and father and shares their respective statuses, the result of a mare mating with a donkey is a mule (*kisora*) that is neither a mare nor a donkey and is given neither of those names since it is born through interbreeding (*vekurañjāya*). The argument is based on the improbability, and *in fact* on the impossibility, of hybridization or crossbreeding between members of separate biological species. That empirical improbability or impossibility constitutes a criterion of distinction between presumed species. It is then insisted that the offspring of an *artificial* hybridization (i.e., one consented by humans) between members of two species is not similar to any of the two parents and is generally sterile. If we complete the Buddhist argument, we find that the offspring of a *kṣatriya* man and a Brahmin woman, contrary to that of a mare forced to mate with a donkey, is not a sterile hybrid. And this shows, once again, that *kṣatriya* and Brahmin individuals do not belong to distinct species.[60]

In the passages that we have analyzed so far, the purpose of the properly biological argumentation is to demonstrate that no organic, physiological or anatomic characteristic could serve as a sign (*liṅga*, VāS, ŚKA and KDAM) that some human individuals belong to a distinct class or species (*jāti*). In the words of the VāS (and ŚKA), it shows that no such characteristic could serve as a class (*varṇa*) discriminant (*viśeṣaṇa*). All the various arguments suggest that contrary to animal, vegetal or mineral/metallic species, no physical characteristic exists among human beings that could make legitimate the fourfold division into classes (*cāturvarṇya*). Consequently, human individuals form one single class (*ekavarṇa*) and that is why, in a very ironic passage, the ŚKA concludes: "[When] each [is taken] separately (*pṛthak pṛthak*), all [the individuals composing the four classes may be]

60 See also Law (1937, 11) and Barua (1959, 145).

blind in one eye, hunchbacked or epileptic, have white leprosy, be leprous, have a clear or dark complexion. For it is indeed as a result of their own actions (*svakarman*) that creatures are determined (*pratiṣṭhita*) to have the same marrow, nails, skin, ribs, stomach and mouth/face. Under such circumstances, oh Brahmin, there is no difference [between them]. What difference due to caste could there be? And since there is no caste discriminant, there is consequently no fourfold division into classes (*varṇacatuṣka*)."[61]

1.3 Genealogical arguments

When we look at Buddhist texts from the *Assalāyana Sutta* (AsS) and *Ambaṭṭha Sutta* (AmbS) to Prajñākaragupta, we find that the Brahmins' effort to justify their brahmanity and the partition of society into castes and classes draws predominantly on a

61 ŚKA M30.8–12/CN630.6–11: *sarve kāṇāś ca kubjāś ca sarve*[1] *'pasmāriṇo 'pi vā / kilāsinaḥ kuṣṭhināś ca*[2] *gaurāḥ kṛṣṇāḥ*[3] *pṛthak pṛthak // pratiṣṭhitāḥ samamajjāna*[4]*khatvacapārśvodaravaktrāḥ*[5] *prajā hi tāḥ*[6] *svakarmaṇā / evaṃgate brāhmaṇa naiva*[7] *bhavati viśeṣaḥ / ko jātikṛto viśeṣaḥ / yasmāc ca jāter na viśeṣaṇo* [sic!] *'sti*[8] *tasmān na vai varṇacatuṣka eva /*. Variant readings: 1: CN om. *sarve*; 2: CN *caivaṃ*; 3: CN *kṛṣṇāś ca*; 4: CN *pratiṣṭhitās te majjāna°*; 5: CN *°vaktrāś ca*; 6: CN *prajahīta*; 7: CN *naivaṃ*; 8: M *yasmān na jāter viśeṣaṇo 'sti*. Also relevant to this problem is KM 16: "Out of ignorance and with an unclear mind, you [Yaśas] said to yourself: 'I am a superior man!' I [Aśoka] am inspired by the light of the teaching of Daśabala, and when I look deep into my heart, I make no difference between the noble and the vile, the skin and the flesh, articulations and bones. The thirty-six parts [of the body] are identical in the noble and the vile man: what other mark of distinction could remain? Their names, their dresses, their clothes and their personal objects alone are different" (English translation of Huber 1908, 95–96). Compare with the *Divyāvadāna* XXVII, CN384.17–21: *śreṣṭho 'smīty aparīkṣako hi gaṇayan mohāndhakārāvṛtaḥ // kāyaṃ yas tu parīkṣate daśabalavyāhāradīpair budhaḥ / nāsau pārthivabhṛtyayor viṣamatāṃ kāyasya sampaśyati // tvaṅmāṃsāsthiśirāyakṛtprabhṛtayo bhāvā hi tulyā nṛṇām / āhāryais tu vibhūṣaṇair adhikatā kāyasya niṣpīḍyate //*.

wide variety of hereditary and genealogical considerations.[62] Among those, at least four are the recurring targets of Buddhist arguments. First, when discussing the question of sacraments (*saṃskāra*), the normative Brahmanic literature asserts that the privilege of being born a Brahmin is acquired under the condition that both direct parents be Brahmins (1.3.1). A second condition is that the purity of Brahmanic ancestry must have been preserved for at least seven generations (1.3.2). In addition to blood filiation, Brahmins also appear to have conceived quite early a second model of filiation based on lineage (*gotra*), where each Brahmanic lineage is traceable to a Vedic seer (*ṛṣi*) from whom its name is derived (1.3.3). The archetype of genealogical legitimacy, however, is to be found in the famous *Puruṣasūkta*, where the origin of the four classes is connected with a cosmic and anthropogonic event: the dismembering of a primeval being (Puruṣa, Prajāpati; 1.3.4). According to that tradition, Brahmins are born from his mouth, *kṣatriyas* from his arms, *vaiśyas* from his thighs and *śūdras* from his feet.[63] We shall now take up the Buddhist reply to each of those arguments.

---

62 Recall the literary theme of the AsS and AgS: *brāhmaṇā, bho Gotama, evam āhaṃsu: brāhmaṇā va seṭṭho vaṇṇo hīno añño vaṇṇo; brāhmaṇā va sukko vaṇṇo, kaṇho añño vaṇṇo; brāhmaṇā va sujjhanti no abrāhmaṇā; brāhmaṇā va brahmano puttā orasā mukhato jātā brahmajā brahmanimittā brahmadāyādā ti. idha bhavaṃ Gotamo kiṃ āhāti?* "Good Gotama, brahmans speak thus: 'Only brahmans form the best caste, all other castes are low; only brahmans form the fair caste, all other castes are dark; only brahmans are pure, not non-brahmans; only brahmans are own sons of Brahmā, born of his mouth, born of Brahmā, heirs to Brahmā.' What does the good Gotama say about this?" Translation by Rhys Davids (1969, 341). On that claim, see Gombrich (1992, 163–164). In the MaS, M.N. II 84, the Buddha qualifies that claim as follows: *ghoso yeva kho eso, mahārāja, lokasmiṃ...* "Sire, this is only a sound in the world..." Translation by Horner (1970, 273). In the AgS, D.N. III 81, the Buddha says that in speaking this way, the Brahmins do not remember the past; see Gombrich (1992, 164) and Collins (1993, 350).

63 For the Buddhist accounts of the *Puruṣasūkta*, see notes 100–101, pp. 42–43, below.

1.3.1 In presenting Brahmins as people who justify the pride that they take in their caste by their having a Brahmin father and mother, Śākyabuddhi, Śāntarakṣita, Kamalaśīla and Prajñākaragupta re-enact the statements of the young Brahmin Bhāradvāja who, as we saw from the VāS, took birth and the purity of ancestry as constitutive elements of brahmanity.

1.3.1.1 In the Brahmanic world, birth governs an important complex of symbols and rituals. As a biological event, it is uniformly considered impure, notably at the time of conception (*jananāśauca*) and delivery (*sūtikāśauca*). It requires, for that reason, the performance of purification sacraments pertaining to the body (*deha-* or *śarīra-saṃskāra*). The relation between biological birth and purification sacraments is therefore conceived as one of continuity and interdependence. That is what allows the *Manusmṛti* (MS II 27) to declare: "By fire oblations during gestation, by the birth ritual, the tonsure ritual and the investiture with the sacred thread made of *muñja* grass, the seminal and uterine fault is removed for the twice-born."[64] Note also that MS V 135 lists sperm and blood among the human body's twelve impurities. Commenting on MS II 27, Medhātithi in fact adds: "The fault [of semen and blood] is the invisible sin, the cause of suffering."[65] Vijñāneśvara also stresses, in his *Mitākṣarā* to *Yājñavalkya Smṛti* I 13, that the fault due to semen and the uterus is "connected with sperm and blood."[66] MS II 26 therefore states: "For the twice-born, the sacrament pertaining to the body must be performed with the holy Vedic rites."[67] Medhātithi comments that passage as follows: "[The expression] 'for the twice-born' has for its purpose the exclusion of *śūdras*. And this is indicating

---

[64] MS II 27: *gārbhair homair jātakarmacauḍamauñjībandhanaiḥ / baijikaṃ gārbhikaṃ caino dvijānām apamṛjyate //.*

[65] Medhātithi (I 119.9) on MS II 27: *enaḥ pāpam adṛṣṭaṃ duḥkhakāraṇam /.*

[66] Vijñāneśvara (4.25) on YS I 13: *śukraśoṇitasambaddham.*

[67] MS II 26ac: *vaidikaiḥ karmabhiḥ puṇyair... dvijanmanām / kāryaḥ śarīrasaṃskāraḥ.*

who must be consecrated. Further, in a secondary sense (*lakṣaṇayā*), intended [by that expression] are members of the [first] three classes. For at that time [i.e., before the consecration], they are not [yet] twice-born."[68]

As those key passages indicate, an unresolved tension thus seems to persist between the claim that brahmanity is acquired by birth (caste and pre-qualification) and the conception that full brahmanity is acquired through sacraments (those of the twice-born and the socio-religious rights and duties). Buddhists will not fail to capitalize on that tension.[69]

In a passage from the AsS, for example, the Buddha gives the following reply to a young Brahmin reciting the verse on the origination of Brahmins in Brahma: "But, Assalāyana, Brahmin wives of Brahmins are known to have their seasons and to conceive and to give birth and to give suck. Yet these Brahmins, born of women like everyone else, speak thus..."[70] That reply

---

68 Medhātithi (I 118.23–24) on MS II 26: *dvijanmanām iti śūdraparyudāsārtham / saṃskāryanirdeśaś cāyam / lakṣaṇayā ca traivarṇikāḥ pratīyante / na hi tadānīṃ dvijanmāno bhavanti /.*

69 Numerous interesting comments on that issue can be found in Kapani (1992, 148–150). The tension seems to subsist between pre-qualification ("birth in such and such a caste, gender, age and the nature of the marriage between the parents constitute the pre-qualification"; English translation of Kapani 1992, 149) and qualification (*adhikāra*). Several legal sources insist on the fact that the newborn is similar to a *śūdra*. "Birth in a pure caste is determining, but not sufficient. One is not born a twice-born, but becomes a twice-born with the sacraments, notably the investiture with the sacred thread (*upanayana*). Inversely, a *śūdra*, since he does not have access to the investiture with the sacred thread, remains in the same caste (*ekajāti*) all his life" (English translation of Kapani 1992, 149). The question asked in the passages here discussed could be formulated as follows: does one become a Brahmin by birth or through the sacraments? Schematically, the critique is as follows: if it is by birth, the sacraments are useless; if it is through the sacraments, every human can be a Brahmin.

70 AsS, M.N. II 148: *dissante kho pana, Assalāyana, brāhmaṇānaṃ brāhmaṇiyo utuniyo pi gabbhiniyo pi vijāyamānā pi pāyamānā pi; te ca brāh-*

will be echoed in the works of Śākyabuddhi and Kamalaśīla. It is found also in the ŚKA and the KDAM: "But your pre-eminence is not justified [merely] by your self-elevation. For indeed, everything that is born from the womb is produced by sperm and blood."[71] In developing the biological argumentation, those passages serve to remind Brahmins that regardless of the genealogies in which they take pride, they are nonetheless born of sperm and blood, like any other human, in the woman's breast. The ŚKA spells this out very clearly: "The Brahmin indeed does not arise from space or from the wind, nor is he born from splitting the ground, like fire (*jātavedas*) from kindling-wood. [No], Brahmins are born from the womb, and *caṇḍālas* are also born from the womb. So what reason do you see, [oh Puṣkarasārin], for [the alleged] pre-eminence [of the first] and wickedness [of the latter]?"[72] Since the biology and obstetric of a Brahmin woman are the same as those of women belonging to other classes or castes, the child to whom she gives birth, from blood and sperm, is just as impure as any other. This means that Brahmins, who are born of blood and sperm in a womb that is polluted by its proximity to urine and feces, as is said in the MS, cannot enjoy any privilege due to their birth.

maṇā, yonijā va samānā, evaṃ āhaṃsu... Translation by Rhys Davids (1969, 341).

71 KDAM, p. LIX, verse 197: *na hy ātmanaḥ samutkarṣāc chreṣṭhatvam iha yujyate / śukraśoṇitasambhūtaṃ yonijaṃ sarvam eva hi //*. ŚKA M41.9–10/CN636.14–16: *na hy ātmanaḥ samutkarṣāc chreṣṭhatvam iha yujyate / śukraśoṇitasambhūtaṃ yonito hy ubhayaṃ samam //*.

72 ŚKA M18.14–17/CN623.16–19: *na hi brāhmaṇa ākāśān maruto vā samutthitaḥ / bhittvā vā pṛthivīṃ jāto jātavedā yathāraṇeḥ // brāhmaṇā yonito jātāś caṇḍālā api yonitaḥ / śreṣṭhatve vṛṣalatve ca kiṃ vā paśyasi kāraṇam //*. The ŚKA M18.18–19/CN623.19–20 goes on: *brāhmaṇo 'pi mṛtotsṛṣṭo jugupsyo 'śucir ucyate / varṇās tathaiva cāpy anye kā nu tatra viśeṣatā //*. "And just like the [members of] other classes, the Brahmin, when he is abandoned to death, is said also to be impure and [therefore] an object of disgust: what is then the difference between them?"

1.3.1.2 The Brahmins depicted in Buddhist sources see a privilege in their being born from Brahmin parents or from Prajāpati's mouth. But as pointed out in the KDAM, this in itself is a refutation of the hypothesis that brahmanity can be acquired through sacraments. For indeed, if Brahmins were born from Brahma, they would not become Brahmins through the sacraments prescribed by dharma.[73] Prior to Śāntarakṣita, Kamalaśīla and Prajñākaragupta, the VSū and the KDAM had already developed a specific argument against the hypothesis that brahmanity results from the sacraments. In brief, the VSū's reply to the Brahmin who claims to come from Prajāpati's mouth is that Brahmins are so numerous that we do not know *which ones* can *legitimately* pride themselves of such ancestry. For we find Brahmins even among people of lower status, such as fishermen and *caṇḍālas*, since some of them received the sacraments and were consequently conferred the denomination of Brahmins.[74] Since those individuals became Brahmins through sacraments and not upon birth, they cannot legitimately be said to be "born

---

73 KDAM, p. LIX, verse 158cd: *brāhmaṇā brahmajā naivaṃ dharmasaṃskārajāḥ khalu //*. "In reality, [insofar as they are] born from Brahma, Brahmins are thus not born [as Brahmins] through the sacraments of dharma."

74 VSū 224.1–4: *atrocyate / brāhmaṇā bahavaḥ / na jñāyate*[1] *ke te*[2] *mukhato jātā brāhmaṇā iti / iha hi kaivartarajakacaṇḍālakuleṣv api*[3] *brāhmaṇāḥ santi / teṣām api cūḍākaraṇamuñjadantakāṣṭhādisaṃskārāḥ*[4] *kriyante / teṣām api brāhmaṇasañjñā kriyate / tasmād brāhmaṇavat kṣatriyādayo 'pīti paśyāma ekavarṇo nāsti cāturvarṇyam iti //*. Variant readings (Dvivedī 1985, 28): 1: *jñāyante*; 2: *kuto*; 3: unsure reading: °*kuleṣv api* against Weber's °*kuleṣṭvapi*; 4: °*daṇḍakāṣṭhādibhiḥ saṃskārāḥ*. "To this we answer that Brahmins being numerous, we do not know which ones among those Brahmins are [really] born from [Brahma's] mouth. In this world, indeed, there are Brahmins even in families of fishermen, washermen or *caṇḍālas*. The sacraments of tonsure, [of investiture with the thread made of] *muñja* grass, of the toothpicks, etc., are also given to those [men] and the name 'Brahmin' is [thus] also given to them. Therefore, since classes such as the *kṣatriyas* are as [questionable] as the Brahmins, we see that [there is only] one class, [and that] there is no fourfold division into classes."

from Prajāpati's mouth." So there are, in the world, individuals reputed to be Brahmins even though they were not born from Prajāpati's mouth. The KDAM reproduces that argument and concludes: "Consequently, one cannot become a Brahmin merely through bodily sacraments. Otherwise (*vā*), if one were a twice-born due to rituals (*saṃskṛta*), even a *śūdra* who has been consecrated would be twice-born, [i.e., a Brahmin]."[75]

1.3.1.3 On the one hand, the Brahmin's biological birth, which is impure and due to sperm and blood *like that of any human*, therefore prevents him from claiming any pre-eminence. On the other hand, his second birth, which is ritualistic and symbolic, also does not guarantee his brahmanity since *many other humans*, such as fishermen and *caṇḍālas*, also receive bodily sacraments. To use a vocabulary that is not yet found in those texts, the evidence is found alternatively in all or in some of the dissimilar instances to the property to be proved.[76]

---

[75] KDAM, p. LXI, verse 211: *tan na śarīrasaṃskāramātreṇa brāhmaṇo bhavet / saṃskṛtena dvijo vā cec chūdro 'pi saṃskṛto dvijaḥ //*.

[76] Several other arguments from the VSū, the ŚKA and the KDAM belong to that *structural type*. This is the case, notably, of the critique of the hypotheses that attempt to make brahmanity legitimate by appealing to the criteria of (1) knowledge (*jñāna*), (2) conduct (*ācāra*), (3) activity (*karman*) and (4) the Veda.

(1) VSū 220.19–20: *jñānam api brāhmaṇo na bhavati / kutaḥ / jñānabāhulyāt / ye ye jñānavantaḥ śūdrās te sarva eva brāhmaṇāḥ syuḥ / dṛśyante ca kvacic chūdrā api vedavyākaraṇamīmāṃsāsāṅkhyavaiśeṣikalagnajīvikā*[1]*disarvaśāstravidaḥ*[2] (/) *na ca te brāhmaṇāḥ syuḥ / ato manyāmahe jñānam api brāhmaṇo na bhavati /*. Variant readings (Dvivedī 1985, 13): 1: °*lagnājīvakā*° (Dvivedī taking *lagna* as the Hindi *jyotiṣ* and *ājīvaka* as the adepts of Makkhali Gosāla, whereas Weber takes *lagnajīvikā* to mean "astrology"; I follow Dvivedī's reading of *ājīvika*, but I am tempted to read *nagna* instead of *lagna*, based on the immediate context); 2: °*sarvaśāstrārthavidaḥ* (knowers of the subjects of all the treatises). "Neither is the Brahmin his knowledge. Why is that? Because knowledge is widely distributed (*jñānabāhulyāt*). [And if this were the case], all the *śūdras* possessing knowledge would be Brahmins. Now, in some cases, *śūdras* are also found who know all the sciences (*śāstra*) such as the Veda, grammar, the Mīmāṃsā, the Sāṅkhya,

the Vaiśeṣika, astrology [/those of the Jains] and [those of] the Ājīvikas's, etc. Those [*śūdras*], however, should not be [considered] Brahmins. Consequently, in our opinion, neither is the Brahmin his knowledge." KDAM, p. LXIII, verses 228cd–230ab: *jñānena yadi vā vipraḥ śūdro 'pi brāhmaṇo bhavet // anye 'pi bahavaḥ santi sakaivartādinīcajā jñānavantaś ca / ye dhīrās te 'pi syur brāhmaṇāḥ khalu // tasmāc ca jñānamātreṇa brāhmaṇo na bhavet khalu /*. "Or if one were a Brahmin because of knowledge, a *śūdra* also could be a Brahmin. Now, there are many other people who are of low birth, down to fishermen, and [yet] possess knowledge. Certainly, those who are erudites (*dhīra*, < PED) would also be Brahmins. And that is why the Brahmin cannot in reality be [a Brahmin] merely because of knowledge." See also the ŚKA, where the argument is related to the question of the origin of humanity (see below). It begins as follows (M41.19–20/CN636.23–24): *teṣāṃ ca jātisāmānyād brāhmaṇe kṣatriye tathā / atha vaiśye ca śūdre ca samaṃ jñānaṃ pravartate //*. "And since they are similar with respect to birth, the same knowledge occurs in the Brahmin and the *kṣatriya*, and also in the *vaiśya* and the *śūdra*." Triśaṅku the Mātaṅgarāja then gives a list of what is known by the people of his class, among which we find the *Ṛgveda, Yajurveda, Sāmaveda* and *Atharvaveda*, as well as the epics (*itihāsa*) and the Vedic glossaries (*nighaṇṭa*).

(2) VSū 221.1–4: *ācāro 'pi brāhmaṇo na bhavati / kutaḥ / yady ācāro brāhmaṇaḥ syāt tadā ye ya ācāravantaḥ śūdrās te sarve brāhmaṇāḥ syuḥ / dṛśyante ca naṭabhaṭakaivartabhaṇḍaprabhṛtayaḥ pracaṇḍataravividhācāravanto na ca te brāhmaṇā bhavanti / tasmād ācāro 'pi brāhmaṇo na bhavati /*. "Neither is the Brahmin his conduct. Why is that? [Because] if the Brahmin were his conduct, all the *śūdras* having conduct would be Brahmins. Moreover, actors, mercenaries, fishermen, buffoons, etc., are seen as having various conducts that are extremely passionate, and yet they are not Brahmins. That is why the Brahmin is neither his conduct." KDAM, p. LXIII, verses 233cd–236: *nāpi svācāramātreṇa brāhmaṇāḥ syus tathā narāḥ // yadi svācārato vipraḥ sarve syur brāhmaṇāḥ khalu / ye ye svācāravantaś ca te te syur brāhmaṇāḥ kila // santi ca bahavaḥ śūdrāḥ śuddhācārasamanvitāḥ / vratopavāsadharmiṣṭhā nīcajā api santi ca / te 'pi syur brāhmaṇāś caivaṃ yady ācārapramāṇatā / tasmād ācāramātreṇa brāhmaṇā naiva mānuṣāḥ //*. "Neither could men be Brahmins merely because of good conduct (*svācāra*), [for] if [one were] a Brahmin (*vipra*) because of [one's] good conduct, all [men] could in fact be Brahmins, and all [men] having good conduct would certainly be Brahmins. Now, there are many *śūdras* endowed with pure conduct, and there are also [men] of vile birth who are very virtuous due to religious observances and fast-

ing. Those [men] also should be Brahmins if conduct were, in this way, the criterion [of brahmanity]. That is why humans are not Brahmins merely because of [their] conduct."

(3) VSū 221.5–7: *karmāpi brāhmaṇo na bhavati / kutaḥ / dṛśyante hi kṣatriyavaiśyaśūdrā yajanayājanādhyayanādhyāpanadānapratigraha-prasaṅgavividhāni*[1] *karmāṇi kurvanto na ca te brāhmaṇā bhavatāṃ sammatāḥ / tasmāt karmāpi brāhmaṇo na bhavati /*. Variant reading: 1: °*prasaṅgavividhāni* (Dvivedī 1985, 13), against Weber °*prasaṅgādi-vividhāni*. "Neither is the Brahmin the activity [that he practises]. Why is that? Because *kṣatriyas*, *vaiśyas* and *śūdras* are found to practise various activities connected with sacrifice [for oneself, performing] sacrifice [for others], studying the Veda, teaching the Veda, giving, receiving, and you do not consider them to be Brahmins. Consequently, the Brahmin is neither the activity [that he practises]." KDAM, p. LXIII, verses 231cd–233ab: *karmaṇā vai dvijāś caivaṃ sarve syur brāhmaṇāḥ khalu / santi hi bahavo loke mahāyajñādikarmiṇaḥ kṣatriyavaiśyaśūdrāś ca / kathaṃ na brāhmaṇā nu te // tasmān na karmamātreṇa brāhmaṇāḥ syur narāḥ khalu /*. "And [if] Brahmins were [Brahmins] precisely because of the activitiy [that they practise], all [men] could indeed be Brahmins. For there are many [people] in the world who partake in activities such as great sacrifices, etc., and who are *kṣatriyas*, *vaiśyas* and *śūdras*. Why are they not Brahmins? That is why men cannot in reality be Brahmins merely because of their activities."

(4) VSū 221.8–11: *vedenāpi brāhmaṇo na bhavati / kasmāt / rāvaṇo nāma rākṣaso 'bhūt / tenādhītāś catvāro vedā ṛgvedo yajurvedaḥ sāmavedo 'tharvavedaś ceti / rākṣasānām api gṛhe gṛhe vedavyavahāraḥ pravartata eva / na ca te brāhmaṇāḥ syuḥ / ato manyāmahe vedenāpi brāhmaṇo na bhavatīti /*. "Neither is the Brahmin [a Brahmin] through the Veda. Why is that? There [once] was a demon named Rāvaṇa. He had learned the four Vedas, i.e., the *Ṛgveda*, the *Yajurveda*, the *Sāmaveda* and the *Atharvaveda*. Therefore, even demons, from household to household, have commerce with the Veda. Now, those [demons] should not be [called] Brahmins. Consequently, in our opinion, the Brahmin is neither [a Brahmin] through the Veda." KDAM, p. LXIII–LXIV, verses 237–239: *vedenāpi tathā naiva brāhmaṇāḥ syur narottamāḥ / yadi vedair bhaved vipro rākṣaso 'pi dvijaḥ khalu // tathā 'bhūd rāvaṇo nāma rākṣaso vedapāragaḥ / sarve 'pi rākṣasāś caivaṃ vedakarmānucārakāḥ // kathaṃ te brāhmaṇā naiva yadi vedād dvijo bhavet / tasmāc ca vedamātreṇa naiva syur brāhmaṇāḥ khalu //*. "Even through the Veda, Brahmins would still (*tathā*) not be the best of men. [For] if [one were] a Brahmin (*vipra*) through the Vedas, even a demon could in fact be a Brahmin. Thus there [once] was a demon named Rāvaṇa who had

1.3.2 According to the norm established by Brahmanic legislators, one further necessary condition of brahmanity is the purity of Brahmanic ancestry over seven generations. One will recall that this was also Bhāradvāja's assertion in the VāS. We must however look at the AsS for a Buddhist critique of that justification, a critique that Śāntarakṣita, Kamalaśīla and Prajñākaragupta will develop anew.

In the AsS, the Buddha first presses Assalāyana with embarrassing questions before telling him the story of a meeting between seven Brahmin seers (*ṛṣi*) and the seer Asita Devala. Upon hearing that seven Brahmins who had retired in their leaf-huts were taking pride in their brahmanity, Asita Devala decided to visit them. Now as the Brahmins tried to humiliate him, Asita Devala became all the more beautiful and this led the Brahmins to doubt the powers they had acquired through practising austerities and chastity.[77] At that point, Asita Devala revealed his celebrated identity and the seven Brahmins paid him respect. Asita Devala then asked them about the ancestral purity in which they took pride and seven questions sufficed to shatter that pride. The first four questions formed a single theme: the Brahmins were asked if they knew whether their mothers as well as the mothers of their mothers had consorted only with Brahmin men, then if they knew whether their fathers as well as the fathers of their fathers had consorted only with Brahmin women.[78] Since the seven seers all answered by the negative, they had to confess their ignorance about their identity.[79]

---

completely mastered the Veda. And all the demons likewise follow the Vedic rituals (*vedakarman*). How could they not be Brahmins if [one were] a Brahmin through the Veda? And that is why Brahmins cannot in reality be [Brahmins] merely through the Veda."

77 AsS, M.N. II 156: *atha kho, Assalāyana, sattānaṃ brāhmaṇisīnaṃ etam ahosi: mogham vata no tapo, aphalaṃ brahmacariyaṃ.* "Then, Assalāyana, it occurred to the seven brahman seers: 'Vain is austerity for us, fruitless the Brahma-faring...'." Translation by Rhys Davids (1969, 348).

78 AsS, M.N. II 156: *jānanti pana bhonto yā janīmātā brāhmaṇaṃ yeva agamāsi no abrāhmaṇaṃ ti?* "But do you, sirs, know whether their

The embarrassment of the Brahmins portrayed in that story betrays their lack of means to prove the purity of their ancestry and, therefore, their uncertainty about their own brahmanity. In the language of Buddhist epistemologists (Śāntarakṣita, Kamalaśīla, Prajñākaragupta), by objecting to personal credibility (*āp-*

---

mothers consorted only with brahmans, not with non-brahmans?" *jānanti pana bhonto yā janīmātu mātā yāvā sattamā mātāmahayugā brāhmaṇaṃ yeva agamāsi no abrāhmaṇaṃ ti?* "And do you, sirs, know whether their mothers' mothers back through seven generations consorted only with brahmans, not with non-brahmans?" *jānanti pana bhonto yo janīpitā brāhmaṇiṃ yeva agamāsi no abrāhmaṇin ti?* "And do you, sirs, know whether their fathers consorted only with brahman women, not with non-brahman women?" *jānanti pana bhonto yo janīpitu pitā yāva sattamā pitāmahayugā brāhmaṇiṃ yeva agamāsi no abrāhmaṇin ti?* "And do you, sirs, know whether their fathers' fathers back through seven generations consorted only with brahman women, not non-brahman women?" Translation by Rhys Davids (1969, 348–349).

79 AsS, M.N. II 157: *evaṃ sante, bho, na mayaṃ jānāma keci mayaṃ homāti.* "This being so, sir, we do not know who we are." Translation by Rhys Davids (1969, 349). Immediately after that passage occurs the famous argument about the being to be reborn (*gandhabba/gandharva*) at the time of conception, i.e., about the passage from the intermediate state of existence (*antarābhava = gandharva*) to rebirth (*upapattibhava*). It is discussed extensively in the AKBh III 10–15b (summarized in Franco 1997, 69–71). See Harvey (1995, 89–108) for the Pali material. In the Pali version, the passage of the AsS says that we do not know whether the being to be reborn is a Brahmin, *kṣatriya, vaiśya* or *śūdra* (AsS, M.N. II 157): *idha mātāpitaro va sannipatitā honti, mātā ca utunī hoti, gandhabbo va paccupaṭṭhito hoti; evaṃ tinnaṃ sannipātā gabbhassa avakkanti hotīti. jānanti pano bhonto yagghe so gandhabbo khattiyo vā brāhmaṇo vā vesso vā suddo vā ti? na mayaṃ, bho, jānāma yagghe so gandhabbo khattiyo vā brāhmaṇo vā vesso vā suddo vā ti.* "'There is here a coitus of the parents, it is the mother's season and the *gandhabba* is present; it is on the conjunction of these three things that there is conception.' 'But do you, sirs, know whether that *gandhabba* is a noble or a brahman or a merchant or a worker?' 'We do not know, sir, whether that *gandhabba* is a noble or a brahman or a merchant or a worker.'" Translation by Rhys Davids (1969, 349). The Sanskrit version of the *Āśvalāyanasūtra* mentioned in the AKBh III 12c also asks if the being to be reborn comes from the east, the south, the west or the north.

tatva), the Mīmāṃsaka Brahmin who denies all perception of supersensible things no longer has any means of valid cognition (*pramāṇa*) at his disposal to justify his genealogical purity.

1.3.3 The preceding arguments were objections to the Brahmanic justifications based on direct blood filiation. But as Renou points out, "added to that limited filiation is the ill-defined filiation of the lineage (*gotra*),"[80] a filiation according to which "every man of a high caste is supposed to be the descendant of such and such old sage."[81] Buddhists will therefore develop a new argumentative strategy to undermine the appeal to lineage, one that partially imitates the preceding strategy, but consists mainly in casting doubt on the brahmanity of the lineages' founding seers. The AmbS, a text that illustrates the pride of caste so disparaged by Buddhists, is the archetype of their polemic on lineages. We shall encounter the same argument in Candrakīrti's works.

Like Yaśas, the minister of Aśoka depicted in other sources,[82] the young Brahmin Ambaṭṭha portrayed in the AmbS only sees vile men of low birth in the Buddhist order (*saṅgha*). This leads

---

80 English translation of Renou (1950, 135).

81 English translation of Renou (1950, 135). There are several interesting passages on lineage in the ŚKA, notably ŚKA M39.9–40.12/CN635.7–25, where Triśaṅku lists seven lineages (*gautamāḥ, vātsyāḥ, kautsyāḥ* [M *kautsnāḥ*], *kauśikāḥ, kāśyapāḥ, vāsiṣṭhāḥ* and *māṇḍavyāḥ*), which are in turn divided into seven subdivisions, so that we get a total of 49 lineages (*ekonapañcāśad gotrāṇi*). See Sharma (1985, 84–87) for an overview of the question. For an extensive Buddhist list of Vedic seers, see MMVR 256.13–257.6.

82 This is notably the case of the sixteenth story of the KM, where Yaśas declares, upon seeing Aśoka honouring the Buddha's disciples: "The religious mendicants come from various castes to enter the religious life. They are not *kṣatriyas* or Brahmins; they are *vaiśyas* and *śūdras*, tanners and weavers, people whose job it is to build bricks and tiles, barbers and hairdressers. There are even vile *caṇḍālas* and others also. Why does the great king honour them?" English translation of Huber (1908, 91). An abridged version of that story appears in the *Divyāvadāna* CN382.4–384.23; see Lüders (1926, 145–147).

the Buddha to ask him: "Ambaṭṭha, what is your lineage?"[83] Ambaṭṭha answers that he is from the Kaṇhāyana lineage, which goes back to the seer Kaṇha, the Black one (= Skt. Kṛṣṇa, so probably the Kārṣṇāyana lineage). The Buddha therefore tells him the story of his alleged ancestor. The seer in that story is the son of Disā, a slave-girl (*dāsī*) of the Sakya king Okkāka. Disā had given birth to a son, a "little black thing" (*kaṇha*, Rhys Davids), who asked his mother immediately after his birth to wash the dirt (*aśuci*) from his body. Now in those days, says the Buddha, people did not speak of demons (*pisāca*), but of *kaṇha* ("a black fellow," Rhys Davids).[84] Those who assisted to the delivery, dumbfounded at the sight of a newborn who spoke as soon as he was born, therefore called him a "*kaṇha.*" This would be the origin of the Kaṇhāyana of which Ambaṭṭha is a descendant by his lineage.[85] But the story continues. For the Brahmins who accompany Ambaṭṭha now despise him. The Buddha then tells how Kaṇha, the son of the slave, later became a powerful seer (*uḷāro isi*). The young Kaṇha would in fact have gone in the Dekkan, where he would have learned the sacred formulas (*brahme mante*) before returning to king Okkāka to ask for his permission to marry his daughter Maddarūpī. When the king and his ministers declined his request because of his low birth, Kaṇha

---

83 AmbS, D.N. I 92: *kathaṃgotto 'si Ambaṭṭhāti?*

84 AmbS, D.N. I 93: *yathā kho pana Ambaṭṭha etarahi manussā pisāce pisācā ti sañjānanti, evam eva kho Ambaṭṭha tena samayena manussā pisāce pi Kaṇhā ti sañjānanti.* "Now just as now, Ambaṭṭha, people call devils 'devils', so then they called devils 'black fellows' (*kaṇhe*)." Translation by Rhys Davids (1969, 115).

85 AmbS, D.N. I 93: *tadagge kho pana Ambaṭṭha Kaṇhāyanā paññāyanti. so ca Kaṇhāyanānaṃ pubbapuriso. iti kho te Ambaṭṭha porāṇaṃ mātāpettikaṃ nāmagottaṃ anussarato ayyaputtā Sakyā bhavanti, dāsiputto tvam asi Sakyānan ti.* "And that is the origin, Ambaṭṭha, of the Kaṇhāyanas. He was the ancestor of the Kaṇhāyanas. And thus it is, Ambaṭṭha, that if one were to follow up your ancient name and lineage, on the father's and the mother's side, it would appear that the Sākyas were once your masters, and that you are the offspring of one of their slave girls." Translation by Rhys Davids (1969, 115).

exposed them to a strong and frightening magic spell, and the king finally accepted to let his daughter Maddarūpī marry him.

This story is significant in several respects. For once, the Brahmin Ambaṭṭha Kaṇhāyana claims to be a descendant of the seer Kaṇha, who according to the Buddha is the son of a slave-girl of the Sakyas, the Buddha's own *kṣatriya* clan.[86] In terms of his direct heredity, the founding seer of the lineage was therefore not a Brahmin and, according to the mixture of classes (*varṇasaṅkara*) theory, *he could not have been one*. Kaṇha only *became* a Brahmin upon learning the Vedic mantras.[87] Finally, once again according to Brahmanic theory, since he married the *kṣatriya* woman Maddarūpī, Kaṇha/Kṛṣṇa could not have had Brahmin children. In other words, whether we look at Kaṇha/Kṛṣṇa's parents or offspring, there is not, and there cannot be, any legitimate Brahmin in his lineage.[88]

The strategy introduced in the AmbS to dismiss the appeal to lineage will be used repeatedly in the VSū, the ŚKA and the KDAM, which are less narrative, but more radical. In order to refute the hypothesis according to which birth makes one a Brahmin, the VSū first considers the motherly ancestry of many legendary persons, including some famous seers. True to its own method,[89]

---

86 On this point, however, see Gombrich (1988, 49–50).

87 See section 1.4, p. 49, below.

88 The dharma literature seems to have foreseen such cases since it spells out the rules for reintegration of caste. In order for the descendance of such a marriage to fully regain its brahmanity, all future children, over the next seven generations, must be born of Brahmin fathers and mothers.

89 That method and its principle are described at VSū 218.3–4: *vedāḥ pramāṇaṃ smṛtayaḥ pramāṇaṃ dharmārthayuktaṃ vacanaṃ pramāṇam / yasya pramāṇaṃ na bhavet pramāṇaṃ kas tasya kuryād vacanaṃ pramāṇam //*. "The Vedas are a means of valid cognition, the *Smṛtis* are a means of valid cognition, [every] statement conform to the [religious] Law and to [worldly] interests is a means of valid cognition; [but] who could make into a means of valid cognition the words of [the person] for whom a [genuine] means of valid cognition would not be a means of valid cognition?" The originality of the VSū rests on the fact

the VSū appeals to the authority of the *Smṛti* (*smṛtiprāmāṇya*), from which it quotes (or pretends to quote) four (unidentified) verses.[90] While many genealogies seem to be more or less fanciful etymological derivations, such as Kauśika who would have been born from *kuśa* grass, Kapila from a brown cow (*kapilā*) and Tittiri from a partridge (*tittirī*), Vyāsa is presented in the VSū as the son of a fisherwoman (*kaivartinī*), Viśvāmitra the son of a *caṇḍāla* woman (*caṇḍālī*) and Kauśika the son of a *śūdra* woman (*śūdrikā*). Farther,[91] the VSū returns to the genealogies

---

that it quotes or pretends to quote, against the Brahmins and their assertions, some texts that are granted a normative value by the Brahmins themselves.

90 VSū 219.13–22, and verses 6–9: *jātir api brāhmaṇo na bhavati / kasmāt / smṛtiprāmāṇyāt / uktaṃ hi smṛtau / hastinyām acalo jāta ulūkyāṃ keśapiṅgalaḥ / agastyo 'gastipuṣpāc ca kauśikaḥ kuśasambhavaḥ // kapilaḥ kapilājātaḥ*[1] *śāligulmāc*[2] *ca gautamaḥ / droṇācāryas tu kalaśāt tittiris tittirīsutaḥ // reṇukā 'janayad rāmam ṛṣyaśṛṅgamuniṃ mṛgī / kaivartiny ajanad*[3] *vyāsaṃ kauśikaṃ*[4] *caiva śūdrikā // viśvāmitraṃ ca caṇḍālī vasiṣṭhaṃ caiva urvaśī / na teṣāṃ brāhmaṇī mātā lokācārāc ca brāhmaṇāḥ / ataḥ smṛtiprāmāṇyāj jātis*[5] *tāvad brāhmaṇo na bhavati /*. Variant readings (Dvivedī 1985, 8): 1: *kapilāj jātaḥ*; 2: *śaragulmāc*; 3: *ajanayad*; 4: *kuśikaṃ*; 5: *ataḥ smṛtiprāmāṇyān manyāmahe jātis*. "Neither is the Brahmin his birth. Why is that? [This is not the case] on the authority of the *Smṛti*. Indeed, it is said in the *Smṛti*: 'Acala is born from a female elephant, Keśapiṅgala from an owl. Agastya [is born] from the *agasti* flower, and Kauśika finds its origin in the *kuśa* grass. Kapila [is born] from a brown cow, and Gautama from a clump of rice. Droṇācārya [is born] from a jar, and Tittiri is the son of a partridge. Reṇukā (Weber: "ein Sandhügel"; sand dune) gave birth to Rāma, and a female deer to Ṛṣyaśṛṅga. A fisherwoman (*kaivartinī*) begot Vyāsa, and a *śūdra* woman Kauśika. A *caṇḍāla* woman [begot] Viśvāmitra, and Urvaśī Vasiṣṭha. Their mothers were not Brahmins, and [yet those sages are known as] Brahmins because of worldy practices.' That is why, on the authority of the *Smṛti*, [to be] a Brahmin first does not consist in birth."

91 VSū 223.2–14, verses 21–26, 28. The issue, while closely related, is here slightly different (see below): *śūdro 'pi brāhmaṇo bhavati / ko hetuḥ / iha hi mānavadharme 'bhihitam / araṇīgarbhasambhūtaḥ kaṭho nāma*[1] *mahāmuniḥ / tapasā brāhmaṇo jātas tasmāj jātir akāraṇam / kaivartī*[2]*garbhasambhūto vyāso nāma mahāmuniḥ / tapasā... // urvaśī-*

---

garbhasambhūto vasiṣṭho 'pi[3] *mahāmuniḥ / tapasā... // hariṇīgarbhasambhūta ṛṣyaśṛṅgo mahāmuniḥ / tapasā... // caṇḍālīgarbhasambhūto viśvāmitro mahāmuniḥ / tapasā... // tāndūlī*[4]*garbhasambhūto nārado hi*[5] *mahāmuniḥ / tapasā... // ... na ca te brāhmaṇīputrās te ca lokasya brāhmaṇāḥ / śīlaśaucamayaṃ brahma tasmāj jātir akāraṇam //*. Compare with the KDAM, p. LI, verses 122–127: 1: *kaṭhinākhyo*; 2: *kaivarti*; 3: *vasiṣṭhākhyo*; 4: *tāṇḍūlī*; 5: *nāradākhyo*. "Even the *śūdra* becomes a Brahmin. For what reason? On this, it has indeed been said in the *Mānavadharma*: 'The great sage named Kaṭha was born from the embryo carried by kindling-wood; through his austerities, he became a Brahmin; that is why birth [as such] is not the cause [of someone being a Brahmin]. The great sage named Vyāsa was born from the embryo carried by a fisherwoman; through his austerities.... The great sage Vasiṣṭha was born from the embryo carried by Urvaśī; through his austerities.... The great sage Ṛṣyaśṛṅga was born from the embryo carried by a gazelle; through his austerities....The great sage Viśvāmitra was born from the embryo carried by a *caṇḍāla* woman; through his austerities.... The great sage Nārada was born from the embryo carried by a *tāṇḍūla* woman* (*tāṇḍūlī*); through his austerities.... Now, those [great sages] were not the sons of Brahmin women, and [still they were known as] Brahmins in the world (*lokasya*). To be a Brahmin (*brahman*) consists in morality and purity, and that is why birth [as such] is not its cause." *According to Weber's translation of *tāṇḍūlī/tāndūlī* (see also Weber 1860, 243 note 2); according to Dvivedī (1985, 24–25), *tāṇḍūlī/tāndūlī* should be understood as a slave-girl (*dāsī*), a woman who prepares rice, separates the bark from the rice through winnowing. The KDAM, p. LII, verse 128 concludes: *evam anye 'pi sarve ca ṛṣayo brahmacāriṇaḥ / tapasā brāhmaṇā bhūtā na brāhmaṇīgarbhasambhavāḥ //*. "Thus it is through their austerities that all the other seers who practised chastity became Brahmins, [but] they were not born from an embryo carried by a Brahmin woman." See also ŚKA M42.7–43.9/CN637.1–12: *asmākam āsīt puruṣā vidyāsv ākhyātapaṇḍitāḥ / maṇipuṣpāś*[1] *ca ṛṣayo bhāsvarāś ca maharṣayaḥ // samprāptā devatā-ṛddhiṃ*[2] *kiṃ cikitsasi vidyayā / aśikṣitāś*[3] *ca caṇḍālā*[4] *brāhmaṇā vedapāragāḥ // kapiñjalādyā janito*[5] *mantrāṇāṃ pāramiṅgataḥ*[6] */ na hy asau brāhmaṇīputraḥ kiṃ vā brāhmaṇa manyase // niṣādy ajanayat*[7] *kālī putraṃ dvaipāyanaṃ munim / ugraṃ tejasvinaṃ bhīṣmaṃ pañcābhijñaṃ mahātapam / na hy asau brāhmaṇīputraḥ kiṃ vā brāhmaṇa vakṣyasi // kṣatriyā reṇukā nāma jajñe*[8] *rāmaṃ mahāmunim / paṇḍitaṃ ca vinītaṃ ca sarvaśāstraviśāradam / na hy asau brāhmaṇīputraḥ kiṃ vā brāhmaṇa vakṣyasi // ye ca te manujā āsan tejasā tapasā yutāḥ / paṇḍitāś ca vinītāś ca loke ca ṛṣisammatāḥ / na hi te brāhmaṇīputrāḥ*

of many seers (here: *mahāmuni, brahmarṣi*), adding Nārada and Kaṭha to the list.[92] All are presented as having a low birth (*nīcakula*), and all *became* Brahmins through their austerities (*tapas*), their morality (*śīla*) and their purity (*śauca*). But none of those unsurpassed Brahmins had a Brahmin mother. The VSū therefore asks: "But who are the seers Kaṭha, Vyāsa, Vasiṣṭha, Ṛṣyaśṛṅga, Viśvāmitra, etc.?"[93] And it answers: "Those were [all] born from lower families, but in the world, they are [considered] Brahmins."[94]

Having considered those genealogies from the mother's side, the VSū then looks at the fatherly ancestry of Brahmins. To

---

kiṃ vā brāhmaṇa vakṣyasi //. Variant readings: 1: CN *maṇipuṣpaś*; 2: CN *devatā ṛddhiṃ*; 3: CN *avaśiṣṭāś*; 4: CN *cācaṇḍālā*; 5: CN *kapiñjalyā janitāḥ*; 6: CN *paramiṃ gatāḥ*; 7: CN *niṣādī janayet*; 8: CN *jahre*. "We [also, the Mātaṅgas], have had men who were respected erudites in the sciences, seers who were flower gems and great radiant seers who acquired the miraculous divine powers; why do you enquire about our science? Some uneducated *caṇḍālas* [became?] Brahmins who mastered the Veda: [this was the case of] a [man] who, born for example from the *cātaka* bird, became perfect in the mantras, though (*hi*) he was not the son of a Brahmin woman, unless (*kiṃ vā*) you think [otherwise], oh Brahmin! [This is the case of] a dark Niṣādī (i.e., an outcast) who gave birth to a son, the sage Dvaipāyana, a great ascetic possessed of the five powers, formidable, bright, terrible, though he was not the son of a Brahmin woman, unless you pretend (*vakṣyasi*) [otherwise], oh Brahmin! [This is the case of] a *kṣatriya* woman named Reṇukā [who] gave birth to the great sage Rāma, who was wise, accomplished and versed in all the treatises, though he was not the son of a Brahmin woman, unless you pretend [otherwise], oh Brahmin! Now those men who were at once possessed with splendour and austerities, who were learned, accomplished and considered as seers in the world, those were not, indeed, the sons of Brahmin women, unless you pretend [otherwise], oh Brahmin!"

92 On some of those genealogies and their parallel development in the epics, see Doniger and Smith (1991, 201, note on MS IX 34 and note on MS X 72).

93 VSū 223.17: *ke punas te kaṭhavyāsavasiṣṭharṣyaśṛṅgaviśvāmitraprabhṛtayo brahmarṣayaḥ* /.

94 VSū 223.17–18: *nīcakulaprasūtās te ca lokasya brāhmaṇāḥ* /.

Brahmins who would argue that a fatherly Brahmanic ancestry is sufficient to grant brahmanity,[95] the VSū first replies, as if to summarize the situation described in the AmbS: "If this were the case, even the sons of slave-girls (*dāsīputra*), [as long as they are] born of Brahmin fathers, would be Brahmins. But you yourself do not accept this."[96] Adding to the argument developed in the AsS against the claim that seven generations of Brahmins were necessary to ensure someone's genuine brahmanity, the VSū then resorts to a motif to which the philosophers will return and that will torment Kumārila. It reads as follows: "Beside, if [only] the son of a Brahmin is a Brahmin, the result is that [that son] is not [necessarily] a Brahmin since, because we find Brahmin women consort [with all kinds of men], from the Brahmin by lineage to the *śūdra*, there is a doubt (*sandeha*) about the [real] father of today's Brahmins."[97] Doubt about the real paternity of Brahmins is therefore due to women's fickleness or, as Āryadeva, Candrakīrti, Śāntarakṣita, Kamalaśīla and Prajñākara-

---

95 That position is developed in the *Mahābhārata* XIII 47.17.

96 VSū 220.1–2: *yady evaṃ dāsīputrā api brāhmaṇajanitā brāhmaṇā bhaveyuḥ / na caitad bhavateṣṭam /*. But the *Bhaddasāla Jātaka* (*Jātaka* IV 144ff), summarized in Fick (1972, 54–56[35–37]), is revealing on this point. The king of Kosala learns that his wife, on her mother's side, is of a slave ancestry (*dāsa*). Irritated by this news, he immediately destitutes her. A few days later, the Buddha comes to visit the king, who tells him the story. Then: "The master replies... that... his wife is a king's daughter and the marriage took place in the house of a khattiya king...: for—he adds—"the old wise men acted according to the principle: *the family of the mother does not matter; the family of the father alone is important* (mātigottaṃ nāma kiṃ karissati, pitigottaṃ eva pamāṇam)..." (Fick 1972, 56[36–37]).

97 VSū 220.2–5: *kiṃ ca yadi brāhmaṇaputro brāhmaṇas tarhi brāhmaṇābhāvaḥ prāpnoti / idānīntaneṣu brāhmaṇeṣu pitari sandehāt / gotrabrāhmaṇam ārabhya brāhmaṇīnāṃ śūdraparyantam abhigamadarśanāt*[1] */*. Variant reading (Dvivedī 1985, 8): 1: *śūdrābhigamanadarśanāt*.

gupta will insist,[98] to the fact that women are continuously love-sick.[99]

1.3.4.1 Buddhist texts discuss two more assertions of the Brahmins: (1) one according to which Brahmins were born from Brahma (*brahmaja*) and (2) one, directly inspired from ṚV X 90, according to which Brahmins were born from the mouth of Puruṣa or Prajāpati. The VSū and KDAM have a similar rendering of the *Puruṣasūkta* teaching that Brahmins were born from the mouth of the dismembered primeval being, *kṣatriyas* from his arms, *vaiśyas* from his thighs and *śūdras* from his feet.[100] The versions of the ŚKA and KVU are slightly different.[101]

---

[98] See sections 2.1.1.2, p. 71, and 2.5.4, p. 146, below.

[99] Contrasting with that type of argument is Buddhaghosa's interesting remark, in his commentary to the AsS (M.A. III 408), that in order to ensure a male descendance, some Brahmins appear to "marry" their wives to men of lower castes/classes. As a conclusion to that section, let it be noted also that if we agree with the MS IX 23 and Candrakīrti (see Lang 1992, 238), the seer Vasiṣṭha had a liaison with the *caṇḍāla* woman Akṣamālā. At least some of the seers were therefore not authentic Brahmins by ancestry, i.e., their genealogy was mixed, and they even perpetuated themselves the mixture of classes. On the story of Vasiṣṭha and Akṣamālā, see the interesting notes of Doniger and Smith (1991, 199, note on MS IX 23). See also Perry (1998, 469 note 44), who refers to the *Taittirīya Āraṇyaka* III 92 and the *Kāṭhaka Saṃhitā* XXXVII 10.

[100] VSū 223.21–22, verse 30: *mukhato brāhmaṇo jāto bāhubhyāṃ kṣatriyas tathā / ūrubhyāṃ vaiśyaḥ sañjātaḥ padbhyāṃ śūdraka eva ca //*. "The Brahmin was born from his mouth, the *kṣatriya* from his two arms; the *vaiśya* was born from his two thighs and the *śūdra* from his two feet." There are several variants in the KDAM, p. LXIV, verse 242 (note the Sanskrit *sambhava* and *samudbhava*, here used adjectively): *mukhato brāhmaṇo jāto bāhubhyāṃ kṣatriyaḥ smṛtaḥ / ūrubhyāṃ sambhavo vaiśyaḥ padbhyāṃ śūdraḥ samudbhavaḥ //*.

[101] ŚKA M22.16–23.2/CN625.24–626.1: *te brāhmaṇāḥ punar vṛṣala brahmaṇaḥ putrāḥ*[1] */ aurasā mukhato jātāḥ / urasto bāhutaḥ kṣatriyāḥ / nābhito vaiśyāḥ / padbhyāṃ śūdrāḥ / brahmaṇāyaṃ*[2] *khalu vṛṣala lokaḥ*[3] *sarvabhūtāni nirmitāni / tasya jyeṣṭhā vayaṃ putrāḥ kṣatriyās tadanantaram / vaiśyas tṛtīyako varṇaḥ śūdro nāma caturthakaḥ*[4] *//*. Variant

The KDAM states at once the Buddhist objection: "If this were indeed the case, the advocates of classes would commit an offence against the norms of morality (*dharmeṣu*).[102] And [since] there would be illicit intercourse between [Brahmin men and women] not to be approached (*agamyāgamana*), how then could there be religious purity (*dharmaviśuddhitā*)?"[103] The VSū, the ŚKA and the KDAM[104] clearly bring to light the disastrous consequences of the above anthropogonic assertion. The three texts

---

readings: 1: CN *brāhmaṇaputrāḥ*; 2: CN om. *ayaṃ*; 3: CN *loke*; 4: M *vaiśyās tṛtīyakā varnāḥ śūdranāmnā caturthakaḥ*. "Brahmins, oh Vṛṣala, are the sons of Brahma, his legitimate sons born from his mouth; the *kṣatriyas* [are born] from his chest, from his arms, the *vaiśyas* from his navel and *śūdras* from his two feet. In fact, this world, oh Vṛṣala, as well as all beings, were created by Brahma. We, [the Brahmins], are his eldest sons and the *kṣatriyas* [appeared] immediately after; the *vaiśya* formed the third class and the one called '*śūdra*' formed the fourth." This is the position of the Brahmin Puṣkarasārin. Note KVU 165.27–31: *kecit tatra sampratipannāḥ / brahmāsya jātiḥ / kecid ākāśyapīyaṃ pūjāḥ keṣāṃcid īśvaraḥ kartā / prajāpatinā sṛṣṭāḥ prajās tasya brāhmaṇo mukham / bāhus tu kṣatriyāḥ / ūrubhyāṃ vaiśyāḥ / padbhyāṃ śūdrāḥ / evaṃ te sampratipannāḥ /*. See the translation by Lévi (1932, 179). The first argument of the KVU covers the biological arguments (KVU 165.32–34): *ye kecana sattvā dvipadāś catuṣpadā vā teṣāṃ yonimukhān nirgamaḥ / kiṃ prāptam / prajāpatiyonicatuṣṭayaṃ ca prathamataḥ / na bhagacatuṣṭayam /*. "All bipeds or quadrupeds were born from a womb. What does that entail? First that Prajāpati has four wombs. But he does not have four sexual organs." See also the translation by Lévi (1932, 179).

102 On the plural use of *dharma*, see Halbfass (1990, 314–315 and 550 notes 22–23).

103 KDAM, p. LXIV, verse 243: *tathā ced dhi bhaved doṣo dharmeṣu varṇavādinām / agamyagamanāc caivaṃ kathaṃ dharmaviśuddhitā //*. The ŚKA, instead of speaking of *doṣo dharmeṣu*, speaks of *paśudharma*, the dharma of cattle. Triśaṅku says to Puṣkarasārin, in the ŚKA M41.11/ CN636.16–17: *cāturvarṇyaṃ pravakṣyāmi paśudharmakathāṃ tava /*. "I will tell you that the fourfold division into classes is a story of dharma of cattle." On the notion of *paśudharma*, see Halbfass (1990, 321 and 552 note 54). MS IX 66 prefers the expression *godharma*.

104 VSū 225.6–8, ŚKA M41.11–16/CN636.16–21 and KDAM, pp. LXIV–LXV, verses 242–249.

begin by asking: if Brahmin men come from the mouth of Puruṣa (or Brahma, ŚKA), what is the origin of Brahmin women?[105] To those upholders of the classes who would reply that Brahmin women were also born from the mouth of the primeval being, the texts answer that if that is the case, then Brahmin women are the sisters of Brahmin men and there follows the disastrous consequence that they are not fit to have sexual intercourse with Brahmin men since this would be an extremely serious violation of the sexual interdict of consanguinity, i.e., a violation of the rules of exogamy.[106] The VSū stops with the incestuous

---

105 VSū 225.6–7: *yadi mukhato jāto brāhmaṇo brāhmaṇyāḥ kuta utpattiḥ* /. KDAM, p. LXIV, verse 244ab: *yadi vipro mukhāj jāto brāhmaṇī kutra sambhavā* /.

106 VSū 225.7–8: *mukhād eveti ced dhanta tarhi bhavatāṃ bhaginīprasaṅgaḥ syāt (/) tathā gamyāgamyaṃ na sambhāvyate* /. "If [you answered that] it is [also] through his mouth, then there would unfortunately be the unwelcome consequence that they would be your sisters, and in this way, [the distinction between] licit and illicit intercourse (*gamyāgamya*) is no longer possible." KDAM, p. LXIV, verse 244cd: *brāhmaṇy api mukhāj jātā svasā bhāryā kathaṃ nanu* //. "[If] the Brahmin woman is also born through his mouth, how [then] is your wife not [also] your sister?" ŚKA M41.12–16/CN636.17–21: *bhavet te bhaginī bhāryā*[1] *naitad*[2] *brāhmaṇa yujyate* // *yadi tāvad ayaṃ loko brahmaṇā janitaḥ svayam* / *brāhmaṇī brāhmaṇasvasā kṣatriyā kṣatriyasvasā*[3] // *atha vaiśyasya vaiśyā vai śūdrā śūdrasya vā punaḥ* / *na bhāryā bhaginī yuktā brahmaṇā janitā yadi* //. Variant readings: 1: CN *bhaginī bhavati te bhāryā*; 2: M *caitad*; 3: CN *kṣatriyasya ca*. "Your sister would be your wife, oh Brahmin, and this is not proper! [For] if, indeed, this world was created by Brahma himself, the Brahmin woman is the Brahmin's sister, the *kṣatriya* woman is the *kṣatriya*'s sister, the *vaiśya* woman the *vaiśya*'s, and the *śūdra* woman the *śūdra*'s. But a sister is not suitable as a wife, [although this is what happens] if [the woman of each class was also] created by Brahma." See also KVU 166.16–17: *yāvad brāhmaṇaputrī brāhmaṇī yady asya mukhato jātā* / *tasmād agamyā* /. "And insofar as the Brahmin woman is Brahma's daughter* if she is born through his mouth, it is then impossible to marry her." See also the translation by Lévi (1932, 180). *Note that I have read *brāhmaṇaputrī* as *brahmaputrī*. Note that for the Buddhists, illicit intercourse (*agamyāgamana*) is the third of ten wrong modes of action leading to an unfavourable destiny (*akuśalakarmapatha*). See AK(Bh) IV 74ab.

case of Brahmin men and women, but the ŚKA and, even more so, the KDAM, draw the same conclusion about *kṣatriya*, *vaiśya* and *śūdra* women. In those three cases, the *Puruṣasūkta* and other similar anthropogonic assertions lead to an interpretation of society's empirical situation in terms of incest and transgression of sexual interdicts on consanguinity for any male Brahmin, *kṣatriya*, *vaiśya* and *śūdra* has his own sister as a wife.[107]

The KDAM presents the same argument as the ŚKA against the hypothesis that Brahmins would be born from Brahma.[108] It concludes: "A sister is not suitable as a wife. How then could there be dharma? Since in that manner there would be illicit

---

107 KDAM, p. LXIV, verses 245–247: *tathā ca kṣatriyā jātā bāhubhyām eva cet tathā / kṣatriyasya bhaved bhāryā kṣatriyā bhaginī khalu // vaiśyāpi hi tathā caivam ūrubhyām eva sambhavā / vaiśyasyāpi bhaved bhāryā vaiśyā tu bhaginī viśaḥ // padbhyāṃ jāto yathā śūdraḥ śūdrī cāpi tathodbhavā / śūdrasyāpi bhaved bhāryā śūdrī hi bhaginī khalu //*. "And just as [it is for the Brahmin man and woman], if, in the same manner, the *kṣatriya* woman were born from [Brahma's] two arms, the *kṣatriya* wife of the *kṣatriya* man would surely be his sister. Likewise, if the *vaiśya* woman were also born from [Brahma's] two thighs, the *vaiśya* wife of the *vaiśya* man would surely be the sister of the *vaiśya* man (*viś*). And [if] the *śūdra* woman also was produced in the same way as the *śūdra* man, who is born from [Brahma's] two feet, the *śūdra* wife of the *śūdra* man would surely also be his sister."

108 KDAM, pp. LIX–LX, verses 198cd–200: *brahmajā brāhmaṇā naivaṁ dharmasaṃskārajāḥ khalu // yadi vā brahmajā viprā brāhmaṇī kutra sambhavā / brāhmaṇy api tathā caiva brahmajā yadi sāmpratam // brāhmaṇasya ca sā bhāryā syāc caivedaṃ na yuktitaḥ / na bhāryā bhaginī yuktā brāhmaṇī brahmajā yadi //*. "[If] Brahmins are born from Brahma, then they are not born from the sacraments [prescribed] by dharma. Alternatively, if Brahmin men (*vipra*) are born from Brahma, where is the Brahmin woman born? Now if we hold that, as in the case [of Brahmin men], the Brahmin woman is also born from Brahma and [that] she is the Brahmin's wife, this cannot not proper (*idaṃ na yuktitaḥ*, see Speyer 1902–1909, p. LX, note 89). [For] a sister is not suitable as a wife, [yet this is what happens] if the Brahmin woman is [also] born from Brahma." VSū 224.1–4, quoted in note 74, p. 29, above, is also related to the problem of the *Puruṣasūkta*.

intercourse [between men and women], there would only be unrighteousness (*adharma*)."[109]

Now such an absurd consequence seems to be largely contradicted by facts. But if the rules of exogamy are not violated within the different classes, it is because their members do not have consanguine relations with their wives. They therefore do not share a common ancestry, neither through lineage nor through family (*kula*). And this is a contradiction of the anthropogonic assertion. The ŚKA can therefore close that discussion with the following important remark: "Beings are not born from Brahma, but are born from defilements (*kleśaja*) and actions (*karmaja*). We observe that beings, each having diverse resting-places, are now in an inferior state, now in a higher state."[110]

1.3.4.2 We can add to the above arguments one final Buddhist critique based on the original unity (*ekatva*) of Puruṣa (VSū), Brahma (ŚKA) and Prajāpati (ŚKA, KDAM); a critique that will reoccur in the work of Prajñākaragupta. For the ŚKA and the KDAM, which present a summary of the argument, nothing should distinguish the so-called castes or classes if, as is professed by Brahmins, Prajāpati were one. "The fruit we obtain is like the seed that was sown.[111] And since Prajāpati is one, he is therefore undifferentiated. And no diversity in the sense faculties, nor any difference in [bodily] operation, is observed in the Brahmin or in [members of] another class. [So] nothing distin-

---

[109] KDAM, p. LXIV, verse 248: *na yuktā bhaginī bhāryā tathā dharmaḥ katham bhavet / agamyagamanāc caivam adharma eva sambhavet //*. Or, as the VSū 225.8 has it: *tac ca loke 'tyantaviruddham /*. "And this is strongly prohibited in the world." See also KDAM, p. LXV, verse 249: *tato 'tyantaviruddhaṃ syād brahmajā brāhmaṇā yadi /*. "Therefore, if Brahmins were born from Brahma, [the resulting situation] would correspond (*syāt*) to what [you] so strongly prohibit."

[110] ŚKA M41.17–18/CN636.21–22: *na sattvā brahmaṇo jātāḥ kleśajāḥ karmajās tv amī / nīcaiś coccaiś ca dṛśyante sattvā nānāśrayāḥ pṛthak //*.

[111] Compare with KVU 166.11: *bījasadṛśaṃ phalam*. See note 114 below.

guishes them."[112] In the ŚKA, Triśaṅku opposes the same argument to the Brahmin Puṣkarasārin, who believes that Brahma is one and that the world and all living beings originated from him. But even if we were to accept that this was the case, if we also accept that inference (*anumāna*) is a means of valid cognition, we must agree that Brahma's creatures were all born in the same manner and, therefore, that they all belong to a single class. "If, oh Brahmin, inference is also a means of valid cognition for you, in that case, [it follows] from what you assert, namely that Brahma is one, that creatures are also only of one kind, and that we are also only of one kind. And [we can draw the same conclusion from] what you assert, namely that this world as well as all living beings were created by Brahma. If this [inference] is for you, oh Brahmin, a means of valid cognition, what you assert, oh you Brahmin, is incorrect, namely that there are four classes: Brahmins, *kṣatriyas*, *vaiśyas* and *śūdras*."[113] The VSū and *Karmavibhaṅgopadeśa* (KVU) use similar arguments when they ask how a fourfold division of classes could be justified of beings born from a single Puruṣa.[114] The VSū illustrates the problem as

112 ŚKA M41.5–8/CN636.11–14: *yādṛśaṃ vāpyate bījaṃ tādṛśaṃ labhyate*[1] *phalam / prajāpater*[2] *hi caikatve*[3] *nirviśeṣo bhavaty ataḥ*[4] *// na cendriyāṇāṃ*[5] *nānātvaṃ kriyābhedaś ca dṛśyate*[6] */ brāhmaṇe vānyajātau vā naiṣāṃ kiṃcid viśiṣyate //*. Compare with the KDAM, p. LIX, verses 195cd–196, and note the variant readings from CN: 1: CN *labhate*; 2: KDAM, CN *prajāpatir*; 3: CN *vaikatve*; 4: KDAM *'bhavad yataḥ*; 5: KDAM *na cendriyeṣu*, CN *sarvendriyāṇāṃ*; 6: KDAM *kriyāvādena dṛśyate*, CN *kriyāvāde na dṛśyate*. The first half-verse from the KDAM (195ab: *yādṛśaṃ sādhyate karma tādṛśī jātitā bhavet /*) has a different function and closes the preceding argument.

113 ŚKA M25.6–10/CN627.6–11: *anumānam api*[1] *te brāhmaṇa yadi pramāṇam / tatra yad bravīṣi* [2]*brahmā eka iti tasmāt prajā apy ekajātyaiva*[2] */ vayam apy ekajātyā bhavāmaḥ / yac ca bravīṣi brahmaṇāyaṃ lokaḥ sarvabhūtāni ca nirmitānīti / sacet te brāhmaṇa idaṃ pramāṇam / tad idaṃ te brāhmaṇa ayuktaṃ yad bravīṣi catvāro varṇā brāhmaṇāḥ kṣatriyā vaiśyāḥ śūdrāś ceti /*. Variant readings: 1: CN *anujānāmi*; 2: CN *brāhmaṇa ekajātya iti / tasmāt prajāpatir apy ekajātyaḥ*.

114 KVU 165.36: *katham ekapuruṣena varṇacatuṣṭayaṃ jātam /*. "How are the four castes born from a single male procreator?" See also the trans-

follows: "Moreover, how could the [individuals] born from a single father be distributed into four classes (*cāturvarṇya*)? [Let us suppose] in this case that with a single woman, a certain Devadatta gives birth to four sons. There is no distinction of class among them [on the basis of which we could say]: 'this is a Brahmin, this is a *kṣatriya*, this is a *vaiśya*, this is a *śūdra*.' Why? Because [those four sons] have a single father. How then, following the same model (*evam*), [could individuals alleged to be] Brahmins, etc., be distributed into four classes?"[115]

---

lation by Lévi (1932, 179). KVU 165.36–166.18, which is too long to be quoted in its entirety, presents many original arguments among which we will retain the following (165.36–166.4, translated in Lévi 1932, 179–180): if the four classes originate from Prajāpati, what is the origin of *caṇḍālas*, barbarians, elephants, oxen, horses, women, demons, wild animals, birds, etc.? For they are indeed not mentioned in the story. Were some of them born through his head and others through the sole of his foot, his toe or his hand? The KVU (166.4–18, translated in Lévi 1932, 180) then lists and criticizes many inconsistencies in the assertion derived from the ṚV X 90. The first argument questions the apparently contradictory idea (*pūrvāparaviruddha*, but the text is incomplete) according to which Prajāpati had four sons while each of his sons had an innumerable quantity of children. Further, each of Prajāpati's children should also have had as his offspring one Brahmin, one *kṣatriya*, one *vaiśya* and one *śūdra*. As is explained in the KVU 166.11–16: *kiṃ kāraṇam / bījasadṛśaṃ phalam / yathā prajāpateś caturvarṇam evaṃ tasya putrāṇāṃ gotrāṇāṃ ca caturvarṇaṃ bhaviṣyati / atha brāhmaṇānāṃ putrāḥ sarve brāhmaṇās tasmāt prajāpates te tu viśiṣṭatarāḥ / yadi ca te prativiśiṣṭatarāḥ prajāpatinā kiṃ prayojanam / atha matam / prajāpatinā brāhmaṇā nyūnatarā iti / tasmād brāhmaṇasya prathamaputraḥ śūdraḥ śeṣā nyūnatarāḥ /*. "Why is that? The fruit is like the seed. Just as Prajāpati had four castes [as his offsprings], his sons and lineages will have four castes [as their offprings]. But if the sons of Brahmins are all Brahmins, they are therefore superior to Prajāpati. And if they are more distinguished than Prajāpati, what is the use [of Prajāpati]? But if it is supposed that Brahmins are inferior to Prajāpati, then the first son of a Brahmin [will have to be] a *śūdra* and all the others [will be even] more inferior." See also the translation by Lévi (1932, 180).

115 VSū 224.5–8: *api ca / ekapuruṣotpannānāṃ kathaṃ cāturvarṇyam / iha kaścid devadatta ekasyāṃ striyāṃ caturaḥ putrān janayati / na ca te-*

According to those three texts, the anthropogonic assertion therefore necessarily implies a unique class since, as is said in the ŚKA, "if the Brahmin were the only one in this [world to be born from Brahma], he would have two tongues, four ears, four nipples, many feet and two heads."[116] At this point, the absurd consequences of the genealogical argument fall in line with some of the conditions set by the biological arguments.

1.4 Unstable brahmanity

1.4.1 Polemical Buddhist texts enjoy quoting or retelling some of the prescriptions and prohibitions codified in the dharma literature. That is the case of the VSū, for example. Among the norms set forth in those treatises, Buddhist authors favoured those that are linked to the prohibition of certain actions on the part of Brahmins, as well as those that concern the four "capital sins" (*mahāpātaka*) that are supposed to cause the loss of caste. For as soon as social statuses are naturalized and considered given at birth, it becomes contradictory to assert that brahmanity can be acquired[117] or lost as a result of performing certain actions. It is on this last point, the loss of brahmanity, that our texts are by far the most prolix.

The legal *Smṛtis* speak of one voice when it comes to identify the four "capital sins": murder of a Brahmin (*brahmahatyā*), absorption of liquor (*surāpāna*), theft of gold (of a Brahmin, Rocher; *stena*) and adultery with the wife of one's own guru

ṣāṃ varṇabhedo 'sty ayaṃ brāhmaṇa ayaṃ kṣatriya ayaṃ vaiśya ayaṃ śūdra iti / kasmāt / ekapitṛkatvāt / evaṃ brāhmaṇādīnāṃ kathaṃ cāturvarṇyam /.

116 ŚKA M28.8–9/CN629.11–13: *yadi brāhmaṇaḥ syād ihaika eva dvijihvaś catuḥśravaṇas*[1] *tathaiva / caturviṣāṇo bahupād dviśīrṣaḥ*[2]... Variant readings: 1: CN *dvijihvāsya catuḥśravaṇas*; 2: CN *bahupādo dviśīrṣaḥ*.

117 See especially VSū 219.2–7 and KDAM, p. XLIX, verses 107–108.

(*gurutalpa*), which is equivalent to incest![118] Those texts, including MS' systematic chapter twelve, promise hell and innumerable rebirths to those who commit those actions, including rebirth "mainly as animals, a few low types of human beings, and especially for 'the violator of a Guru's bed,' plants."[119] As many as twelve verses from the ŚKA develop an argument based on the four "capital sins."[120] The ŚKA motif is identical in every case: the Brahmin who would steal gold, and/or drink liquor, and/or commit adultery with his guru's wife, and/or murder a Brahmin, would become a non-Brahmin.[121] The text goes further, how-

---

[118] See MS XI 55ff. On those "generic" crimes and other equivalent crimes, see MS XI 55–59; on their respective expiation, see MS XI 72–90 (brahmanicide and murder of a twice-born; important remark in MS XI 90), MS XI 91–99 (intoxication; MS XI 98, decline to the level of the *śūdra*), MS XI 100–103 (stealing gold) and MS XI 104–107 (adultery and incest).

[119] Rocher (1983, 61–89). On the possible rebirths mentioned in the MS and *Yājñavalkya*, see the exhaustive tables 5 and 6 in Rocher (1983, 70–71).

[120] ŚKA M19.19–20.2/CN624.8–12: *anyac cāhaṃ pravakṣyāmi brāhmaṇair yat prakalpitam / pātakā hi samākhyātā brāhmaṇeṣu caturvidhāḥ // suvarṇacauryaṃ madyaṃ ca gurudārābhimardanam / brahmaghnatā ca catvāraḥ pātakā brāhmaṇesv amī //*. "I will expose another thing that Brahmins believe. For Brahmins, indeed, the capital sins [leading to their fall] are declared to be of four types: theft of gold, intoxication, adultery with the wife of [one's own] guru and, [finally], murdering a Brahmin. Those are, for Brahmins, the four capital sins [causing their fall]."

[121] ŚKA M20.3–12/CN624.12–20: *suvarṇaharaṇaṃ varjyaṃ steyam anyan na vidyate / suvarṇaṃ yo hared vipraḥ sa tenābrāhmaṇo*[1] *bhavet // surāpānaṃ na pātavyam anyat pānaṃ*[2] *yatheṣṭataḥ / surāṃ tu yaḥ pibed vipraḥ... // gurudārā na gantavyā anyadārā yatheṣṭataḥ / gurudārāṃ tu yo gacchet sa... // na hanyād brāhmaṇaṃ hy ekaṃ hanyād anyān anekaśaḥ / hanyāt tu brāhmaṇaṃ yo vai sa... // ity ete pātakā hy uktā brāhmaṇeṣu caturvidhāḥ / bhavanty abrāhmaṇā yena tato 'nye 'pātakāḥ smṛtāḥ //*. Variant readings: 1: M *tenābrāhmaṇaṃ*; 2: M *anyapānaṃ*. "Theft of gold is to be avoided, but there is no other theft [for a Brahmin]. The Brahmin who would [nonetheless] steal gold would by this [very fact] become a non-Brahmin. Drinking liquor is prohibited (*na pātavya*) [to the Brahmin, but all] other beverage is [permitted] as

ever, and caustically stigmatizes the bad faith of Brahmins as they appear to allow for expiating procedures (*niḥsaraṇa*).[122]

But for the normative literature, a decline and dire destiny is not only the result of committing a "capital sin." In a society where interactions are largely ruled by interdicts of purity,

---

desired. The Brahmin who would nonetheless drink liquor would by this [very fact] become a non-Brahmin. The wife of [his own] guru is not approachable [by the Brahmin] for sexual intercourse, [but] the wife of another [is accessible] as desired. He who would nonetheless have sexual intercourse with the wife of [his own] guru would by this [very fact] become a non-Brahmin. [A Brahmin] cannot kill a single Brahmin, but he can kill others in large numbers (*anekaśas*). He who would nonetheless kill a Brahmin would by this very fact become a non-Brahmin. Those [crimes] are said among the Brahmins to be the four capital sins due to which [Brahmins] become non-Brahmins, [but crimes] other than those are considered (*smṛta*) non-capital sins." And the text goes on (ŚKA M20.13–15/CN624.20–22): *kṛtvā caturṇām ekaikaṃ bhaved abrāhmaṇas tu saḥ / labhate na ca sāmīcīṃ*[1] *brāhmaṇānāṃ samāgame / āsanaṃ codakaṃ caiva vyutthānaṃ sa*[2] *na cārhati //*. Variant readings: 1: CN *sāmītiṃ/samitiṃ*; 2: CN *ca*. "But having committed only a single one (*ekaika*) of those four [capital sins leading to his fall], the [Brahmin] would become a non-Brahmin, no longer receives praises in the meeting of Brahmins, and is no longer worthy of a seat, of water and of rehabilitation (*vyutthāna*, < PED / BHSD)."

122 ŚKA M20.16–21.2/CN624.22–27: *tasya niḥsaraṇaṃ dṛṣṭaṃ brāhmaṇaiḥ patitasya tu / vrataṃ vai sa samādāya punar brāhmaṇatāṃ vrajet // asau dvādaśavarṣāṇi dhārayitvā kharājinam / khaṭvāṅgam ucchritaṃ kṛtvā mṛtaśīrṣe ca bhojanam // etad vrataṃ samādāya niścayena nirantaram / pūrṇe dvādaśame varṣe punar brāhmaṇatām vrajet /*. "Nonetheless, Brahmins foresee an expiation for the fallen [Brahmin]. He can regain his brahmanity after fulfilling a vow. Having worn for twelve years the skin of an ass, raised the staff topped with a skull (*khaṭvāṅga*) and eaten in a skull, having [therefore] fulfilled that vow, he could assuredly regain his brahmanity as soon as the twelfth year is over." The more moderate MS, *Yājñavalkya* and *Baudhāyana* notably prescribe the re-initiation (*punarupanayana*). See Kapani (1992, 150 and note 342) for references; see also MS XI; compare MS XI 73 and 106 with Doniger and Smith (1991, 261 note on MS XI 106). See note 118, p. 50, above, for references to MS. On the observance designed for caste reintegration in the case of the killer of a Brahmin, see Lorenzen (1991, 13).

Brahmins must also submit to many interdicts. Claiming to follow the authoritative Manu, the VSū and the KDAM then assert that if a *śrotriya* Brahmin were to accept the donation of a *śūdra*, he would be reborn as an ass twelve times before being reborn sixty times as a hog and seventy times as a dog.[123] And if he were to "drink" the saliva of a *vṛṣālī*, meet her sigh or have a *vṛṣālī* for mother (KDAM: sleep with her), a Brahmin could no longer expiate his fault (*niṣkṛti*). If he were to eat from a *śūdra* woman's hands, he would become a *śūdra* within one month and, after his death, would be reborn as a dog. Finally, if a Brahmin lived around *śūdra* women or had a *śūdra* for his housewife, he would be abandoned by the Manes and would go to hell.[124]

---

[123] VSū 219.8–11, verses 4–5: *adhītya caturo vedān sāṅgopāṅgena*[1] *tattvataḥ / śūdrāt pratigrahagrāhī brāhmaṇo jāyate kharaḥ // kharo dvādaśa janmāni ṣaṣṭijanmāni sūkaraḥ / śvānaḥ saptatijanmāni ity evaṃ manur abravīt //*. Compare with the KDAM, p. L, verses 112–113: 1: *°āṅgaś ca*. "Thus Manu has declared that the Brahmin who, having thoroughly learned the four Vedas with their auxiliary and secondary parts, accepts donation from a *śūdra* is born as an ass; an ass he remains for twelve lives, a hog for sixty lives and a dog for seventy lives." The Manu who is mentioned here is probably not the one from the MS, but the Manu from a *Mānavadharma(sūtra)*, which is now lost but which would have inspired the MS. On that issue, see Bronkhorst (1985).

[124] VSū 222.17–22, verses 18–20: *vṛṣālīphenapītasya niḥśvāsopahatasya ca / tatraiva*[1] *prasūtasya niṣkṛtir nopalabhyate // śūdrīhastena yo bhuṅkte māsam ekaṃ nirantaram / jīvamāno bhavec chūdro mṛtaḥ śvānaś ca jāyate*[2] *// śūdrīparivṛto vipraḥ śūdrī ca gṛhamedhinī / varjitaḥ pitṛdevena*[3] *rauravaṃ so 'dhigacchati //*. Compare with the KDAM, pp. XLIX, verses 110–111 (and p. LX, verse 208) and p. LXI, verse 209: 1: *tayaiva saha suptasya* (better and metrically correct); 2: *mṛtaś ca sa prajāyate* (111) and *mṛtaḥ sa śvā prajāyate* (208); 3: *pitṛdevaiś ca*. "No expiation is perceived for [a Brahmin] who absorbs the saliva of a *vṛṣālī*, contacts her sigh, or is born of her (VSū) / sleeps with her (KDAM). [A Brahmin] who eats in the hand of a *śūdra* woman may in his life, immediately, within one month, become a *śūdra*, and, once dead, is reborn as a dog. A Brahmin who surrounds himself with a *śūdra* woman or (*ca*) [whose] house-wife [is] a *śūdra* woman goes to hell, abandoned by the Manes and the gods." On some of those prohibitions, see MS III 12–19. See the references provided by Dvivedī (1985, 23): verse 19 refers to the *Aṅgirasa Smṛti* I 48, *Āpastamba Dharmasūtra* VIII 7 and *Vyāsa*

Following MS X 92, the VSū and the KDAM also reproduce the prescription according to which a Brahmin is immediately deprived of his status if he deals meat, lac or salt,[125] and becomes a *śūdra* within three days if he sells milk.[126] The VSū concludes—

Smṛti IV 67; verse 20 refers to the *Mahābhārata* XIII 47.9 and to the *Vyāsa Smṛti* IV 68.

125 The KM knows and criticizes also those prescriptions; KM 77: "Selling salt destroys pure conduct, and [yet] drinking or touching the water of the Ganges would be called right conduct? ... By selling meat, one is bringing every evil upon oneself. ... Selling salt destroys good conduct, while touching the river washes every sin; is selling salt therefore a great sin and touching the river a great merit? What is the reason for calling this good and that evil? If a Brahmin sells meat,* he immediately loses his caste. By handling weapons,** he also loses his caste. If he sells meat, of a mass of thirty-six pounds, he destroys his brahmanity. Selling lac and honey,*** this is also called losing one's caste." (English translation of Huber 1908, 439 and 439–440). Skt. fragments in Lüders (1926, 188/306). *See MS X 92; **see MS III 61; the *Bhūridattajātaka* no. 153 (Alsdorf 1977, 44 and 51) makes some allusion to Brahmin arms dealers; ***see MS X 92 and X 89; Dvivedī (1985, 12) also refers to the *Yājñavalkya Smṛti* III 40. On the jobs that prevent sacrifice to Brahmins, see Fick (1972, 9–10 note 1[7 note 1]) and MS III 151ff.

126 VSū 220.6–7, verse 10: *sadyaḥ patati māṃsena lākṣayā lavaṇena ca / tryahāc chūdraś ca bhavati brāhmaṇaḥ kṣīravikrayī //*. "By [selling] meat, lac and salt, [the Brahmin] instantly falls; and the Brahmin who is selling milk becomes a *śūdra* within three days." The verse is found also in Candrakīrti's CŚV$_{Tib}$ on CŚ IV 23, P *ya* 95b6–7: *rgya skyegs dang ni lan tshwa dang // sha yis 'phral du nyams par byed // 'o ma 'tshong ba'i bram ze gang // nyi ma gsum gyis dmangs rigs 'gyur [zhes bya ba la sogs pa smras pa yang yin no] //*. KDAM, p. LXI, verse 214 is very different: *sadyaḥ patati māṃsena dhātvannakṣīravikrayī / brāhmaṇo 'pi bhavec chūdraḥ surāpo lavaṇena ca //*. "By [selling] meat or by selling minerals/metals (*dhātu*), food or milk, [the Brahmin] instantly falls. Though a Brahmin, he will become (*bhavet*) a *śūdra* if he drinks liquor and [sells] salt." Also VSū 220.8–9, verse 11 and KDAM, p. LXI, verse 215: *ākāśagāmino viprāḥ patante* [KDAM *patitā*] *māṃsabhakṣaṇāt / viprāṇāṃ patanaṃ dṛṣṭvā tato māṃsāni varjayet //*. "Brahmins who travel in space fall as a result of eating meat. Seeing the Brahmins' fall, one should avoid meat!" Finally KDAM, p. LXI, verses 216–217: *bhakṣyante yena māṃsāni bhakṣyeta* [for *bhakṣyate*, according to Speyer (1902–

and it would be difficult to conclude otherwise: "if [to be] a Brahmin consisted of birth, then he could not take the status of a *śūdra* upon his fall (*patana*). Indeed, how could even a vile horse become a hog?"[127] Such illustrative return to the biological argument is a constant feature of the Buddhist argument.

1.4.2 Quoting from the *Mānavadharma(sūtra)*, the author of the VSū concludes on three different occasions that the quality of a Brahmin is indeterminate (*aniścita* or *aniyata*).[128] Even though those two Sanskrit terms are conceptually very rich, especially among the epistemologists, the context of their usage in the VSū suggests an ontological, rather than epistemological, meaning even if, as is said in the texts, brahmanity is difficult to *recognize with certainty*. With the first quotation, the text wants to demonstrate that a Brahmin may fall from his caste, and therefore become a non-Brahmin. With the second, it suggests that such paradigmatic Brahmins as the seers of the Veda have a non-Brahmanic ancestry certainly on the mother's side, and possibly also on the father's side. Finally, it is said that brahmanity may be acquired by virtue and may be lost as a result of breaking the prescriptions. Brahmanity is therefore unstable, lacking fixity or regularity, indefinite. None of the advanced discriminating criteria leads to a well-defined class that is coextensive with the ordinary denotation of the word "Brahmin." None is free of con-

---

1909, LXI note 94)] *tena kiṃ na hi / abhakṣyabhakṣaṇāc caiva brāhmaṇaḥ patito bhavet // patito brāhmaṇaś caivaṃ saṃskāraṃ nārhati punaḥ / tasmāj jñānaṃ vinā naiva śarīro* [sic!] *brāhmaṇo bhavet //*. "What would he who eats meat not eat? Now, through eating what should not be eaten, the Brahmin may fall. And the fallen Brahmin is thus no longer worthy of sacraments. That is why, without knowledge, the body itself [does] not [make one] a Brahmin."

[127] VSū 220.10–11: *yadi hi jātir brāhmaṇaḥ syāt tadā patane śūdrabhāvo nopapadyate / kiṃ khalu duṣṭo 'py aśvaḥ sūkaro bhavet /*.

[128] See VSū 222.15 (*aniścita*), 223.1 and 18 (*aniyata*). Weber translates both *aniścita* and *aniyata* as "unbestimmt" (uncertain), and *brāhmaṇaprasaṅga* as "Brâhmaṇaschaft," i.e., "brahmanity," "quality/condition of a Brahmin."

tradiction or fallacy, for if we rely on those criteria, some individuals commonly called "Brahmins" are non-Brahmins, while some individuals commonly called "*śūdra*s" are Brahmins. No criteria can therefore refute the conclusions drawn from the biological argument that underlies all discussions.

Chapter 2

Dharmakīrti and his successors

> "[Believing in] the authority of the Veda, claiming that a certain [being] is an agent, looking for religious merit in ablutions, showing pride with reference to caste, and undertaking austerities in order to eliminate sins, those are the five signs of stupidity, whence [all] intelligence has disappeared."
>
> Dharmakīrti[1]

2.1 Before and around Dharmakīrti

2.1.1 Introduction

Very little attention was given to the problem of caste in the scholastic productions that punctuated, with the *Abhidharmas*, the different doctrinal systematizations of Indian Buddhism. In fact, it does not seem to have been addressed at all in that literature.

Such silence is not so surprising, however, when one considers that the development of the *Abhidharma* literature probably did not follow the same proselytizing and edificatory intentions

---

1 PV I 340: *vedaprāmāṇyaṃ kasyacit kartṛvādaḥ snāne dharmecchā jātivādāvalepaḥ / santāpārambhaḥ pāpahānāya ceti dhvastaprajñāne pañca liṅgāni jāḍye //*. I will present later the commentaries of Śākyabuddhi and Karṇakagomin on this verse. Note the compound *jātimadāvalepa* in the *Divyāvadāna* CN383.12. See also note 45, p. 17, above.

as the *Sūtra, Avadāna* and *Jātaka* literature. It is indeed those intentions, also at play in the KM, that justified the long arguments against caste and the Brahmins' symbolic and ritualist prerogatives. In other words, the presence or absence of anti-Brahmanic developments and critiques of the caste theory is generally conditioned, in Buddhist literature, by its intended audience. Now, the *Abhidharmas* reflect internal/sectarian divisions and are therefore less concerned with attacking the various Brahmanic theories. In their different *Abhidharmas*, which are in fact only vaguely similar,[2] each school thus developed and defended a sectarian doctrine that was in every case presented as the correct and definitive interpretation of the Buddha's teachings. "As the *Abhidharma* literature serves merely to organize and explain doctrines presented in a relatively unstructured form in the sutras, *Abhidharma* texts provided the means by which the position of one group could be defined and defended against the divergent interpretations and criticisms of others."[3] The various *Abhidharma* traditions thus developed their doctrinal identity in opposition to other Buddhist groups, not in opposition to non-Buddhist movements (although there are a few exceptions). And since they all offered an exhaustive systematization of the Buddhist doctrine through an "investigation of *dharmas*" (*dharmāṇāṃ pravicayaḥ*), it was more natural for *Abhidharma* texts to defend the internal interests of a community, rather than the edificatory or proselytizing interests of Buddhism as a whole.

When one looks at the majority of the scholastic and philosophical productions of the Madhyamaka and Yogācāra schools, one also finds that their arguments are more concerned with providing a correct interpretation of the Buddhist doctrine than with attacking the views of non-Buddhist schools. Despite some notable exceptions (e.g., works like [pseudo] Nāgārjuna's *Vaidalyaprakaraṇa* and Āryadeva's *Catuḥśataka*), that tendency seems

---

2 See Lamotte (1976, 198).

3 Willemen, Dessein and Cox (1998, 10).

to be the rule up to the end of the fifth century (Buddhapālita, Vasubandhu, Saṅghabhadra).

Throughout the period of doctrinal systematizations, and in the texts that we will investigate below, the problem of the naturalization of social statuses therefore only received marginal attention. The situation changed only in the second half of the sixth century with Dharmapāla, and even more so when Dharmakīrti gave a new direction to the polemic.[4] Close comparison between the roughly contemporary thinkers Candrakīrti and Dharmakīrti shows that a break and reorientation seems to occur in the Buddhist argumentation. Candrakīrti made what is perhaps the best contribution to the polemic against the naturalization of caste, but he did so by presenting his argument in the "old style," i.e., by integrating and arranging systematically all the canonical materials. While he integrated some aspects of those materials, Dharmakīrti concentrated instead on the question of the perceptibility of class (*jāti*). In so doing, he was the first to consciously move the polemic to the level of epistemology and ontology.

2.1.1.1 Vasubandhu against the homogeneous character (*sabhāgatā*/*nikāyasabhāga*)

The efforts toward a systematization of the Buddhist doctrine however did not entirely dismiss the polemic against the naturalization of the social statuses connected with caste. For the polemic can be found, discreetly and indirectly, in the Sautrāntika critiques of the Sarvāstivādin-Vaibhāṣika notion of "homogeneous character" (*sabhāgatā*).[5]

---

4 On the historical conditions that led to a new agenda in 6th–7th century Buddhist philosophy, see Eltschinger (2007, 25–65), Eltschinger (2010) and (forthcoming). On the historical context, see Davidson (2002, 25–112) and Sanderson (2009).

5 The brief discussion that follows is based on primary sources only when they have been preserved in Sanskrit, i.e., in the AK(Bh), the AbhD and the AKVy. My discussion of the *Abhidharmas* preserved in Chinese

In the enumeration of the factors dissociated from the mind (*cittaviprayuktasaṃskāra*) presented in their different *Abhidharmas*, the Sarvāstivādin-Vaibhāṣikas include what they call a *sabhāgatā* or *nikāyasabhāga*,[6] which van den Broeck translates as *espèce*, La Vallée Poussin as *genre*, and Cox as "homogeneous character." AK II 41a and NAS define the *sabhāgatā* as the resemblance or uniformity of sentient beings (*sattvasāmya*). The Sarvāstivādin-Vaibhāṣikas thus restrict the homogeneous character to sentient beings, and they do so on the authority of various sutras,[7] as well as by means of some interesting arguments in the case of Saṅghabhadra. And in every case, the homogeneous character is uniformly presented as a substantial entity (*dravya*, AKBh, AbhD, NAS), as a *dharma* having causal efficiency (AbhD, NAS).

For the Sarvāstivādin-Vaibhāṣikas, the homogeneous character (*nikāyasabhāga*) is therefore the *cause* of the resemblance of sentient beings who share a common state of existence.[8] In his

---

is based on modern translations and essentially follows that of Cox (1995).

6 AbhD 89.5 and 6: *sabhāgatā nāma dravyam /... nikāyasabhāga ity asya śāstrasañjñā /*. AKVy 157.9–10: *jñānaprasthānādike śāstre nikāyasabhāga ity anayā sañjñayāyaṃ cittaviprayukto nirdiśyate /*.

7 See LVP (1980, II 198 note 1). Xuanzang's critique in the *Siddhi* reads: "... The sutra does not say that it is different from form, mind and mental factors (*rūpa-citta-caitta*)" (English translation of LVP 1928–1929, 58). As for Xuanzang's own position, it reads as follows in the *Siddhi*: "With the expression 'homogeneous character' (*sabhāgatā*), the scripture designates the mental and physical *dharmas* that are common among the living beings of such and such a category. It does not refer to some reality distinct from form, mind and mental factors (*rūpa-citta-caitta*)" (English translation of LVP 1928–1929, 59).

8 AbhD 89.5: *sabhāgatā nāma dravyam / sattvānām ekārtharuciḥ sādṛśyahetubhūtam /*. And then 89.10–11: ... *ity asti sabhāgatā nāma dharmaḥ, ekārtharucihetur iti /*. See also Xuanzang's presentation, in the *Siddhi*, of the position of the Sarvāstivādin-Vaibhāṣikas: "3. It is said that the homogeneous character is the cause of all men having the same occupations, of all gods having the same wishes (*chanda*); it is therefore a real entity" (English translation of LVP 1928–1929, 58–59).

etymological explanation of the term, Saṅghabhadra insists on that causal nature of the entity: "[In accordance with the above interpretation, the first element] *sa*, [or, 'homogeneous,' of the compound *sabhāgatā*] indicates the 'mutual similarity' of the body, the appearance, the modes of behavior and the aspirations [of sentient beings]. [The second element] *bhāga*, [or 'part,'] has the meaning of 'cause.' There exists a discrete real entity that is the 'cause of this mutual similarity'..."[9] In the course of defining the *nikāyasabhāga* in his *Abhidharmāmṛtarasa*, Ghoṣaka also declares: "The similarity (*sādṛśya*) in terms of body, mind and speech with other beings in the various realms of rebirth (*upapattisthāna*) is the species of beings."[10] Finally, Yaśomitra has given us the original Sanskrit of Saṅghabhadra's definition of the *sabhāgatā* stated in the NAS: "The homogeneous character of the group refers to the cause (*kāraṇa*) of the mutual similarity (*sābhāgya*) of the body (*śarīra*), the appearance (*saṃsthāna*), the various controlling faculties (*indriya*), the modes of behavior (*ceṣṭa*), the sustenance (*āhāra*), and so on or to the cause of the mutually similar aspirations (*abhisambandha*) of the various categories of sentient beings born in the same rebirth state."[11]

As the cause of similarities and distinctions among sentient beings of a given category, the homogeneous character is a substantial entity that, from the very beginning, seems to entertain a complex relation with the retribution of actions (i.e., with karma), with which it *cooperates* in determining the future rebirth state.[12] For contrary to Vasubandhu, Saṅghabhadra refuses

9 Translation by Cox (1995, 230); see also Cox (1995, 235 note 7).

10 English translation of van den Broeck (1977, 231).

11 AKVy 159.9–11: *śarīrendriyasaṃsthānaceṣṭāhārādisābhāgyakāraṇam anyonyābhir abhisambandhanimittaṃ ca sabhāgatety ācāryasaṅghabhadraḥ* /. Translation by Cox (1995, 229).

12 According to Cox (1995, 107), the "*Dharmaskandha, Saṅgītiparyāya* and *Jñānuprasthāna* discuss the role of homogeneous character in reference to the rebirth process and list it among the causes that determine the specific rebirth state of sentient beings." Still according to Cox (1995, 110), "for the Sarvāstivādin-Vaibhāṣika, homogeneous charac-

to grant only to karma the power to fully determine that state.[13] One could suppose that for the Sarvāstivādin-Vaibhāṣika, the specific state and situation of the new existence would be determined by karma, while the homogeneity or uniformity of the physical, psychic and behavioural characteristics, etc., of all sentient beings within a given state would be determined by the homogeneous character. Elsewhere in the AK(Bh), Vasubandhu in fact makes a correlation between karma and the homogeneous character when, under AK IV 95ab, he ascribes to the Sarvāstivādin-Vaibhāṣikas the idea that an action projects (*ākṣipati*) a new existence (*janman*) and then goes on to equate existence with the homogeneous character. The result of the projecting action (*ākṣepakakarmaphala*), in this case, seems to be the state of existence and its internal homogeneity, while the result of the fulfilling actions (*paripūrakakarmaphala*) consists in the contingent and accidental determinations of each individual born in that rebirth state.

Many such determinations correspond to each state. We have seen that Ghoṣaka mentioned the body, the mind and speech, and that Xuanzang spoke of wishes and occupations. Late Abhidharmic sources are more generous. The AKBh and the AbhD successively mention the realm of existence (3 *dhātus*), the level (*bhūmi*) within those realms, destiny (5 *gatis*), the mode of birth (4 *yonis*), feminity and masculinity (*strīpuruṣa*), the fact of being a lay follower (*upāsaka*), a monk (*bhikṣu*), one in training (*śaikṣa*), an Arhat, etc. Finally, in addition to the body, Saṅghabhadra mentions the configuration (*saṃsthāna*), the faculties (*indriya*), the modes of behaviour (*ceṣṭa*), the sustenance (*āhāra*) and

---

ter functions together with previous action (*karman*) to produce the similarities and distinctions that determine the genera of sentient beings."

13 Saṅghabhadra in Cox (1995, 230): "Even though it is observed that the body and appearance are effects projected by [previous] similar action, since there are [also] distinctions among the controlling faculties, modes of behavior, sustenance, and so on, [one should acknowledge that these distinctions are caused by homogeneous character]."

the aspirations (*abhisambandha*). But more importantly, and this warrants our discussion of the homogeneous character, the AKBh and AbhD mention the caste (*jāti*)[14] as one type of homogeneous character, although no reference to caste is made by Saṅghabhadra himself. For the Sarvāstivādins, therefore, "each sentient being is characterized by several types of homogeneous character."[15] Or as Saṅghabhadra has said: "There are innumerable varieties of homogeneous character of sentient beings (*sattvasabhāgatā*) in accordance with distinctions in realm (*dhātu*), rebirth state (*gati*), mode of birth (*yoni*), region (*bhūmi*), body, and so on."[16]

The notion of "homogeneous character" is therefore another manifestation of the Sarvāstivādin-Vaibhāṣika moderate realism. Every sentient being, regardless of the state of existence, belongs to a multitude of genus or species that each constitutes a really existing substantial entity and is the cause of resemblances and differences among sentient beings. According to the AK and the AbhD, caste is therefore one of the homogeneous characters. The social status is thus reified with the consequence that caste, which is real, appears to be one aspect of karmic retribution. Now Vasubandhu did notice the similarity of the homogeneous character with some of the Vaiśeṣika categories (*padārtha*, e.g., the universal, the particular). And because of that, we are justified in reading his Sautrāntika critique of the homogeneous character as a polemic against, *inter alia*, the naturalization and reification of the social statuses connected with caste, even though this is not its explicit purpose.

A few words shall be sufficient to show the modifications introduced by Vasubandhu in the Sarvāstivādin-Vaibhāṣika doctrine of the homogeneous character. Let it first be noted that

---

14 AKVy 157.16: *jātayo brāhmaṇādayaḥ* /.

15 Cox (1995, 108).

16 Translation by Cox (1995, 230). See also AKBh 67.17–19: *bhinnā punas teṣām eva sattvānāṃ dhātubhūmigatiyonijātistrīpuruṣopāsakabhikṣuśaikṣāśaikṣādibhedena pratiniyatā dharmasabhāgatā* /.

Vasubandhu does not consider this factor dissociated from the mind as a cause of resemblance amongst the sentient beings of a given category of existence, but rather as a class or a universal. Moreover, Vasubandhu makes a distinction between a general homogeneous character (*abhinna*, properly *sattvasabhāgatā*) characterizing all sentient beings *qua sentient beings*,[17] and a particular (*bhinna*) homogeneous character that includes several subdivisions (i.e., those mentioned above).[18] Contrary to Sanghabhadra, the AbhD appears to accept this twofold division of the homogeneous character.[19] Finally, according to Vasubandhu, the Sarvāstivādin-Vaibhāṣikas speak of the homogeneous character in order to provide some ground and to justify general notions (*buddhi*) and designations (*prajñapti*).[20]

Adopting the Sautrāntika positions, Vasubandhu presents five objections against the homogeneous character. But I will not analyze them all.[21] In the three objections that I find of interest,

---

17 AKVy 157.12–13: *yā sarvasattvavartinī sā pratisattvam anyā 'nyāpy abhinnety ucyate sādṛśyāt /.*

18 AKVy 157.14: *bhinnā yā kvacid vartate kvacin na vartate /.*

19 AbhD 89.6–9: *sā punar abhinnā bhinnā ca / abhinnā sarvasattvānāṃ sattvasabhāgatā / sā pratisattvaṃ sarveṣv ātmasnehāhāraratisāmyāt / bhinnā punas teṣām eva sattvānāṃ dhātubhūmigatiyonijātistrīpuruṣopāsakabhikṣuśaikṣāśaikṣādīnām ekārtharucitvabhedapratiniyamahetuḥ /.*

20 AKBh 67.19–20: *yadi sattvasabhāgatā dravyam aviśiṣṭaṃ na syād anyonyaviśeṣabhinneṣu sattveṣu sattvaḥ sattva ity abhedena buddhir na syāt prajñaptiś ca /.* The AbhD does not seem to agree with this justification. The NAS, however, seems to accept the principle of a justification of notions and designations by the homogeneous character: "[This function] is precisely the cause for [our] notion and provisional designation of their mutual similarity as constituting the same category." Translation by Cox (1995, 233). See also Xuanzang, *Siddhi*: "2. The Sarvāstivādin formulates a causal argument. The homogeneous character (*sabhāgatā*) is the cause of the generic or collective notions and expressions...: we use the collective names 'man,' 'god,' 'realm,' etc., to designate individual beings, men, etc." (English translation of LVP 1928–1929, 58).

21 Objection (1) reads as follows (AKBh 67.25–26): *yadi pṛthagjanasabhāgatā nāma dravyam asti kiṃ punaḥ pṛthagjanatvena / na hi manu-*

Vasubandhu successively criticizes (2) the unknowability of the homogeneous character, (3) its restriction to sentient beings and (5) its proximity to the Vaiśeṣika categories. In each case, the Sautrāntika critique is facilitated by the fact that it distorts the Sarvāstivādin-Vaibhāṣika position, for in dismissing the causal nature of the homogeneous character it treats the latter as a universal that lacks causal efficiency.

Vasubandhu nonetheless begins by addressing the unknowability of the homogeneous character and, consequently, its superfluity in the process of knowing a universal. The homogeneous character, as a substantial entity, is indeed apprehensible neither through perception (*pratyakṣa*), nor through inference

---

ṣyasabhāgatāyā anyan manuṣyatvaṃ kalpyate /. "If there is a substantial entity called 'homogeneous character of the ordinary person,' then what is the use of [positing] the quality of being an ordinary person? Indeed, no humanity is conceived other than the homogeneous character of human beings." The Sarvāstivādin-Vaibhāṣikas find in the "quality of the ordinary person" one of the factors dissociated from the mind, and define that quality as the non-possession (*aprāpti*) of the noble ones' *dharmas* (AKBh) or as the non-acquisition of the pure path of saints (*anāsravamārga*, Ghoṣaka). For Vasubandhu, there is a redundancy between the quality of the ordinary person and the homogeneous character of the ordinary person. By accepting the homogeneous character of the ordinary person, the quality of the ordinary person becomes superfluous. Compare with the objection of the NAS, in Cox (1995, 231). Saṅghabhadra there makes a distinction between the homogeneous character of the ordinary person as the cause of mutual resemblances, and the quality of the ordinary person as the cause of the *state* of the ordinary person. Objection (4) reads as follows (AKBh 68.3–4): *tāsāṃ ca sabhāgatānām anyonyabhinnānāṃ katham abhedena sabhāgatāprajñaptiḥ kriyate* /. "Moreover, how is it that [all] those homogeneous characters that are distinct from one another are designated without any distinction as 'homogeneous character'?" Compare with the objection of the NAS, in Cox (1995, 233), and see Saṅghabhadra's answer in Cox (1995, 233–234). See also Xuanzang, *Siddhi*: "Still, we have collective notions and expressions about the homogeneous characters that are all homogeneous characters. The homogeneous characters must therefore, in turn, have a homogeneous character. Or, and this is our position, similar beings (*sabhāga*) are not similar because of a homogeneous character" (English translation of LVP 1928–1929, 58).

(*anumāna*). In other words, it cannot be accessed by any means of valid cognition (*pramāṇa*). Vasubandhu then insists on the fact that everyone *can* tell the difference or lack of difference in a given group of individuals. It is therefore not necessary to postulate a distinct entity responsible for the resemblance of entities. Later on, using the same kind of arguments, Dharmakīrti and Prajñākaragupta will argue that everyone knows those differences independently, without prior instruction (*anupadeśam*).[22] In the words of Vasubandhu: "Moreover, it is certainly not the case that people perceive the homogeneous character, for [the latter] is incorporeal. Neither do they ascertain this [homogeneous character] by [inferential] discernment (*prajñā*). And yet, [people] know the absence of class distinction among sentient beings. Consequently, even if the [homogeneous character] existed, what function would it play in the [cognition of a universal][23]?"[24] Saṅghabhadra, for whom the homogeneous char-

---

22 See sections 2.3.2, p. 107, and 2.4.2–3, pp. 123–137, below.

23 AKVy 158.19–21: *jātyabhedapratipattau jātyabhedapratipattir asti / sā tu na sabhāgatayā dravyāntarakalpitayā kṛtā pramāṇenānupalabhyamānatvena tasyā vyāpārāsambhavāt /*. "One cognizes a non-distinction of class [only] when one cognizes a non-distinction of class. But the latter does not result from a homogeneous character conceived as a distinct substantial entity, because that [homogeneous character conceived as a distinct substantial entity] has no function [in the process of knowledge] since it is not apprehended through a means of valid cognition." Yaśomitra adds, in AKVy 158.21–24: *brūyās tvam / na nirnimittā sāmānyabuddhir bhavitum arhati / tena yan nimittaṃ tasyāḥ sāmānyabuddhes tat sabhāgatā nāma dravyam iti / vayam api tāṃ sāmānyabuddhiṃ sanimittāṃ brūmaḥ / sādṛśyakṛtā hi sā buddhiḥ / tac ca sādṛśyaṃ na dravyāntaram iti brūmaḥ /*. "You could say: there cannot be a cognition of a universal without a cause. The substantial entity called 'homogeneous character' is therefore the cause of the cognition of a universal. As for us, we also claim that the cognition of a universal possesses a cause. That cognition is indeed the result of a resemblance, but we do not say that this resemblance is a distinct substantial entity."

24 AKBh 67.26–68.2: *naiva ca lokaḥ sabhāgatāṃ paśyaty arūpiṇītvāt (/) na caināṃ prajñayā paricchinatti pratipadyate ca sattvānāṃ jātyabhedam iti satyā api tasyāḥ kathaṃ tatra vyāpāraḥ /*. Compare with the objection of the NAS, in Cox (1995, 232).

acter is a cause prior to being a class, will answer that its efficiency is established by means of an *inference* based on its observed effects, "just as one knows that there was an action performed in a former life, because one observes a present effect attained through action."[25] Saṅghabhadra is moreover not ready to renounce the perceptibility of the homogeneous character. According to him, the homogeneous character is in fact apprehensible through yogic perception (*yogipratyakṣa*).

Since Vasubandhu only interprets the homogeneous character of the Sarvāstivādin-Vaibhāṣikas as a universal and not as one of the causes co-presiding the determination of a new existence, it is not surprising to find him ask his opponent why the homogeneous character only applies to sentient beings. As I said in the first chapter, any entity, by means of its discriminants and criteria, instantiates at least provisionally a given class.[26] Vasubandhu therefore asks: "Moreover, why don't you also accept a homogeneous character for those things that are not sentient beings (*asattvasabhāgatā*)? Indeed, [plants like] rice, barley and the *mudga* and *māṣa* beans, [trees like] the mango tree and the bread-fruit tree, [metals like] copper and gold, etc., resemble those of their own class (*svajātisādṛśya*)."[27] Saṅghabhadra offers

---

[25] Translation by Cox (1995, 232).

[26] See section 1.2, p. 17, above.

[27] AKBh 68.2–3: *api cāsattvasabhāgatā*[1]*pi kiṃ neṣyate / śāliyavamudgamāṣāmrapanasalohakāñcanādīnāṃ svajātisādṛśyāt /*. Variant reading: 1: Pradhān reads *asattvasattvasabhāgatā*, contrary to AKVy 158.24–25 and the text reproduced in Jaini (1977, 90 note 4). See also the objection of the NAS, in Cox (1995, 232). See also Xuanzang, *Siddhi*: "The Sarvāstivādin will have to admit a homogeneous character for trees (*vṛkṣasabhāgatā*), a homogeneous character for grass (*tṛṇasabhāgatā*), since we call all trees 'tree,' just as we call all men 'man.' However, he reserves the homogeneous character (*sabhāgatā*) for sentient beings" (English translation of LVP 1928–1929, 58). Explanation by Yaśomitra, AKVy 158.25–28: *na dravyāntarasabhāgatānimittā sattvaḥ sattva iti sāmānyabuddhiḥ / sāmānyākārapravṛttatvāt / śāliyavamudgamāṣādisāmānyabuddhivat / śāliyavasvajātisādṛśyakṛtā hy eṣā sāmānyabuddhiḥ / na ca teṣāṃ svajātisādṛśyaṃ svato 'rthāntaraṃ bhavati /*. "The cognition of a universal, such as '[this is a] sentient being' [and 'this too

numerous, and sometimes complex, answers to Vasubandhu's question. Let us note here that according to him, there are two causes to the obtention or loss of a homogeneous character in this life (AKBh ordinary person → saint) or in another life (AKVy human beings → gods), namely past efforts (*prayatna*) and past actions, which are applicable to sentient beings alone and not to things that are not sentient beings.[28] The latter therefore do not have a homogeneous character.

The fifth and last of Vasubandhu's critiques has to do with the similarity, manifest at least in his own presentation, between the homogeneous character posited by the Sarvāstivādin-Vaibhāṣikas and the universals (*sāmānya*) or classes (*jāti*) asserted by the Vaiśeṣikas: "[Vasubandhu/Sautrāntika:] But in this manner, the Vaiśeṣikas find their voice (*dyotita*) [in your position], for this is indeed also their doctrine (*siddhānta*): what they call the 'category of universal' [truly] exists through which general ideas appear even with reference to [things] with dissimilar fea-

is a] sentient being,' does not have as its cause a homogeneous character that is a distinct substantial entity, since [that cognition] occurs due to the aspect of a commonality, as in the case of the cognition of the universal of rice, barley, and the *mudga* and *māṣa* beans, etc. Indeed, the cognition of a universal results from the fact that rice and barley resemble those of their own class. Now, the fact that they resemble those of their own class is not something different from themselves." The conclusion is that since there is no variation in the cognition of the universals of sentient beings and things that are not sentient beings, either none of them have a homogeneous character, or they all have one. The Sarvāstivādin-Vaibhāṣikas, who put forward the homogeneous character of sentient beings as a premise, must accept the second possibility.

28 Along those lines, see the clarification provided in Vasubandhu's tetralemma in AKBh 67.20–24, which is repeated in AbhD 90.1–4. The loss of the homogeneous character, when it is not the result of effort, is often identified with death (see van den Broeck 1977, 36–38 for references). We have seen, moreover, that in his discussion of the results of projecting and fulfilling actions (*ākṣepaka*° and *paripūrakakarmaphala*), Vasubandhu identifies *janman* and *nikāyasabhāga* as having a sense close to that of existence (*bhava*).

tures (*atulyaprakāra*). [The Sarvāstivādin-Vaibhāṣika:] This, however, is their difference [with our position]: whether they find their voice [in our position] or not, that [category of universal] subsists in many [individuals], although it is one."[29] It is interesting to note that both in Vasubandhu's opponent and in Saṅghabhadra, the very principle of a universal is accepted and its similarity with the Vaiśeṣika doctrine is claimed. Accepting the existence of universals is not equivalent, however, to adhering to the Vaiśeṣika understanding and theory of universals. Among the points of discordance, one must certainly note that contrary to the Sarvāstivādin-Vaibhāṣikas, the Vaiśeṣikas consider the universal to be one (*eka*) and permanent (*nitya*). In the NAS, Saṅghabhadra takes up, and further develops, the contrasting summary of that affinity with the Vaiśeṣika: "If the Vaiśeṣika school maintained that these two categories [of generality and particular generalities] were not singular, were momentary and impermanent, were without support, and were distinguished [from the object to which they apply], we would accept their opinion and suffer no categorical fault (*atiprasaṅga*)."[30]

---

29 AKBh 68.4–7: *vaiśeṣikāś caivaṃ dyotitā bhavanti / teṣām api hy eṣa siddhāntaḥ / sāmānyapadārtho nāmāsti yataḥ samānapratyayotpattir atulyaprakāreṣv apīti / ayaṃ tu teṣāṃ viśeṣaḥ / sa eko 'py anekasmin vartate yadi dyotitā yadi na dyotitāḥ /*. AKVy 159.3–5: *yadi dyotitāḥ sāmānyapadārthavāditvāt / yadi na dyotitā ekānekanityānityatvādiviśeṣavāditvāt /*. "If they find their voice [in our position], it is because they profess a category of universal. And if they do not find their voice [in our position], it is because we profess different things such as the oneness and multiplicity, permanence and impermanence [of this category of universal]."

30 Translation by Cox (1995, 234). In the NAS, Saṅghabhadra answers the following objection: "This [homogeneous character] would seem to be the category of generality (*sāmānyapadārtha*) or the category of particular generality (*sāmānyaviśeṣa*) maintained by the Vaiśeṣika school." Even though the word *viśeṣa* appears twice in the passage from the AKBh, I do not believe that the Vaiśeṣika category of "particularity" is what Vasubandhu has in mind, as LVP (1980, II 198) would have it. According to the AbhD (90.10–11), only the "class" category would be questioned: *kośakāraḥ punas tāṃ [sabhāgatāṃ] vaiśeṣikaparikalpitajā-*

To conclude this section, let it be noted that in his critique of the homogeneous character, Vasubandhu never directs any of his arguments against social statuses. The polemic remains very general and its subject is the homogeneous character itself, as well as its different types. But in identifying the homogeneous character of the Sarvāstivādin-Vaibhāṣikas with the universal of the Vaiśeṣikas, Vasubandhu criticizes the reality of classes and universals. Since caste is one of the particular homogeneous characters, Vasubandhu is therefore *de facto* criticizing the hypostasis of class in a social sense. Even though the AbhD also includes caste among the homogeneous characters, it is very difficult to determine to what extent the Sarvāstivādin-Vaibhāṣikas, whose ontology is realist in many respects, developed a notion of caste similar to the Brahmanic thematizations.[31] The Sautrāntika po-

---

tipadārthena samīkurvan vyaktaṃ pāyasavāyasayor varṇasādharmyaṃ paśyatīti /. "But when he identifies the [homogeneous character of our doctrine] with the 'class' category as it is conceived by the Vaiśeṣikas, [Vasubandhu], the author of the [*Abhidharma*]*kośa*, obviously sees an identity of colour between milk and a crow!"

31 In the context of his discussion of possession (*prāpti*) and non-possession (*aprāpti*), the Vaibhāṣika Saṅghabhadra (NAS 399c7–14) addresses the following question: can the distinction between the nature of an ordinary person (*pṛthagjanatva*) and the nature of a noble one (*ārya-tva*) be accounted for in the same way as the distinction between a Brahmin and a non-Brahmin? In answering that question, Saṅghabhadra resorts to the three criteria of discernment (= wisdom), activity and morality: "If one objects: 'Why is [this difference between the nature of an ordinary person and that of a noble one] not like that between the nature of a Brahmin [and the nature of those of other castes?]' [We would respond that these two cases are not similar] because no established distinction is observed [between a Brahmin and those of the other castes] as there is between the noble one and the ordinary person. There is a particular established distinction between a noble one and an ordinary person because [the noble one has] no force that instigates [actions that result in bad rebirth states] and no proceeding toward [the effect of actions that result in bad rebirth states, while] an ordinary person has both this instigating force and this proceeding. [In the case of a Brahmin and those of other castes], there is no particular established distinction in terms of insight [into dharma],

lemic against the homogeneous character as a factor dissociated from the mind is nonetheless a notable chapter in the history and development of the Buddhist argumentation against the naturalization of social statuses and had many implications on the problem of the relation between social status and the retribution of actions. The fact that the polemic remains strictly internal to Buddhism is all the more interesting.

2.1.1.2 Āryadeva and Candrakīrti

Composed long before the works of Bhāviveka/Bhavya and Dharmapāla, Āryadeva's *Catuḥśataka* (CŚ) is one of the key scholastic works among those that did not pursue strictly systematic purposes. Two of the work's features moreover paved the way for possible developments on the question of caste: firstly, an important part of its content is directed against non-Buddhist positions (Sāṅkhya, Vaiśeṣika); secondly and, I believe, consequently, it attempts to formulate evaluation criteria of Buddhist and non-Buddhist scriptures (*āgama*).[32] One is therefore not surprised to find, upon reading the CŚ, that Āryadeva questions the notion of "caste" when, in CŚ IV (a chapter entitled "Rejecting the illusion of egotism" [*ahaṅkāraviparyāsaprahāṇa*]), he describes

---

skill in the creative arts, suppression [of evil], and dexterity [in the cultivation of virtue]. If the Brahmin alone among the various castes were able to perform these actions and those of other [castes] were not able to perform them, it would then be possible, for this reason, to posit a nature of the Brahmin [as distinct from the nature of those of other castes]. [However, such a distinction is not possible because these actions are not performed by Brahmins alone]. Even though certain distinctions between [Brahmins of the] central and surrounding regions are observed, they do not have separate intrinsic natures. Since we allow that this [observed] distinction [between Brahmins of different regions] is based on the fact that they have separate homogeneous characters (*sabhāgatā*), [we are not forced into the] erroneous position [of maintaining that these various groups of Brahmins have, in each case, a discrete intrinsic nature]." Translation by Cox (1995, 206–207).

32 See Tillemans (1986).

the king as the paradigm of egoism and self-feeling.[33] In attacking the pride (*darpa, mada, māna*) of kings, and therefore at least indirectly the *kṣatriyas*, Āryadeva reformulates many Buddhist arguments previously used to question the legitimacy of the Brahmin's pride. As we shall see, with the notable exception of the biological arguments, all the arguments presented in the first part of this book reappear in Āryadeva and in Candrakīrti's important commentary (*Catuḥśatakavṛtti/ṭīkā*, CŚV) to CŚ IV 21–23. In particular, all the main features of a Buddhist position *explaining* the phenomenon of caste are there synthesized: its conventionality, occupationality and processuality. After reviewing several hypothetical justifications for the pride of kings, Āryadeva begins to criticize an argument based on caste, according to which the fact of being a *kṣatriya* and the duties incumbent on him justify his arrogance.[34] Similarly to the texts examined earlier (VāS, KDAM, those derived from the AgS, etc.), Āryadeva first replies that caste is occupational in nature and that it is named after people's different means of livelihood. As he writes: "All methods of livelihood are designated in society as caste. Consequently, no distinction due to caste is found among all human beings."[35] In other words, professional activities and means

---

33 On the problematic and the general structure of the chapter, see Lang (1992 and 2003, 88 and 108).

34 CŚV$_{\text{Tib}}$ on CŚ IV 21, P *ya* 93b6–7: *gang gi phyir rgyal srid yongs su skyong ba'i chos ni rgyal rigs kho na la bshad kyi / gzhan rigs gsum la ni ma yin te / de'i phyir rigs dang ldan pa'i rgyal rigs kho nas rgyal srid bya dgos te / gzhan dag gis ni ma yin no // de'i phyir 'di'i rgyags pa rigs pa nyid do //*. "Objection: Since it is taught that the duty of protecting the kingdom* (*rājya*) belongs just to the royal class (*kṣatriya*) and not to the other three, kingship must be exercised solely by the *kṣatriyas* who possess [this] caste [by birth], and not by any others. For this reason, his pride** (*mada*) is appropriate." Translation (slightly modified) by Lang (2003, 203). *See Suzuki (1994, 66.11 and 68.10): Tib. *rgyal srid* as equivalent of Skt. *rājya*; **see Suzuki (1994, 42.12 and 70.15): Tib. *rgyags pa* as equivalent of Skt. *mada*.

35 CŚ$_{\text{Tib}}$ IV 21, P *ya* 93b7–8: *'tsho ba'i thabs so cog la'ang // 'jig rten na ni rigs shes bsnyad // des na sems can thams cad la // rigs las dbye ba yod ma yin na //*. Translation by Lang (2003, 203).

of livelihood have no ontological incidence on the individuals by whom they are practised. Since they do not affect their mode of being, they do not justify any real differentiation of individuals into classes.

I have already said above that in his summary of the teachings of the AgS and the likes, Vasubandhu, at AK III 97cd–98ab, stripped those texts of their ironical and, especially, polemical character. In the CŚV, Candrakīrti also refers to the events of the first cosmic period, but this time with a clear polemical intention in mind. As was the case with Vasubandhu's presentation, in the beginning living beings are said to be sexually and socially undifferentiated. Candrakīrti's picture, while abridged, is standard: "[I]n the first eon all beings that arose were self-generating (*upapāduka*) because their birth did not depend on external factors, such as semen.[36] Because they were generated only from mind, they were born from the mind (*manomaya*),[37] had their own luminosity (*svayamprabha*),[38] had magical powers (*ṛddhi*-

---

36 AKBh 186.22: *prāthamakalpikā manuṣyā rūpāvacarā ivāsan*. "Human beings from the first cosmic age were like the beings from the material realm." See LVP (1980, III 28) on their apparitional character and LVP (1980, II 132) on their asexual character. AgS, D.N. III 85: *tena samayena... na itthipumā paññāyanti. sattā sattā tv eva saṅkhyaṃ gacchanti.*

37 AKBh 153.13–14: *sa eva manonirjātatvān manomaya uktaḥ / śukraśoṇitādikaṃ kiñcid bāhyam anupādāya bhāvāt /*. "The [intermediary being] is called 'born from the mind' because he comes forth from the mind, because he is constituted without depending on any external element like semen, blood and so on." On beings born from the mind, see AgS, D.N. III 85; LP 204.9; MVastu I 338.19.

38 According to AKBh 186.23–24; LVP (1980, III 204). Bodies will lose their luminosity (hence the obscurity and then the appearance of the sun and the moon) as a result of eating in lumps (see below), and this will make them coarse and heavy (LVP 1980, III 205). AKVy 339.13: *ādityādiprabhānapekṣatvāt svayamprabhāḥ*. On self-luminous beings (*sayampabha / svayamprabha*) see AgS, D.N. III 84/85 and LP 204.9, and MVastu I 338.18 respectively. Episodes of loss of luminosity and the appearance of the stars and calendar divisions are found in the AgS, D.N. III 85–86, LP 205.7–14 and MVastu I 339.1–340.6.

mat), flew through the sky (*ākāśagāmin*),[39] and were nourished by bliss (*prītibhakṣa*).[40] Having bliss as their food, they were lacking male and female sexual organs (*strīpuruṣendriya*). It was therefore impossible for caste to differentiate them because they all arose from a self-generated source. When, later, these beings began to eat in lumps (*kavaḍīkārāhāra*) and became accustomed to very coarse food (*audārika*), channels of urine and excrement (*mūtrapurīṣamārga*) developed as a result so that their natural excreta could be expelled (*niṣyandanirvāha*). When they saw the different physiques (*saṃsthāna*) created by male and female sexual organs, beings who had the desire for sexual pleasures (*kāmarāga*) set about doing together what was wrong because they had been accustomed to it in their past lives (*pūrvābhyāsavaśāt*).[41] For this reason, birth from the womb (*jarāyuja*) developed."[42]

---

39 AKBh 186.24: *vihāyasaṅgama*. AgS, D.N. III 84/85 and LP 204.9: *antalikkhacara*; MVastu I 338.19: *antarīkṣacara*.

40 According to AKBh 186.24; LVP (1980, III 204). AKVy 339.14: *kavaḍīkārāhārānapekṣatvāt prītibhakṣāḥ*. On beings who feed on delight (*pītibhakkha / prītibhakṣa*), see AgS, D.N. III 84/85 and LP 204.8–9, and MVastu I 338.19 respectively.

41 Compare with the episode as it is told in the AgS, D.N. III 88–89; LP 208.3–15; MVastu I 342.8–12. Compare also with Vasubandhu's sequence at AKBh 187.6–10; LVP (1980, III 205).

42 CŚV$_{Tib}$ on CŚ IV 21, P *ya* 94a1–5: *bskal pa dang por ni sems can thams cad phyi rol gyi rkyen sa bon la mi ltos par skye ba nyid kyi phyir brdzus te skye zhing / yid tsam las skyes pa'i phyir yid las byung ba rang gi 'od can / rdzu 'phrul dang ldan pa / nam mkha' la 'gro ba dga' ba za zhing dga' ba'i zas can pho dang mo'i dbang po dang bral ba ste / de'i phyir 'di dag thams cad brdzus te skye ba'i skye gnas las byung ba nyid kyi phyir rigs las tha dad pa nyid mi srid do // de'i dus phyis ni khams kyi zas la zhugs shing zas ches rags pa la goms par byed pa na / de'i rgyu mthun dbyung bar bya ba'i gcin dang phyi sa'i lam byung ba / phan tshun pho dang mo'i dbang pos byas pa'i dbyibs tha dad pa lta ba na / tshe snga mar goms pa'i dbang gis 'dod pa'i 'dod chags skye ba rnams la phan tshun log par zhugs pas mngal nas skye ba'i skye gnas 'byung bar 'gyur to //*. Translation by Lang (2003, 203–204). The Sanskrit terms and notes are my additions and are mostly taken from the AKBh 186.22–187.10, which is very close to the above.

Standard also is Candrakīrti's narration of the events that led to a gradual social differentiation: "Then, because they were at fault in hoarding grain,[43] some among their society began to take what was not given to them (*adattādāna*). As a result, different classes came about due to the acceptance of different livelihoods. This is how a large group of people (*mahājanakāya*)[44] commissioned a capable man to protect the fields.[45] By accepting that work, he became known as a person of the royal class (*kṣatriya*).[46] Those people who, eager to restrain their senses, turned their backs on the villages (*gṛhyebhyo bahirmanas*)[47] in order to perform austerities, came to be known as Brahmins. Those who served the kings came to be known as the class of commoners (*vaiśya*). Those who engaged in harmful actions such as plowing were known as the lower classes. And among the [latter], various castes such as that of the wageless employees (*karmakāra*) appeared from the different parts of a given activity. Because this is so, in society there are no [permanent] distinctions created by class. Because of the absence of such a distinction, class is not an appropriate reason for pride. Consider the example of classifying new pots [according to their contents]. By classifying the new pots' [contents], one labels them accordingly, from a pot of sesame oil to a pot of melted butter. Similarly, that work which was done in the first eon became known

---

[43] Compare with the description of the episode found in the AgS, D.N. III 89–92; LP 209.13–212.6; MVastu I 343.4–344.15.

[44] According to AKBh 187.16.

[45] CŚV (Suzuki 1994, 46.10–11): *kṣetraparirakṣārtham*; AKBh 187.15: *kṣetrāṇi pālayitum*.

[46] Compare with the description of the episode found in the AgS, D.N. III 92–93 (see section 1.1.3, p. 4, above); LP 212.6–213.3; MVastu I 347.16–348.7. The MVastu discusses only the aetiology of the *kṣatriya*, the person elected by the people (*mahāsammata*) and the king. See Senart (1882, I 621 note on I 348).

[47] According to AKBh 187.17–18.

as caste."[48] For Candrakīrti, therefore, the aetiology of social divisions and subdivisions goes back to the first cosmic period. Based on a centrifuge dynamic, the processual explanation does not allow for the introduction of any ontological differentiation between social divisions. And here again, only the appearance of new aspirations, interests and occupations accounts for the process. But according to the aetiological explanation of the AgS and the likes, the events responsible for the various human institutions happened too far in the past to have been remembered. And that is why the value, and especially the original malignity of those institutions, are no longer perceived by today's men.

Candrakīrti closes his commentary on this passage with a very interesting verse where he integrates the occupational and dynamic aspects of caste: "Whether born lower-caste or upper caste, based upon that work by which one makes a living one will become [a member] of that caste over time."[49]

---

[48] CŚV$_{\text{Tib}}$ on CŚ IV 22, P *ya* 94a5–94b3: *de nas 'jig rten du sogs 'jog gi skyon gyis ma byin par len pa la sogs pa la zhugs pas rang gi 'tsho ba'i bya ba'i khyad par khas blangs pa las rigs tha dad par 'gyur to // 'di ltar skye bo'i tshogs phal po ches zhing bsrung ba'i phyir mi spus la bab pa zhig bskos pa dang las de khas blangs pas de la rgyal rigs zhes bya bar grags so // thul bar 'dod pa gang dag dka' thub bsgrub par bya ba'i phyir / grong las yid phyir phyogs par gyur pa de dag ni bram ze zhes bya bar grags so // rgyal po bka' bzhin byed pa rnams ni rje'u rigs so // rmod pa la sogs pa las ngan pa la sbyar ba rnams ni dmangs rigs te / de dag la yang las kyi khyad par gyi nang tshan tha dad pa las las byed pa la sogs pa'i rigs tha dad par 'gyur to // ... gang gi phyir 'di de ltar yin pa de'i phyir sems can rnams la rigs kyis byas pa'i dbye ba yod pa ma yin no // de'i phyir khyad par med pas rigs rgyags pa'i rgyur mi rigs te / bum pa gsar ba'i rnam grangs bzhin no // ji ltar bum pa gsar ba rnam grangs kyis ji ltar 'dod pa bzhin byed de / 'dod pa'i sgo nas 'bru mar gyi bum pa dang mar gyi bum pa'i bar du 'gyur ro // bum pa ji lta ba de bzhin du bskal pa dang por las gang byed pa de la rigs zhes brjod do //*. Translation (modified) by Lang (2003, 204). The Sanskrit terms and notes are my additions.

[49] CŚ$_{\text{Tib}}$ IV 21, P *ya* 94b3: *rigs ngan nam rigs ldan yang [b]la // las gang gis ni 'tsho 'gyur ba // de nas bzung ste de de yi // rigs su dus kyis 'gyur ba'o //*.

As we saw in the first chapter, a good part of the Brahmanic legitimizations of caste rested on various genealogical claims that appealed especially to the purity of the Brahmin's ancestry, both at the level of the family (*kula*) and the lineage (*gotra*). In response to those claims, the AmbS and the VSū argued that the purity of a genealogy was difficult to establish over a long period of time due to women's near legendary fickleness. Āryadeva takes up those arguments in CŚ IV 22, which may be the source of Śāntarakṣita's, Kamalaśīla's and Prajñākaragupta's later developments on this theme: "Since the past is far gone and the minds of women are fickle, consequently, it is not due to birth (*jāti*) that someone is called a *kṣatriya*."[50] As Prajñākaragupta will do later on, Candrakīrti here makes a connexion between the theme of women's fickleness and the issue of mixed caste. For nobody can prove that anywhere along the genealogy no woman has had sexual relations with a man belonging to another social group, thus breaking the class or caste endogamy and giving birth, as a result, to a child of mixed caste. He says: "To call 'caste genealogy' [the fact that] the [future] fathers and mothers [were] successively born pure [with regard to caste], this is a difficult thing to arrive at, for sin (*vyabhicāra*) is observed among women. Because of the long time that has gone since, and also because women's mind is fickle, those [women] may have had [sexual] encounters with [men from] other classes[51] (*rus* = *varṇa*?) and children may have been born [of those mixed unions]. Therefore, the caste may have been totally corrupted. Consequently, because of the corruptions of caste due to unfaithful women, the pride (*māna*) of caste genealogy that arises from birth is unjustified. Therefore, being called a '*kṣatriya*' does

---

50 CŚTib IV 22, P *ya* 94b5: *'das dus shin tu ring ba dang // mi mo rnams yid g.yo ba ste // de phyir rgyal rigs shes bya ba // rigs las 'ga' yang yod ma yin //*. CŚ IV 22ab comes very close to TS 3579ab: *atītaś ca mahān kālo yoṣitāṃ cāticāpalam /*. See section 2.5.4.1, p. 146, below.

51 I read the Tib. *rus* as equivalent to the Skt. *varṇa* (1) based on Suzuki (1994, 66-9–10) where the Tib. *rus* renders the Skt. *varṇa*, and (2) based on CŚVTib on CŚ IV 22, P *ya* 94b4: *rus bzhi po bram ze'i rigs dang / rgyal rigs dang / rje'u rigs dang / dmangs rigs dag rnam par gnas te /*.

not proceed from birth (*jāti*)."[52] Candrakīrti then makes a generalization out of the example of the *kṣatriya* and concludes: "Because time is endless and because the majority of women are fickle, an intelligent person in this world does not take pride in class."[53] Let it be noted that in his critique of genealogy, Candrakīrti also introduces the argument already encountered in the AmbS, the VSū and the KDAM which is based on the motherly ancestry of the Vedic seers, a motherly ancestry that is now animal, now of vile social origin. For example, since Vyāsa's mother belonged to the caste of fishermen (*kaivarta*), a paradigmatic Brahmin turns out to be of a mixed caste.[54]

In CŚ IV 23, finally, Āryadeva and Candrakīrti take up the theme of the instability and relativity of classes that we already discussed. CŚ IV 23 spells out the unwelcome consequences of a position that would attempt to find in the legitimate or normal activity of the classes what could not be established by genealo-

---

52 CŚV$_{\text{Tib}}$ on CŚ IV 22, P *ya* 94b5–8: *pha dang ma dag cing skyes shing skyes pa la rigs brgyud ces bya bar bsnyad na de ni rnyed par bka' ste / bud med rnams la 'khrul pa mthong ba'i phyir ro // de las 'das pa'i dus ring ba nyid kyi phyir la / bud med rnams kyi yid kyang g.yo ba can yin pa'i phyir de rnams la rus gzhan dang phrad pa la bu tsha dag skye ste / de'i phyir rigs yang dag par sun phyung bar 'gyur ro // de'i phyir g.yem ma rnams kyis rigs sun phyung ba rnams kyis rigs kyis byas pa'i rigs brgyud kyi nga rgyal mi rigs so // de'i phyir de ltar na rgyal rigs zhes bya ba rigs las yod pa ma yin no //*.

53 CŚV$_{\text{Tib}}$ on CŚ IV 22, P *ya* 95a8–95b1: *dus la mtha' med nyid phyir dang // bud med tshogs ni g.yo phyir te // de yi phyir na mkhas pas 'dir // rigs kyis nga rgyal bya min nyid //*. Translation by Lang (2003, 205).

54 CŚV$_{\text{Tib}}$ on CŚ IV 22, P *ya* 95a7–8: *rgyas pa yang spos ldan du rtsibs logs skyes kyis snga dro khug rna dkrigs nas nya ba'i bu mo las bskyed par grags te / de ni gling du skyes pas gling skyes shes kyang bya la / rig byed la chags pas rgyas pa zhes bya'o //*. "Also, it is known that Vyāsa was born from a fisherman's daughter after the [sage] Parāśara covered Gandhavatī(/Satyavatī) with a dense early morning fog. Since he was born on an island, he was also known as Dvaipāyana, and he was called Vyāsa because of his attachment (*vyasana*) to the Veda." Translation (modified) by Lang (2003, 205).

gies and the claims to innateness, i.e., the fixity of classes:[55] "If even a *śūdra* becomes a *kṣatriya* by his activity, I wonder why a Brahmin does not become a *śūdra* also by his activity?"[56] The activity therefore does not guarantee the fixity of social classes.

Already in the VSū, brahmanity was very explicitly regarded as relative, unstable and indeterminate. By means of an analogy, Candrakīrti describes the classes as unestablished (*asiddha*), or according to a Tibetan version that may be an interpretation of Candrakīrti, as unestablished *per se* (*svataḥ*). Just as the opposite bank (*pāra*) of a river is not established *per se*, but is instead relative to the person who describes it as opposite, the fact of being a Brahmin or a *kṣatriya* is not established *per se*; it is relative. The analogy, as far as I understand it, is not linear, however: brahmanity is in fact not so much relative to the situation of the speaker as it is to the adopted criterion, here the person's activity. Moreover, the fact that belonging to a class is accidental rather than essential, relative rather than established *per se*, is all the more evident to Candrakīrti that it corresponds to what the most authoritative normative sources seem to suggest. For

---

55 CŚV$_{\text{Tib}}$ on CŚ IV 23, P *ya* 95b1: *gal te rigs kyis rgyal rigs su mi 'gyur na / de'i tshe skye dgu skyong ba'i las kyis rgyal rigs su 'gyur ro //*. "If someone does not become a member of the royal class because of his class at birth, then he will become a member of the royal class because of his actions in protecting the people." Translation by Lang (2003, 205). Before this passage, Candrakīrti had already insisted on the ephemeral character of caste. CŚV$_{\text{Tib}}$ on CŚ IV 22, P *ya* 95a6–7: *'jig rten gyi rigs rje ba yang yin no //*. "Similarly, the classes of society also undergo change." Translation by Lang (2003, 205).

56 CŚ$_{\text{Tib}}$ IV 23, P *ya* 95b1–2: *gal te las kyis dmangs rigs kyang // rgyal rigs shes byar 'gyur na ni // las kyis dmangs kyang bram zer ni // gang gis 'gyur ba min par sems //*. Sanskrit fragment of CŚ IV 23cd in Suzuki (1994, 64, 8–9): ... [*ka*]*rmaṇā / vipro 'pi karmaṇā śūdrāḥ kena manye na jāyate //*. This Sanskrit fragment and Candrakīrti's commentary (see note 58) both clearly show that the Tibetan translators of CŚ IV 23 inverted the roles of Brahmins and *śūdras* in the proposition, for whereas the Tibetan text suggests that *śūdras* may become Brahmins through their activity, the Sanskrit says that Brahmins may become *śūdras*.

like the VSū and, less clearly, the KM and the KDAM, Candrakīrti bases his argument on the MS X 92.[57] Here is Candrakīrti's commentary: "Now if even a non-*kṣatriya* becomes a *kṣatriya* when he performs the activity of a *kṣatriya*, even the person that we call a *śūdra* will become a Brahmin when, receiving [a donation] and reciting [the Veda], he is performing the activity of a Brahmin. Thus, any [person] performing the activity of another [person] would be [of the class of] that [other person]. In this case, what is accepted [by the opponent] is false (*tan na*), namely that one will be a *kṣatriya* through [one's] activity. Consider the example of a boat going to the opposite bank (*pāragamana*): a boat goes to the opposite bank and comes back. In this case, [each of] the two [persons] standing on [each] bank of the river says, 'The boat has reached the other bank!' and 'The boat has reached the other bank!' But no opposite bank is established [by itself (Tib.)]. [Likewise, whether we are considering] a Brahmin or a *kṣatriya*, he is not established [by himself]. If it is through his activity that a *śūdra* becomes a *kṣatriya*, [then] in the same way the Brahmin himself will become a *śūdra* through his activity, and [that is precisely what Manu] has said, for instance: 'By [selling] meat, lac and salt, [the Brahmin] immediately falls. And the Brahmin who sells milk becomes a *śūdra* within three days.' And to this we add: if classes stem from [people's] activity, birth (*jāti*) cannot be their cause, and those [classes] do not stem from both [the activity and birth] since birth was refuted earlier."[58] Let the fol-

---

[57] See section 1.4, p. 49, above, note 126, p. 53.

[58] Sanskrit fragment of CŚV on CŚ IV 23 in Suzuki (1994, 64.10–66.10): *yadi hīdānīm akṣatriyo 'pi kṣatriyakarma kurvan kṣatriyo bhavati / śūdro 'pi hi n[ām]a brāhmaṇakarma kurvan brāhmaṇo bhaviṣyati / pratigṛhṇann adhīyāṃś ca / tathāpy anyo 'py anyadīyaṃ karma samācaran sa eva syāt / tatra yad iṣṭaṃ karmaṇā kṣatriyo bhaviṣyatīti tan na / naupāragamanavat / yathā nau[ḥ] pāraṃ gacchaty āgacchati / tatra nadyā ubhayakūlasthitau bruvāte nauḥ pāraṃ gatā nauḥ pāraṃ gateti / na ca kiṃcit siddhaṃ pāram asti / sa [e]vāsiddho brāhmaṇaḥ kṣatriyo vā / yadi śūdraḥ karmaṇā kṣatriyo bhavaty evaṃ vipro 'py karmaṇā śūdro bhaviṣyati / āha ca / sadyaḥ patati mā[ṃ]sena lākṣayā lavaṇena ca / tryaheṇa śūdro bhavati yo vipraḥ kṣīravikrayī // ityādi /*

lowing of Candrakīrti's concluding statements be remembered: if it is the activity that defines the class, then birth is of no incidence, and that is the conclusion that is promoted by all the Buddhist texts analyzed so far.

One of Āryadeva's merits is therefore to have brought to the philosophical tradition some of the arguments scattered in the canonical Buddhist literature and probably already well established, if not in the VSū, at least in the ŚKA. He in fact does more than present arguments, for he also updates the Buddhist explanation of the empirical facet of caste. As for Candrakīrti, who provides very useful supplements to Āryadeva's work, he prolongs up to the seventh century the aetiological explanations derived from the AgS, and in contrast with Vasubandhu, he restores their polemical content. Philosophers from the post-systematic period, whether Mādhyamika (Śāntarakṣita) or not, could thus find in Āryadeva a model for presenting arguments against the naturalization of caste to a non-Buddhist audience.

2.1.1.3 Dharmapāla and the Brahmanic usurpation

The critique of caste and the outrageous pretensions of Brahmins is typical of the polemic against non-Buddhists. Until the sixth century, it was almost entirely absent from the scholastic and systematic literature. In the first half of the sixth century, however, with Dignāga, Bhāviveka/Bhavya, Dharmapāla and probably Dharmakīrti (even though, to my knowledge, the first two do not express their views on caste),[59] there seems to be a considerable change of attitude with regard to the intended audience of Buddhist philosophical discourse. Clearly, the heated debate that went on between Dharmapāla and Bhāviveka/Bhavya shows that the dogmatic and philosophical problems internal to Buddhism were still quite important. But parallel to those

āha cātra / karmaṇā yadi va[rṇ]āḥ syur jātis tatra na kāraṇam / na ca dvābhyāṃ bhavanty ete jātiḥ prāg dūṣitā yataḥ //. Compare with CŚV$_{\text{Tib}}$ on CŚ IV 23, P *ya* 95b2–7.

59 See note 76, p. 87, below.

problems, these philosophers go very far beyond the framework of an internal dispute either to include non-Buddhist schools and positions in their polemic, or to leave internal controversy nearly out of consideration. Bhāviveka/Bhavya and Dharmapāla in particular appear to feel the need to defend, or at least to set, *a Buddhist doctrinal identity* that will be Madhyamaka for the one, and idealist for the other. This attitude is particularly clear in chapters VI to X of Bhāviveka/Bhavya's MHK, where the Sāṅkhya,[60] Vaiśeṣika,[61] Vedānta[62] and Mīmāṃsā[63] doctrines are systematically examined and criticized, although Dharmapāla also attacks on several points the Sāṅkhya and Vaiśeṣika positions, as well as positions close to those of the Mīmāṃsā. But what is perhaps no less significant is that Dharmapāla, Dharmakīrti and Bhāviveka/Bhavya were the first to really put to the test, against well-defined evaluation criteria and procedures, the pretensions to authority of Buddhist and non-Buddhist scriptures (*āgama-prāmāṇya*).[64] And their arguments were clearly intended to be acceptable also to a non-Buddhist audience. For while Buddhist scriptures may not need to be submitted to a critical evaluation (*parīkṣā*) by Buddhists themselves in order to be considered authoritative, they must nonetheless resist the critique of non-Buddhists. In that sense at least, and in the light of the first two chapters of PV, Dharmakīrti's attitude seems closer to that of Bhāviveka/Bhavya and Dharmapāla[65] than to Dignāga's.

---

60 See Honda (1967).

61 See Hattori (1994).

62 See Gokhale (1958), Nakamura (1958) and Qvarnström (1989 and 1990).

63 See Kawasaki (1992a, 407–471) for the Sanskrit and Tibetan texts of MHK IX and X. On MHK IX in general, see Lindtner (1997). On some aspects of the Mīmāṃsaka position, see Eltschinger (1998) and the English translation in Kawasaki (1976).

64 For Dharmapāla, see Tillemans (1986 and 1990, I, 23–35). For Bhāviveka/Bhavya, see Eltschinger (1997 and 1998). For Dharmakīrti, see Eltschinger (2007, 67–114) and Krasser (2011).

65 On that matter, see also Tillemans (1990, I, 18–22).

In his commentary to Āryadeva's CŚ XII (廣百論釋論 *Guǎng bǎi lùn shì lùn*, IV), Dharmapāla goes into a long diatribe against the Brahmin and Jain outsiders. He draws a picture of the Brahmin that is free of complacency and perhaps unique in its severity. For him, the Brahmin's path is nothing but an endless recitation of meaningless formula. And if Brahmins are at all venerated, it is because the majority of them try successively to fool others by reciting mantras, by worshipping fire or by purifying themselves through austerities. They in fact earn a living by abusing women and *śūdras*. For Brahmins from the distant past invented the whole of the Veda, according to Dharmapāla, and then claimed that they were natural instead of the creation of human imagination. Brahmins even describe themselves, in those texts, as the most venerable among men and recommend non-Brahmins who wish to acquire incommensurable merits to take care of their needs. Dharmapāla concludes by comparing the Brahmin's behaviour to that of greedy lepers, and holds that they are venerated because of their knowledge and because the Veda is difficult to recite.[66] According to Dharmapāla, then, the Brahmins created, and continue to keep in place, symbolic instruments of violence and domination. The creation of the Veda simply results from the necessity to make that domination natural.[67]

Like so many other authors and texts, from the VSū to Candrakīrti, Āryadeva maintains, in CŚ XII 22, that birth or caste are

66 See Āryadeva's CŚ XII 21, the Chinese and Tibetan versions of which differ. See respectively Tillemans (1990, I, 110) and (1990, I, 132).

67 On those matters, see Tillemans (1990, I, 108–111). Candrakīrti is more reserved than his predecessor Dharmapāla in his attack of Brahmins and, contrary to Dharmapāla, he *here* does *not* present any argument to undermine the legitimacy of the glory that falls upon Brahmins because of their birth. For Candrakīrti, Brahmins simply perform the recitation of formulas and fire oblations. And since they seek profit and worldly honours, Brahmins have to be hypocrites. Their doctrine, which is "mostly an outward show" (*phyi 'chos*), fits well in *saṃsāra*, and is therefore an obstacle to liberation. See Tillemans (1990, I, 130–132).

a purely karmic product that does not lead to liberation.[68] Dharmapāla offers two arguments against the superiority of the Brahmin's birth in his commentary on that verse. Developing the "biological" arguments found in the canonical literature, and anticipating later philosophers,[69] he first asserts that the *dharmas* that serve as sense faculties and sensory objects to Brahmins are not different from those that fulfil the same functions among individuals of other castes. The second argument then claims that since Brahmins and *śūdras* live together on the same continent (*dvīpa*), Brahmins cannot claim any superiority over the *śūdras*.[70] While this second argument may seem over simple, it plays on the pan-Indian cosmological belief that a common set of characteristics is shared by the inhabitants of each of the four continents: average life expectancy, height, physiognomy, etc. And as Dharmapāla is quick to point out, whereas cosmological determinants may justify a qualitative gradation among the inhabitants from one continent to another, no such gradation may be justified within a given continent.

Dharmapāla's refutation of the Brahmanic argumentation is often convincing. But he offers no explanation for the partition of Indian society into castes. His rather fiery remarks on the motivations that led to the composition of the Veda are nonetheless extremely interesting.

2.1.2 Dharmakīrti and the reformulation of the polemic

At this stage we must formulate a hypothesis to explain why it is only with Dharmakīrti that the Buddhist polemic on caste took on a partially new turn; one that would also engage his successors Śākyabuddhi (c. 660–720?, PVṬ), Śāntarakṣita (c. 725–788, TS), Kamalaśīla (c. 740–795, TSP), Karṇakagomin (c. 800, PVSVṬ)

---

68 See Tillemans (1990, I, 111).

69 See section 1.2, p. 17, above, and sections 2.3.2, p. 107, and 2.5.1, p. 138, below.

70 I am not aware of any other instance of that cosmological argument.

and Prajñākaragupta (c. 800, PVA).[71] I will here present only two possible explanations for this: one internal to the works to be examined, the other external.

2.1.2.1 Internal explanation: the theory of exclusion (*apoha*)

With the philosophers, the problem of caste quickly crystallized into the ontological debate and the problem of universals (*jāti, sāmānya*). Whether we look at one or any of the specific positions adopted by every given school or individual thinker, the break is clear between the realism of Brahmanic philosophers and the nominalism/conceptualism of the Buddhist schools. Starting with Dignāga, the core Buddhist arguments on universals are based on the theory of exclusion (*apoha*) or exclusion of others (*anyāpoha*).[72] Despite some important variations and developments brought by the philosophers discussed below, the theory attempts to explain, in anti-realist terms, the genesis and formation of concepts (classes, genus, universals, etc.). And it does so, in Dharmakīrti at least,[73] by appealing to the causal efficiency (*arthakriyāsāmarthya*) of entities or particulars (*svalakṣaṇa*). In showing that particulars irreducibly distinct from one another can produce identical effects, notably conceptual judgements, the theory of exclusion claims that universals have only a conceptual or notional existence. According to that theory, we come to believe in the extra-mental and extra-linguistic reality of classes and universals because of the superimpositions (*samāropa*) and the unifications (*ekīkaraṇa*) (relayed by beginningless latent impregnations, *vāsanā*) of those conceptual materials with sensory data.

---

71 On those authors and their works, see Steinkellner and Much (1995).

72 On Dignāga's theory of exclusion, first refer to Hayes (1985) and Pind (forthcoming). On the form that the theory took in the work of Dharmakīrti, see Frauwallner (1932, 1933a and 1933b) and Dunne (2004, 113–144).

73 On the important differences between the theories of Dignāga and Dharmakīrti, see Katsura (1991).

In so far as Brahmanic philosophers took both meanings of the word *jāti* (class, universal; caste, [social] class, birth) to belong to the same realist ontology, and therefore accepted that all Brahmins are instantiations of the class "brahmanity" (*brāhmaṇatva*) in the same way that all cows are instantiations of the class "cowhood" (*gotva*), the Buddhist epistemologists were justified to test the social valorization of class against the exclusion approach, just as they did with its epistemological valorization.[74] With the theory of exclusion, they possessed a new instrument to reject a separation of the social and epistemological argumentations; an instrument that proved to be very powerful in their critique of the realist legitimizations of caste. Śākyabuddhi, Karṇakagomin and Śāntarakṣita clearly understood this. For prior to going into a discussion of class in the social sense, they will all say that it has already been the object of detailed refutations in the sections of their works dealing with the theory of exclusion. Their subsequent discussions of the naturalization of caste are then reducible to an argumentation against the pride that Brahmins take in their caste.[75]

---

[74] This is especially true if we adopt Dumont's structural interpretation of caste, which includes strong *apoha* elements. That interpretation indeed "de-substantializes" caste as much as possible, so that in the end it only has a relative existence within a system of "distinctive oppositions" (Dumont 1972, 79[62]). Under that interpretation, caste essentially seems to be the sum of everything that it is not and does not allow. See Dumont (1972, §§ 23–26, 76–103[59–90]).

[75] PVṬ P *ñe* 27a3–4 ≈ PVSVṬ 558.3–4: *sāmānyaniṣedhān niṣiddhaiva jātiḥ / kevalam abhyupagamyocyate /*. "Although [Dharmakīrti] already refuted the class by refuting the universal, he simply accepts [it provisionally] and says [what follows]." TS 3575ab: *śataśaḥ pratiṣiddhāyāṃ jātau jātimadaś ca kim /*. "And why [show such] a pride in caste when the class has [already] been refuted hundreds of times?" See also PVṬ P *ñe* 85a3–4 = PVSVṬ 618.27 on PV I 340: *vastubhūtasāmānyaniṣedhān na pūrvaḥ pakṣaḥ /*. "[Your] first hypothesis does not [hold], since we have [already] refuted real universals." On the value of that "first hypothesis," see section 2.5.1.1, p. 138, below.

2.1.2.2 External explanation: Kumārila and the principle of *vedamūlatva*

Now the fact that Dharmakīrti's commentators and successors recognized and stressed the strong polemical *potential* of the theory of exclusion does not explain away the fact that none of the chapters or sections dealing with exclusion in the works of Dignāga, Dharmakīrti and Śāntarakṣita (PS[V], chap. V, PV[SV], chap. I and TS, chap. XIII, *sāmānyaparīkṣā*, and XVI, *śabdārthaparīkṣā*) include a discussion of the problems related to the social aspect of class. A first hypothetical explanation only begins to take form when we consider that *all* the critiques formulated by Buddhist epistemologists against the Brahmanic realist thematizations of caste appear in chapters or sections *directed against the Mīmāṃsā*. As I shall argue, starting with Dharmakīrti, the Buddhist polemical efforts against the naturalization of caste are closely linked to the critique of Mīmāṃsaka positions. More precisely, Dharmakīrti and his successors bring back all the canonical arguments previously directed at Brahmins in general in their polemic against the Mīmāṃsā.

Compared to Dignāga, Bhāviveka/Bhavya and Dharmapāla,[76] Dharmakīrti in fact entirely rewrites the Buddhist critique of the

---

[76] As far as I know, Dignāga does not discuss the authorlessness of the Veda, nor the "social" valorization of classes. And Bhāviveka/Bhavya, while he dedicates a chapter to the Mīmāṃsaka positions, does not say a word about caste despite the objector's opening position presented in MHK IX 11 (Kawasaki 1992a, 410): *devarṣijuṣṭaśiṣṭeṣṭaṃ purāṇaṃ vartma śobhanam / vedārthabāhyaiḥ strīśūdrair yuktaṃ yat tyajyate trayī //*. (Translated in English in Kawasaki 1976, 11, together with TJ *ad loc.*, note 10). More than that: according to de Jong's (1988, 429–430) interpretation of Avalokitavrata on *Prajñāpradīpa* I, the great Mādhyamika doctor would even have favoured the first two classes. Kawasaki (1992b, 10; other elements in Eltschinger 1998, note 22) was able to show, however, that the Mīmāṃsā criticized by Bhāviveka/Bhavya looks like a non-systematic collection of ideas and doctrines probably current in his days and, for the last two thirds of the text, often having nothing to do with the Mīmāṃsā of Śabara and Kumārila. As for Dharmapāla, we have seen that he does not so much attack the Mīmāṃsā as

Mīmāṃsā. For once, only 6 verses (= PV I 218–223) go to an examination of the Naiyāyika and perhaps also the Jain legitimizations of scriptural authority, while no less than 115 verses (= PV I 224–338) go to his critique of the authorlessness of the Veda as a logical reason for its authority (*vedaprāmāṇya*). The Naiyāyika's and the Jain's acceptance of the principle of a trustworthy person (*āpta*) capable of perceiving supersensible things (*atīndriyadarśipuruṣa*) may have stopped Dharmakīrti from going into a more thorough critique of their positions, for their criteria of authority may have seemed sufficiently close to his own. But this probably does not fully account for his decision. I believe that a more satisfactory explanation is to be found elsewhere, more specifically in Kumārila.

Three of Wilhelm Halbfass' publications[77] have contributed to build an image of Kumārila as a champion of Brahmanic orthodoxy.[78] The whole Mīmāṃsā tradition centres on the notion of dharma, a term which is first understood to refer, in the normative literature, to "the dharma of (social) classes and the stages of life" (*varṇāśramadharma*). But the Mīmāṃsā is more an orthopraxy than an orthodoxy.[79] For its intent, stated in its open-

---

the Brahmins, whom he accuses of having confiscated the symbolic power by creating the whole of the Veda.

77 Halbfass (1976; 1983, 1–26 = chap. I, "Kumārila on Ahiṃsā and Dharma"; and 1990, 310–333 = chap. 17, "*Dharma* in the Self-Understanding of Traditional Hinduism").

78 On many occasions, Halbfass describes the Mīmāṃsā, and more specifically that of Kumārila, as a restoration (Halbfass 1990, 321, 329 and 331). For him (1990, 325), "'orthodox' Hinduism found [in the Mīmāṃsā] its most uncompromising expression." Verpoorten (1987, 23) also describes the Mīmāṃsā as the "ambassador of Brahmanic orthodoxy in its most rigorous form" (English translation of Verpoorten).

79 For example, Śabara's comments on the *codanāsūtra* support this claim (ŚBh I 1.2/I 20.5–21): *yo hi yāgam anutiṣṭhati taṃ dhārmika iti samācakṣate* /. "Is called '*dhārmika*' the [man] who performs the sacrifices." See also ŚV, *codanāsūtra*, 192: *anyat sādhyam adṛṣṭvaiva yāgādīn anutiṣṭhataḥ / dhārmikatvasamākhyānaṃ tadyogād iti gamyate* //.

ing sutra, is to materialize the "desire to know the dharma"[80] (*dharmajijñāsā*). The definition of dharma proposed in Jaimini's second sutra in fact makes it the object (*artha*) of Vedic injunctions (*codanā*).[81] Already in its foundational text, the Mīmāṃsā thus finds in the Veda the exclusive source of knowledge of dharma, which is now intimately linked to the practice of sacrifice. In his radicalization of the Mīmāṃsā position, Kumārila tries to undermine all attempts to establish the norms of dharma on commonly accepted empirical criteria, even the conduct of learned men (*śiṣṭācāra*) or eminent ones (*mahājana*).[82] And in so doing, he rejects all identifications of dharma with harmlessness (*ahiṃsā*) or with benefitting others (*parānugraha*), as well as all identifications of unrighteousness (*adharma*) with hurting others (*parapīḍā*).[83] In other words, Kumārila equally objects to the relativization of Vedic prescriptions, to the universalization of one or more specific norms, and to the empiricalness of the norms of dharma. For him, dharma and unrighteousness are ultimately and exclusively related to Vedic injunctions (*vidhi*) and prohibitions (*ni°/pratiṣedha*).[84] His approach, which is already clearly expressed in the ŚV, finds its full expression in the TV on MīSū I 3.1–29, where he describes in details the criteria for the "vedicity" of the Brahmanic and non-Brahmanic *Smṛtis*. His position culminates in the principle that dharma is rooted in the Veda (*dharmasya vedamūlatvam*). And on that principle, he remains strictly intransigent.

Kumārila will vehemently reject a juxtaposition of relative dharmas. Because only the Veda is authoritative when it comes to dharma, only Vedic prescriptions guarantee that people's socio-

---

80 MīSū I 1.1: *athāto dharmajijñāsā* /.

81 MīSū I 1.2: *sa hi niḥśreyasena puruṣaṃ saṃyunaktīti pratijānīmahe / tad abhidhīyate codanālakṣaṇo 'rtho dharmaḥ* /.

82 On those different matters, see ŚV, *codanāsūtra*, 195–196ab and 243–247; *autpattikasūtra*, 1–6; TV on MīSū I 3.7.

83 In addition to the references given above, see primarily Halbfass (1983).

84 See ŚV, *codanāsūtra*, 242 and 248.

religious conduct meets the norms. In fact, as a treatise on epistemology and linguistic theory, the *Tarkapāda* is nothing but an apology of the Veda and, as such, a propaedeutic to founding the norms that logically follow from the Veda.[85] It is in that sense that we must establish a closer connection than we have so far between the authorlessness of the Veda as a criterion of their authority, and the principle that dharma is rooted in the Veda as a criterion of dharma.

Everyone will agree that Kumārila's thought, more than Śabara's, is mainly directed at Buddhism. As Halbfass has very acutely pointed out: "The orthodox efforts to exclude Buddhism from the domain of the true and real dharma were predominant and ultimately prevailed, and the restorative philosophy of dharma contained in the Mīmāṃsā is to a large degree an answer to the Buddhist challenge."[86] It is therefore not surprising to find Kumārila add a series of very severe critiques of the Buddha and Buddhism to his long examination, in MīSū I 3.4, of the principle that dharma is rooted in the Veda.

Dharmakīrti, I believe, was very aware of the possible consequences, for Buddhism, of the "radicalization of the *vedamūlatva* principle"[87] operated by Kumārila. He was also aware of the profoundly apologetic nature of the commentary to the *Tarkapāda*. I have noted above the continuity between the authority of the Veda and the principle that dharma is rooted in the Veda. As clearly stated in PV I 224, when Dharmakīrti criticizes the authorlessness of the Veda, he criticizes one of the logical reasons put forward by the Mīmāṃsaka to establish the Veda's authority. For the Veda's authority on unempirical (*adṛṣṭa*) matters pro-

---

85 This is confirmed by the opening sentences of TV on MīSū I 2.1/II 1.14–18: *siddhapramāṇabhāvasya dharme vedasya sarvaśaḥ / vidhyarthavādamantrāṇām upayogo 'dhunocyate // sāmānyataḥ prāmāṇye siddhe 'dhunā vibhājya viniyogaḥ pratipādyate / avadhṛtaprāmāṇyasya vā vedasyedānīṃ samastasya vidhyarthavādamantranāmadheyātmakasya yathāvibhāgaṃ dharmaṃ praty upayogaḥ pratipādyate /*.

86 Halbfass (1990, 321).

87 Halbfass (1990, 328).

vides its full legitimacy to the principle that dharma is rooted in the Veda, and that it is because the Veda is authoritative that Kumārila can both refute any relativization of the norms of dharma with more intransigence than his predecessors, and justify his strict exclusion of Buddhism. In other words, ruining the notion of the authorlessness of the Veda is for Dharmakīrti to weaken the whole of Kumārila's "restorative" enterprise.

These points shall enable us to explain why, starting with Dharmakīrti and after a long period of silence on the issue, the Buddhist efforts to fight the naturalization of caste were uniformly directed against the Mīmāṃsā, even though Bhartṛhari and the Naiyāyikas,[88] for example, had made some vigorous attempts to naturalize and ontologize the class. If Dharmakīrti, Śāntarakṣita and Prajñākaragupta reintegrate the canonical positions and arguments against caste in their polemic against the Mīmāṃsā, it is because the Mīmāṃsā, starting with Kumārila, is perceived by everyone as the philosophical expression *par excellence* of Brahmanic orthodoxy. The Mīmāṃsā, by conferring their full vedicity, and therefore also their full authority, to the juridical *Smṛtis, ipso facto* guarantees their normativity. For our purpose, it is moreover especially important to note that we also owe it to Kumārila to have developed, beginning with the TV, a specific argumentation in favour of the reality and direct perceptibility of class. Later Naiyāyikas will themselves often repeat that argumentation without any substantial modification.[89] Kumārila is therefore the first to support with strong philosophical arguments the social norms set by the juridical literature and that he wants to restore. It is not surprising, therefore, to find the late Buddhists integrate their arguments against the naturalization of caste to their general polemic against the Mīmāṃsā.

Dharmakīrti both formally systematizes the meta-religious evaluations of his predecessors and proposes, in the *Pramāṇa-*

---

88 On this point, see Halbfass (1976) and, for Bhartṛhari, (1976, 300[28] and note 95).

89 See section 2.4.1, p. 116, below.

siddhipariccheda, a Buddhism that is unified and reduced to its minimal axioms, i.e., to axioms that most Buddhists will accept.[90] In PV I and PV II, he first proposes (= PV I 213–217) a formal method to evaluate the different scriptures. He then (= PV I 218–340) goes into a critical examination of the criteria considered to grant their reliability to scriptures. And finally (= PV II), he offers a systematic and argued presentation of the inherent authority of the Buddha's teachings on soteriological matters. Those two chapters, I believe, first reflect a strong preoccupation with the multiplication of schools and movements that come in competition with Buddhism as such, and also a strong proselyte concern to build a unified Buddhist doctrinal identity. This had become necessary to counteract the growing institutional precarity that was certainly underway in Dharmakīrti's time.

A long transition occurs however between those two sections of PV. It consists in an analysis in 115 verses of the authorlessness of the Veda. I have sketched above a hypothesis to account for that third and final part of the *Svārthānumānapariccheda*. Its size and systematic character show alone how important it was for Dharmakīrti to provide a critique of the Mīmāṃsā's dogmatic pillar. But Dharmakīrti's intent was not limited to attacking Kumārila and the authorlessness of the Veda. Even more so, he wanted to undermine the epistemological foundation it pro-

[90] Hayes (1984, 662–663): "... Dharmakīrti ends up offering an elaborately argued apology of the central core of Buddhist doctrine, that set of doctrines accepted by nearly all Buddhist *āgamas*, whether Śrāvakayāna, Bodhisattvayāna or Tantrayāna in orientation. It was this apologetic quality of Dharmakīrti's work, along with his attempts to justify the teachings of Buddhist scripture without explicitly citing scriptures as his authority, that provided the model for many of the subsequent generations of Buddhist intellectuals." I now (2009) consider Hayes' statement a bit too radical. Considered in detail, Dharmakīrti's buddhology is unambiguously mahāyānistic. There are, moreover, reasons to believe that Dharmakīrti showed reluctance with regard to certain doctrines (natural efficacy of mantras, soteriological relevance of initiation) of the contemporaneously developing (Buddhist) esotericism (see Eltschinger 2001, 121–123 and 2008, 286).

vided to the Veda's unconditioned validity and credibility as the exclusive authority on dharma for the different social classes and stages of life (*varṇāśramadharma*). On that hypothesis, then, Dharmakīrti primarily intends to neutralize the threat—one of many, perhaps—to the very existence and tolerability of the Buddhist community that would result from a radicalization of the principle that dharma is rooted in the Veda. Having said that, Dharmakīrti's text validates in no way that hypothesis since he focuses on the technical and theoretical aspects of the debate without ever turning to its practical implications. Is there then no justification, in Dharmakīrti, for the connexion proposed between the principles of the authorlessness of the Veda and the necessary Vedic origin of dharma? To answer that question, it is necessary to look at one of Śākyabuddhi's brief comments on PVSV 126.4–5. That comment is capital in so far as it very clearly indicates that Śākyabuddhi, for one, understood that the epistemological aspect of the Veda's authorlessness could serve to legitimize the restoration or perpetuation of a dharma of social classes (*varṇadharma*). Let us consider that passage. The italics correspond to Śākyabuddhi's comment: "Even though the authorlessness is accepted [by the Mīmāṃsakas] because it is reliable, [*but not because it secures the Law of the (social) classes*], that [authorlessness] applies also to some belying (*visaṃvādaka*) [mundane practices] since [the latter also] are beginningless.[91] Why, therefore, [speak of this] authorlessness?"[92] Despite its neg-

---

[91] In PV I 243 and below, Dharmakīrti rejects the claim that "every Vedic recitation is preceded by [one's] guru's Vedic recitation" (*vedasyādhyayanaṃ sarvaṃ gurvadhyayanapūrvakam*). ŚV, *vākyādhikaraṇa*, 366 is a justification for the authorlessness of the Veda. PV I 244–246ab are a sub-section of that critique, one which questions more specifically the claim that having no beginning (*anāditva*) is a reason for the authorlessness of the Veda.

[92] PVSV 126.4–5: *kāmam avisaṃvādakam ity apauruṣeyatvam iṣṭam / tad visaṃvādakānām api keṣāṃcid anāditvād astīti kim apauruṣeyatvena /*. PVṬ P *je* 346b4–5: *de ltar na rnam pa gang gis mi slu ba'i phyir skyes bus ma byas pa nyid du 'dod kyi rigs kyi chos bsrung ba'i phyir ni ma yin na /*. There is no equivalent for this comment in Karṇakagomin.

ative formulation, the comment is fairly clear: the Mīmāṃsakas are trying to hide their social conservatism behind their epistemology. Behind the theoretical effort, Śākyabuddhi unmasks a practical interest, a socio-political motivation.[93] In other words, Śākyabuddhi here uncovers an effort to naturalize the hierarchical social order that the Mīmāṃsaka Brahmins believe they can derive from some non-human Veda that they take to be the sole authority on dharma and are the only ones capable of interpreting.

That important comment, it is true, only engages Śākyabuddhi. But it has the merit of exposing an explicit awareness of the presuppositions and motivations attributable to the Mīmāṃsā. A few words by Śākyabuddhi are of course not sufficient to validate a schematic hypothesis on Dharmakīrti's 107 verses and his difficult auto-commentary. They nonetheless show that the general explanation here developed is not illegitimate, for it finds its confirmation in at least one part of the tradition.

2.2 Context and problematic of Dharmakīrti's discussion

Dharmakīrti's brief discussion of the unreality of class comes in the general context of his critique of the authorlessness of the Veda propounded by the Mīmāṃsā. Its immediate context consists in an argument for the conventionality of Vedic mantras.[94] For Dharmakīrti, as we shall see, the efficiency of Vedic mantras

---

93 The properly political dimension of the dharma of social classes is even clearer when we consider that in the normative literature, the king is responsible for enforcing the Law of classes and the stages of life. It is not therefore surprising to find that dimension in Kumārila, ŚV, *vanavāda*, 29cd: *kvacid ācārataś ca samyag rājānupālitāt* /. "Moreover, in some [places, brahmanity] can also [be determined] by the rule of conduct since it is well protected by the king."

94 On the general question of mantras, see Gonda (1975), Alper (1989) and Padoux (1989).

comes in contradiction with the authorlessness of the Veda.[95] For him, to claim that mantras have a natural efficiency[96] (*bhā-*

[95] Dharmakīrti's discussion is problematic from the very beginning. Indeed, while it falls very well in the general context of a critique of the Mīmāṃsā, it shows a lack of understanding of the Mīmāṃsā position on mantras. In PVSV 123.15–17, Dharmakīrti presents his own definition of a mantra: *na mantro nāmānyad eva kiṃcid / kiṃ tarhi / satyatapaḥprabhāvavatāṃ samīhitārthasādhanaṃ vacanam /*. Now, everything tends to indicate that in the passage with which we are concerned here (= PVSV 155.18–157.28), Dharmakīrti does not in any way adjust that very general conception to the quite specific conception of the Mīmāṃsā. The latter, indeed, never isolates the mantra from the context provided by a given ritual sequence. And while for the Mīmāṃsā one will use a mantra for a precise purpose, that purpose remains strictly subordinated to the prescribed ritual act. The mantra, by itself, has no purpose or result. The realization of its purpose depends on the correct performance of a given ritual which *does* have a purpose or result. The Mīmāṃsā subdivides the Vedic corpus into mantras and *brāhmaṇas*, then into mantras on one side and religious injunctions (*vidhi*), descriptive statements (*arthavāda*) and names (*nāmadheya*) on the other. Whether they are recited, chanted or whispered, the mantras are, in theory, a verse or passage from the Ṛgveda (*ṛc*), Sāmaveda (*sāman*) or Yajurveda (*yajus*), and their choice vary with the adopted procedure (*itikartavyatā*). On this point, see Keith (1978, 79–82). In MīSū I 2.32, Śabara says of the mantras that they are indicative (*abhidhānasamartha*; Taber 1989, 149): "Indeed, the Mīmāṃsā, in its formal definition of mantra, MīSū I 2.32, is careful to specify that a mantra is what *expresses* (literally, activates) an indication of a ritual element (*abhidhānasya codaka*); it is not the indication itself. That is to say, mantras imply references to ritual details" (Taber 1989, 150). Spoken by the officiant simultaneously with the different elements constituting the ritual sequence, the mantras indicate to him, or remind him what he is doing or remains to be done in the procedure. On the mnemonic function of mantras, see Taber 1989, 161–162 note 14. Mantras, as Taber writes (1989, 149), "provide a running narrative of the rite."

Dharmakīrti, in PVSV, devotes two passages of unequal length to mantras (PVSV 123.14–124.26 and 155.18–164.24; translated in Japanese in Omae 1989, 62–65, and Wakahara 1988, 2–21). Both passages appear in the context of the polemic against the Mīmāṃsā. Since I have discussed elsewhere (Eltschinger 2001 and 2008) the function and content of those passages, I here only give an outline of Dharmakīrti's position. As we saw above, a mantra consists in an expression (*vacana*,

vaśakti) is to accept that mantras bestow results (*phalada*) on *all* their users (*prayoktṛ*), Brahmins and *śūdras* alike. For when the mantra's efficiency is considered to be permanent and "natural" (i.e., depending on the mantra's intrinsic nature), it cannot be limited to the three classes (*varṇa*) of the twice-born or the authorized sponsors of a sacrifice (*yajamāna*), at the exclusion of *śūdras*. Moreover, even if we abandoned the premise that the mantra is permanent and yet accepted that it is a real entity (*bhāva*), that entity will be exposed to the same law of causality as any other real entity. In order for a mantra to acquire the additional property (*atiśaya, viśeṣa*) of being efficient exclusively with Brahmins and their kin, its cause, here its users, will have to *really* differ from those who are excluded, and not only differ *conventionally*. In other words, the real entity called "mantra"

---

etc.), i.e., in a succession of phonemes (*varṇa*), revealed by a person possessing power (*prabhāvavatpuruṣa*) or by a cognitively superior person (*puruṣātiśaya*). There is little doubt that for Dharmakīrti that person is identical with the author of scriptures. It is therefore a person capable of perceiving supersensible things (*atīndriyārthadarśipuruṣa*), whom Kamalaśīla identifies with the Buddha (see TSP 904.7–8 and 904.11–13 on TS 3487). That person is the author of tantras or treatises in which are formulated the ritual and/or moral prescriptions, as well as the religious observances (*vidhi, vidhāna, vrata*, etc.) to be followed by anyone who hopes to use a mantra successfully. The man who meets the conditions described therein *ipso facto* meets the conditions of the convention (*samaya*) or promise (*pratijñā*) formulated by the author of the ritual treatise. As long as the prescriptions are observed by the user (*mantraprayoktṛ*), the mantra is empowered (*adhiṣṭhāna*) by the person who composed the mantra (*mantrapraṇetṛ*). It should finally be noted that (1) some karmic considerations are present in Dharmakīrti's discussion and that, capital to an understanding of the general structure of PV I 224ff, (2) the two passages constitute proofs of the existence of cognitively superior persons, i.e., in the final analysis, of the strictly human character of the scripture (*āgamapauruṣeyatā*).

96 I freely translate *bhāvaśakti* as "natural efficiency." PVṬ P *ñe* 23b3 = PVSVṬ 553.27 glosses: *bhāvaśaktiḥ śabdasvabhāvasyaiva... śaktiḥ*. "*bhāvaśakti* refers to the efficiency belonging to the nature of [verbal] sounds [that constitute the mantra]." *bhāvaśakti* is therefore the essential or intrinsic capacity of the mantra.

will only acquire differentiated properties if Brahmins and *śūdras*, like cows and horses, belong to different classes.[97] If, on the other hand, the difference of class (*jātibheda*) is only due to worldly usage and social conventions (*lokavyavahāra*), Brahmins and *śūdras* will equally benefit from the mantra's efficiency (as long as the mantra's efficiency depends on the entity itself and not, as Dharmakīrti holds, on a wish or convention established by the author of the mantra).

The underlying context of this argument is to be found in the absolute prohibition for *śūdras* to use mantras or have access to the Veda. That prohibition, like the exclusion of *śūdras* from the initiation (*upanayana*) sacrament (*saṃskāra*) and, therefore, from the condition of the twice-born (*dvija*), is repeated in all the dharma literature, including of course the Mīmāṃsā. However liberal the different legislators may have been in allowing *śūdras* to access Vedic rituals and sacraments other than the initiation sacrament, all were equally intransigent about the Veda itself, i.e., about the memorization, recitation, muttering (*japa*) or hearing of mantras.

In MS X 126, for example, *śūdras* are precluded from accessing sacraments and disqualified from dharma.[98] *Laghuviṣṇu* I 15 says of the fourth class, the class of the *śūdras*, that it is "excluded from all sacraments"[99] (*sarvasaṃskāravarjita*). Śaṅkha, Vedavyāsa and Haradatta allow *śūdras* to access some sacraments, but under the significant condition that no Vedic mantra be used.[100] So even if some authors are more liberal than others, *śūdras* remain excluded from the initiation. According to Śabara commenting on MīSū VI 1.33, the Veda only speaks of the initiation of the three superior classes: Brahmins receive the initia-

---

97 As we noted above, Dharmakīrti does not accept the reality of classes. Here he only provisionally does so. See section 2.1.2.1, p. 85, above and section 2.3.2, p. 107, below.

98 See Kane (1974, 158). For nuances based on MS IV 80, see Kane (1974, 159).

99 See Kane (1974, 159 and note 372).

100 See Kane (1974, 159).

tion in the spring, *kṣatriyas* in the summer and *vaiśyas* in the fall. But in being forbidden from receiving the initiation, *śūdras* are excluded also from studying and from all contact with the Veda, in whatever form. Hence *Vasiṣṭha* XVIII 13 proscribes the recitation or memorization of the Veda near a *śūdra* (*śūdrasamīpe*).[101] *Gautama* XII 4 in fact describes several punishments awaiting the *śūdra* according to the degree to which he may come in contact with the Veda. If he intentionally listens to the Veda, the *śūdra* will have his hears filled with tin or lac (*trapujatubhyāṃ śrotrapūraṇam*). If he pronounces a portion of the Veda, his tongue will be cut (*jihvāccheda*). If he learns the Veda, he will be put to death (*śarīrabheda*).[102] In MīSū VI 1.35, Śabara also forbids *śūdras* to study the Veda.[103] In MīSū I 3.2, he in fact specifies that contact with the Veda is restricted to the three superior classes.[104] Any contact with the Veda being forbidden to the *śūdra*, he can however listen to the narrative literature (*itihāsa*) such as the *Mahābhārata*, as well as to the *Purāṇas*. A passage from the *Mahābhārata* in fact seems to allow the four classes to access the epic, which will nonetheless preferably be recited by a Brahmin.[105] Along those lines, the *Bhāgavatapurāṇa* declares that the Veda (*trayī*) cannot be heard by women, *śūdras* and those who pretend to be Brahmins (*dvijabandhu*), and explains that this is the reason why the sage Vyāsa, out of compassion, composed the *Mahābhārata*.

---

[101] See Kane (1974, 154 and note 358). The prohibition is found in the ŚBh on MīSū VI 1.38.

[102] See Kane (1974, 155 and note 361).

[103] ŚBh VI 1.35/V 213.3–5: *tasmād vedādhyayane brāhmaṇādayaḥ śrutāḥ / śūdrasya na śrutaṃ vedādhyayanam / ato 'vedatvād asamarthaḥ śūdro nādhikriyata iti /*. See Verpoorten (1987, 25).

[104] ŚBh I 3.2/II 77.4–5: *tenopapanno vedasaṃyogas traivarṇikānām /*. See also *Praśastapādabhāṣya* §311: *brāhmaṇakṣatriyavaiśyānām ijyādhyayanadānāni /*.

[105] *Mahābhārata* XII 328.49; see Kane (1974, 155 and note 362).

It is easy to understand, under such conditions, that the *śūdra* is prohibited from any contact with Vedic mantras.[106] According to MS X 127, any rite performed for a *śūdra* is done without Vedic mantras, except for the mantra *namaḥ*, the only authorized exception. While the *śūdra* is allowed to think about the divinity, about Agni for example, and to pronounce that mantra, he is not allowed to say: "May a blessing rest on Agni" (*agnaye svāhā*).[107] According to Aparārka commenting on MS IV 80, the *śūdra*s may perform religious observances (*vrata*), but exclusively through a Brahmin, and so long as no muttering prayers are used and no oblations (*homa*) are offered to the gods. *Atri* XIX 137 even lists the practice of mantras among the six mortal sins for women and *śūdras*, and requires their execution by the king in case of a violation of the interdict.[108] On the other hand, *śūdra*s are authorized to recite some non-Vedic mantras, the Purāṇic mantras, for example.[109]

When we turn to Dharmakīrti, we find that the argument developed at PVSV 155.18–157.28 may be divided in three parts.[110]

---

106 See Gonda (1975, 261). The *Praśastapādabhāṣya* §311 authorizes the *śūdra* to involve in ritual activities devoid of mantras (*śūdrasya... amantrikāś ca kriyāḥ*).

107 See Kane (1974, 158 and note 371).

108 See Kane (1974, 119 and note 258).

109 See Kane (1974, 156) and Gonda (1975, 264–265).

110 According to Śākyabuddhi (PVṬ P *ñe* 23a3) and Karṇakagomin (PVSVṬ 553.12), the position here defended by Dharmakīrti follows from the proposition that if, or because, some Vedic expressions are mantras, (then) they have a human origin, i.e., they depend on the convention or promise established by a person possessing power. In other words, mantras will be productive as long as they are conventional. In PVSV 155.26–156.22, Dharmakīrti elaborates a twofold argumentative strategy to show that authorless expressions could never be mantras. Each of those two strategies is in turn composed of two parts.

As he had done in his critique of the permanence of sound (*śabdanityatā*), Dharmakīrti plays in his first series of arguments (= PVSV 155.26–156.10) on the Mīmāṃsaka dialectic stating that words are phonemes (*varṇa*) in a specific order (*krama*). For his opponent (= PVSV 155.27–28), the fact that the mantra bears results is due solely to the intrinsic

---

nature of the entity (*bhāvasvabhāva*), i.e., solely to the mantra's phonemes according to Śākyabuddhi and Karṇakagomin. Dharmakīrti's answer (= PVSV 155.28–156.2) follows from the principle that enables him to assert on various occasions, in the footsteps of Dharmapāla, that if words are only phonemes, then the words *rasaḥ* (taste) and *saraḥ* (lake, pool), since they are made of the same phonetic components, will refer to the same object. But this is obviously false (see *Guǎng bǎi lùn shì lùn*, chap. V (223b6), on CŚ XIII; Tillemans (1990, I, 140–141) and (1990, I, 250 note 230); PVSV 119.14–16 on PV I 238, where, in addition to PV I 301 and according to Śākyabuddhi and Karṇakagomin, the issue is implicit). Furthermore, if mantras are nothing but phonemes and if their productivity is due solely to their nature, they will bear results independently of the prescriptions on how to use them, regardless of the order in which the atomic phonemes that constitute the nature of mantras are produced. And this is also obviously false. In his critique of the second objection (= PVSV 156.2–3), according to which the mantra consists in phonemes that follow a determined order and not in phonemes only, Dharmakīrti arrives at the same conclusion (PV I 293ab and PVSV 156.5–7) since, referring once again to some of his prior arguments (notably to PV I 259), he rejects the claim that the phonemes' order is something different (*arthāntara*) from the phonemes.

In the second strategy (= PVSV 156.10–22), Dharmakīrti moves the discussion to the area of causality, his favourite subject against the eternalist Mīmāṃsā, where the problematic of caste will also reappear. Here again, Dharmakīrti adopts the structure and conclusion of the previous discussions against the word's semantic capacity (*śabdaśakti*), the permanence of sound (*śabdanityatā*) and the *sphoṭa* (the non-phonetic element that, according to Sanskrit grammarians, functions as the meaning bearer of a word or sentence). If one holds that it is part of a mantra's nature to be the *cause* of a benefit (*arthahetu*) for the person using it, then productivity is a defining characteristic of the mantra. But if the mantra is permanent (*nitya*) because it has not been produced (*akṛtaka*), it will follow from the fact that it exists permanently, that the mantra will bear its results (*arthasiddhi*) permanently (*nityam*).

Against an opponent arguing (= PVSV 156.16–17) that the productivity of a mantra depends on rules (*vidhānāpekṣa*) and that the mere fact of using a mantra (*mantraprayoga*) cannot be its only cause, Dharmakīrti (= PV I 293d and PVSV 156.19–22) reiterates the principle according to which a permanent entity cannot be provided with an additional property (*anādheyātiśaya*) by a cooperating cause (*sahakārin*) that is

And in the last part, PVSV 156.23–157.28, he demonstrates that the Mīmāṃsaka postulate about the Veda having no human author, and therefore also the postulate about the natural efficiency of Vedic mantras, have for their necessary consequence that Vedic mantras must bestow results on *all* humans without exception, including *śūdras*.

In so doing, Dharmakīrti may be developing two ancient Buddhist literary themes, one belonging to the *Bhūridattajātaka*, the other to the *Assalāyana Sutta*. For already in the *Bhūridattajātaka*, we find an interrogation as to why non-Brahmins are excluded from the recitation of Vedic mantras. According to that *Jātaka*, Brahmins believe that Brahma (here: *vasin*) created this world in such a way that Brahmins (*ariya*) would dedicate their lives to study (*ajjhena*), *kṣatriyas* (here: *jan'inda*) to control of the land (*paṭhavī*), *vaiśyas* to agriculture (*kasī*) and *śūdras* to serving (*pāricariya*).[111] Subhoga's interlocutor is first worried that, if this were the case, no non-Brahmin (*abrāhmaṇa*) could learn the mantras' verses (*mantapada*).[112] Later on, however, he affirms that a *caṇḍāla* (*caṇḍālaputta*) could also speak the mantras after having learned the Veda (*adhicca vede*), as long of

---

part of a causal process, since it does not depend on anything (*anapekṣa*). If the entity were to receive an additional property by the cooperating cause that is here the rules, that entity would depend on that cause and would *ipso facto* lose its permanence. Dharmakīrti can therefore conclude (PVSV 156.21–22): ... *ity anapekṣāḥ sadā kuryur na vā kadācid anatiśayāt* /. "It follows from this that [since they] depend on nothing, [mantras] should either produce [their effect] permanently [if they are efficient by nature], or [they should] never [produce it] since, [if they are inefficient by nature, they can] not, [in so far as they are permanent, receive] the additional property [that would enable them to produce their effect]."

111 *Bhūridattajātaka*, verse 150: *ajjhenam ariyā, paṭhaviṃ jan'indā, vessā kasiṃ pāricariyañ ca suddā upāgu paccekā yathāpadesaṃ: katāhu ete vasinā ti āhu*. Translated in Alsdorf (1977, 51).

112 *Bhūridattajātaka*, verse 151: *etañ ca saccaṃ vacanaṃ bhaveyya yathā idaṃ bhāsitā brāhmaṇehi, nākhattiyo jātu labhetha rajjaṃ, nābrāhmaṇo mantapadāni sikkhe, nāññatra vessehi kasiṃ kareyya, suddo na muñce parapessitāya*. Translated in Alsdorf (1977, 51).

course as his intelligence would allow him to do so. And his head would not split in seven parts as a result.... The text finally questions why the recitation of Vedic mantras by non-Brahmins should lead them to commit suicide (*attavadha*).[113]

Now while the content of the *Bhūridattajātaka* offers a precedent to Dharmakīrti's argument, the *Assalāyana Sutta* is one of its distant ancestors in terms of its *structure* and conclusion. The Buddha there tells the following story. A king assembles one hundred men of various social origins and first asks those among them who are of higher extraction (i.e., of *kṣatriya*, Brahmin and royal extractions) to light a fire using noble woods in order to produce heat. The king then also asks those among them who are of low extraction (*caṇḍālakula, nesādakula, veṇakula, rathakārakula, pukkusakula*) to light a fire to produce heat, but this time using vile materials.[114] The Buddha then asks Assalāyana if one of the two fires will be more radiant and have more flames than the other, and if one fire will better fulfil the function of fire (*aggikaraṇīya*).[115] To both questions, Assalāyana gives a negative answer.[116] The conclusion to this argument therefore goes as follows: whatever difference of appearance there may be between the two causes (men and fuel) of each fire, none of the fires are different in their nature, nor in their function.

---

[113] *Bhūridattajātaka*, verse 177: *caṇḍālaputto pi adhicca vede bhāseyya mante kusalo mutīmā, na tassa muddhā pi phaleyya sattadhā – mantā ime attavadhāya katto?* Translated in Alsdorf (1977, 54).

[114] AgS, M.N. II 151–152. Translated in Rhys Davids (1969, 344).

[115] AgS, M.N. II 152. Translated in Rhys Davids (1969, 344–345).

[116] AgS, M.N. II 152–153. Translated in Rhys Davids (1969, 345).

2.3 Dharmakīrti against the class (*jāti*)

2.3.1 Immediate context

As I have already indicated, Dharmakīrti's treatment of caste appears in the immediate context (= PVSV 156.23–157.28, including PV I 294–296ac) of a discussion that essentially deals with problems of causality. Straightaway, Dharmakīrti asserts, in PV I 294ab, that "if the natural efficiency [of mantras] were as [you describe], those [mantras] would be for everyone a means of attaining (*sādhana*) [a desired result]."[117] Dharmakīrti therefore begins his critique of caste by attacking the prohibitive use of Vedic mantras affecting *śūdras*. Central to his argument is the opponent's notion of a natural efficiency that would be permanent and, consequently, immune from the intervention of man as a cooperating cause of the mantra's efficiency. At this stage, Dharmakīrti thus reproduces the schema according to which no additional property may be added to permanent mantras to account for their productivity. In so far as they are permanent and independent, mantras cannot, therefore, be subjected to any human conditioning (*saṃskāra*) that would result in their being effective for the authorized sponsors of sacrifices (*yajamāna*), but ineffective for *śūdras* or *caṇḍālas*. Dharmakīrti very clearly asserts that the mantra's productive essence does not disappear with the *śūdra* anymore than it increases with the Brahmin or the authorized sponsors of sacrifices,[118] "for the causality [of mantras] is not [in any way] linked to a certain [person at the expense of another]."[119] In other words, in so far as no coopera-

---

[117] PV I 294ab: *sarvasya sādhanaṃ te syur bhāvaśaktir yadīdṛśī* /. Commentators disagree in their explanations of the word *īdṛśī*. PVṬ P *ñe* 25b2: *gal te dngos nus te 'dra na zhes bya ba skyes bu'i byed pa la bltos pa med pa'i rang bzhin nyid rang gi 'bras bu sgrub par nus pa yin na*; PVSVṬ 556.12: *samayanirapekṣā yadīdṛśī*; PVV 396.20: *īdṛśī kāryaviśeṣasādhikā*.

[118] PVSV 156.27–157.1: *tasya tenānapakarṣaṇād anyena cānutkarṣaṇāt* /.

[119] PVSV 157.1: *kenacit saha kāryakāraṇabhāvāyogāt* /.

tion is possible in the form of a human conditioning, the permanent character of a mantra's natural efficiency cannot be modified to introduce a differentiation in its productivity. As Dharmakīrti will later say, such a differentiation can only be justified under the strict condition that the mantra be a human convention with restrictions as to its usage and field of application.[120]

In the remaining part of his argument, Dharmakīrti abandons the premise that the mantra is permanent and addresses the problem from the perspective of the causality of real entities (*bhāva*). This is the approach used in his terse verse I 295: "[But since] even for an entity that can be conditioned, [such as an impermanent mantra, only] a [real] difference in the causes[121] is differentiating, [the purely conventional[122]] difference among [Brahmin and *śūdra*] users [can]not restrict the [mantra's] efficiency.

---

[120] See PVSV 157.20–22: *yadā tu samayād ebhyaḥ phalaṃ tadāyam adoṣaḥ / samayakārasya ruceḥ phalotpattiniyamāt /*. This is also what Karṇakagomin is saying (PVSVṬ 557.11–13) when commenting on PV I 295d: *samaye bhavet / yadā samayo mantras tadā samayasya kartā vastusvabhāvānapekṣaḥ samayaṃ karoti / yathā loke ye brāhmaṇāḥ prasiddhās tebhya eva prayoktṛbhyaḥ phalaṃ dāsyāmi nānyebhya iti syāt samayaḥ /*. Compare with PVṬ P *ñe* 26a7–8. On this kind of *samaya*, see Eltschinger (2001, 22–27) and Eltschinger (2008, 275–276).

[121] PVṬ P *ñe* 26a5 = PVSVṬ 556.26: *vastubhedo hi kāraṇabhedaḥ*. On the use of the word *vastu* in the sense of "cause," see AK II 286–287, where the fourth sense of *vastu* is *hetu*.

[122] According to PVSVṬ 556.27–28: *na ca brāhmaṇaśūdrādīnāṃ svabhāvabhedaḥ paramārthato 'sti / kevalaṃ lokavyavahārakṛto vipraśūdrādibhedaḥ / tena lokavyavahārabhinnānāṃ prayoktṝṇāṃ bhedāt...* Compare with Śākyabuddhi's introduction to PV I 295 (PVṬ P *ñe* 26a3–5): *gzhan yang 'di ni bram ze yin la 'di ni dmangs rigs yin no zhes bya ba'i khyad par 'di ni 'jig rten gyi tha snyad tsam du byas pa yin gyi / bram ze la sogs pa'i blo'i dbang po la sogs pa la bram ze nyid la sogs par byas pa don dam pa'i khyad par ni yod pa ma yin no // de bas na brda tsam du byas pa yin pa'i phyir / bram ze la sogs pa sbyor ba po'i khyad par 'bras bu'i dngos po'i khyad par yang rigs pa ma yin no //*.

[But such a restriction] might occur in a convention [i.e., in a promise on the part of the one who reveals the mantra]."[123]

Since real entities acquire additional properties through their causes, they will only behave differently if there is a difference in the nature of their causes. The discussion that follows verse I 295 is therefore based on the principle that no difference in the effect is justified without a difference in the cause. For our purpose, a differentiation in the productivity of a mantra will only be justified if, as persons who may benefit from using a mantra, the authorized sponsors of sacrifices and the *śūdras* have distinct modes of being. In other words, both in Dharmakīrti and in the argument about fire that occurs in the AgS, the problem of caste is reduced to the question of determining whether the effects—the functions of fire or the results of mantras—vary if their causes are Brahmins or *śūdras*. And let it be clear that those effects will vary only if there is a *real* difference in their causes, but will remain strictly identical if that difference is merely *nominal* or conventional.

Now, Dharmakīrti's position is clear on this point: "Consequently, even as products (*kārya*), those mantras that bestow the [expected] results due to an additional property of their nature (*svabhāvātiśaya*) should [never act] differently even when they are used by *śūdras*, etc., because there is no difference, [whether in thought, sense faculties or body],[124] in the nature of the two men named [respectively] '*śūdra*' and 'Brahmin'."[125] An opponent may argue that in addition to making a nominal distinction between the *śūdra* and the Brahmin, people also have different attitudes toward those two alleged types of humans,

---

[123] PV I 295: *saṃskāryasya hi bhāvasya vastubhedo hi bhedakaḥ / prayoktṛbhedān niyamaḥ śaktau na samaye bhavet //*.

[124] PVṬ P *ñe* 26b6 = PVSVṬ 557.22–23: *puruṣayos tayor buddhīndriyadeheṣu svabhāvabhedābhāvāt /*.

[125] PVSV 157.9–11: *tad ime mantrāḥ svabhāvātiśayāt phaladāyinaḥ kāryā api na śūdrādiprayoge 'py anyathā syuḥ / śūdraviprābhidhānayoḥ puruṣayoḥ svabhāvābhedāt /*.

respectively disdain and respect.[126] To this, Dharmakīrti replies: "[Real] things, which [only] comply with differences in nature, are indeed not [made to behave] differently by nominal or conventional differences that [merely] conform to human arbitrariness."[127] In referring to the prevalent antinomy between intrinsic nature and human arbitrariness, Dharmakīrti here anticipates on the distinction that he will later make in his argument between the domain of direct perception and the domain of conventions. That opposition is at the core of his philosophy, which is marked by the constant conceptual interplay between perception (*pratyakṣa*), the particular (*svalakṣaṇa*) and the real thing (*vastu*) on one side, and conventions (*saṅketa, samaya*), instruction (*upadeśa*) and the speaker's intention (*vivakṣā*) on the other. Involved in this opposition are concepts close to those of necessity and contingency. But it also embraces the classical Buddhist antinomies between substantially real (*dravyasat*) and nominally real (*prajñaptisat*), or between ultimately real (*paramārthasat*) and conventionally real (*saṃvṛtisat*). I will say more on those oppositions below.

We know at this point that for Dharmakīrti, nothing in their intrinsic nature distinguishes those people that are called "Brahmins" from those that are called "*śūdras*," and that those designations ultimately issue from social conventions and human arbitrariness. As was the case in the "canonical" literature, Dharmakīrti's task is now to develop an argumentation that will both address the naturalization of those statutory divisions and account for their existence as a social fact. Dharmakīrti meets that double obligation in a short passage[128] (= PVSV 157.13–18) intended to answer the following objection: "Between those two,

---

126 PVṬ P *ñe* 26b7–8 ≈ PVSVṬ 557.25–26: *nanv ayaṃ brāhmaṇo 'yaṃ śūdra iti loke nāmabhedo 'sti / tathā sammānādivyavahārabhedaś ca / tataḥ svabhāvabhedo 'vasīyata iti cet /.*

127 PVSV 157.11–13: *na hi puruṣecchānuvidhāyino nāmavyavahārabhedāt svabhāvabhedānubandhinām arthānām anyathātvam asti /.*

128 That passage has been translated by Ono (1993, 45 note 317).

[the Brahmin and the *śūdra*], there exists a [real] difference of class (*jātibheda*)."[129]

2.3.2 The argument

We have seen already that Śākyabuddhi and Karṇakagomin immediately correlate Dharmakīrti's position (at PVSV 157.13–16) with the refutation of universals (*sāmānyaniṣedha*), as it occurs in the section of PV dealing with conceptual exclusion. For them, despite the fact that the class has already been refuted, its principle is here provisionally admitted in order to show to the opponent that even if the reality of classes and universals were accepted, the social distinctions associated with denominations would have no ontological basis.[130] If a class existed, says Dharmakīrti, it would share with its individual instantiations three differentiating characteristics: "Indeed, this [difference of class] is observed when, as in the case of cows and horses, [there is in each individual of each class] a [shared] difference [pertaining to] specific form, property and function (*ākṛtiguṇaśaktibheda*)."[131] Let us recall that the expression "specific form" (*ākṛti*) appeared in the arguments of the VSū, the ŚKA and the KDAM, together with "configuration" (*saṃsthāna*) and "external physical aspect" (*ākāra*), where it corresponded to one of the class discriminants (*liṅga, viśeṣaṇa*) examined and rejected by those texts.[132] It is therefore not surprising to find Karṇakagomin gloss "specific form" by "configuration," an identification that had been very vigourously criticized by Kumārila in his ŚV and TV.[133] But ac-

---

129 PVSV 157.13: *tayor jātibheda iti cet* /.

130 PVṬ P *ñe* 27a3–4 ≈ PVSVṬ 558.3–5: *sāmānyaniṣedhān niṣiddhaiva jātiḥ / kevalam abhyupagamyocyate / sa khalu bhavann api jātibhedas tridheṣṭaḥ* [*dṛṣṭaḥ* PVṬ] / *ākṛtiguṇaśaktibhede sati* /.

131 PVSV 157.13–14: *sa khalv ākṛtiguṇaśaktibhede dṛṣṭo gavāśvavat.*

132 See section 1.2, p. 17, above. See also Halbfass (1976, 294[22]–295[23] and 295[23] note 71).

133 See ŚV, *vanavāda*, 16ff together with NRĀ 438.1–3; TV on MīSū I 3.30/ II 237.8ff together with *Nyāyasudhā* on TV on MīSū I 3.30/I 645.23–24.

cording to Śākyabuddhi and Karṇakagomin, a shared difference pertaining to specific form occurs in every individual cow while it is absent from all individual horses.[134] And the shared difference pertaining to property occurs also in all individuals instantiating a given class (*samānajātīyāsu vyaktiṣv anugāmī*), for example the difference pertaining to the (strength of) taste and degree of cooking of their milk or flesh (PVṬ *māṃsa*).[135] The shared difference pertaining to function is finally defined by Karṇakagomin as the capacity to produce an effect that corre-

---

Someśvara attributes to Akṣapādādi the position according to which the word *ākṛti* refers to the configuration. Śāntarakṣita, in his *Vipañcitārthā* on the *Vādanyāya* (reference in Halbfass 1992, 112), seems to know and criticize that Naiyāyika position. In his *Mahābhāṣyadīpikā* (IV 3.7–9), Bhartṛhari also criticizes that identification when he writes: *ākṛtir iti na tat saṃsthānam*. On the Naiyāyika (Uddyotakara, Aviddhakarṇa, Śrīdhara, Vyomaśiva, etc.) version of substance (*dravya*) as mere configuration (*saṃsthānamātra*), see Halbfass (1992, 103–105). On the Buddhist side, the Vaibhāṣikas hold that visibles (*rūpa = cakṣurindriyaviṣaya*) consist in colour (*varṇa*) and configuration (*saṃsthāna*). See the Sautrāntika critique of that position in AK I 10 and IV 3, as well as Matilal (1986, 250–254). On specific form as a sign of class (*jātiliṅga*), see Biardeau (1964, 176 notes 1–2). On the definition of specific form as a sign of class in the *Vaiśeṣikasūtra*, see Oberhammer (1991) s.v. *ākṛti*.

134 PVṬ P *ñe* 27a5: *de la dbyibs kyi khyad par ste de ni gsal ba po'i khyad par dang ldan pa'i ba lang dag la rjes su 'gro ba yod kyi rta'i gsal ba dag la ni ma yin no //*. PVSVṬ 558.5–6: *tatrākṛtibhedaḥ saṃsthānaviśeṣaḥ sa prativyakti bhedavatīṣv api goṣv anugāmī vidyate / nāśvavyaktiṣu /*. Śākyabuddhi says: **vyañjakaviśeṣayukteṣu goṣu*. Kumārila, in ŚV, *vanavāda*, 4–5, declares: *na caite vyañjakās tasya guṇavad vā viśeṣaṇam / tathā hi nāgṛhīteṣu teṣu syād gotvabodhanam // teṣāṃ ca vyañjakaiḥ svaiḥ syāt punar grahaṇakalpanā / tathā saty anavasthā syān na syād gotvāvadhāraṇam //*. According to Pārthasārathimiśra, the position criticized by Kumārila is that of the Kāśyapīyas, i.e., the Vaiśeṣikas.

135 PVṬ P *ñe* 27a5–6 ≈ PVSVṬ 558.7–8: *guṇabhedaḥ kṣīrādīnāṃ rasavīryavipākādibhedena / sa ca samānajātīyāsu vyaktiṣv anugāmī dṛṣṭo na vijātīyāsu /*. PVṬ with no equivalent for *vīrya*.

sponds to each of them. Thus cows share the capacity of being milked, contrary to horses.[136]

Already at this stage of the argument, Śākyabuddhi and Karṇakagomin are quick to draw the following conclusion: "Consequently, since in this way [shared] differences pertaining to specific form, etc., are observed to co-occur in the individuals belonging to the same class, we may accept a class difference between cows and horses. On the contrary, no [shared] difference pertaining to specific form, etc., is strictly limited to Brahmins, etc., so that one could posit a difference of class [between them]."[137] Dharmakīrti's initial approach is therefore similar to that of the biological arguments on animal and vegetal species developed in the texts analyzed previously. Contrary to animal, vegetal or mineral species, no differentiating feature or class discriminant can justify the division of human individuals into classes, so that all individual Brahmins would instantiate the universal "brahmanity" and all individual *śūdras* would instantiate the universal "*śūdra*hood" (*śūdratva*).

Dharmakīrti's argumentation does not stop here, however, for he goes into a critique of the position that was only apparent in the texts examined in the first chapter, namely, the position defended by the Mīmāṃsā, the Vaiśeṣika and the Nyāya on the perceptibility of classes and universals. He writes: "Moreover, people recognize (*prati√PAD*) the [difference of class] independently of [all] teaching (*anupadeśam*)."[138] According to Śākyabuddhi and Karṇakagomin,[139] this must be interpreted to mean that

---

136 PVSVṬ 558.9–10: *śaktibhedo 'nurūpakāryasāmarthyalakṣaṇaḥ / yathā gavāṃ dohādisāmarthyaṃ nāśvānām /*. PVṬ P *ñe* 27a6–7 with no equivalent for *anurūpa*.

137 PVṬ P *ñe* 27a7–27b1 ≈ PVSVṬ 558.9–11: *tad evaṃ samānajātīyavyaktyanugāminām ākṛtyādibhedānām upalambhāt kāmaṃ gavāśvādiṣv astu jātibhedo naivaṃ brāhmaṇādiṣu pratiniyata ākṛtyādibhedo 'sti yena jātibhedaḥ kalpyeta /*.

138 PVSV 157.14: *anupadeśaṃ cainaṃ lokaḥ pratipadyate /*.

139 PVṬ P *ñe* 27b1–2 ≈ PVSVṬ 558.11–13: *sakṛc ca gavādiṣu* (*gavāśvādiṣu* PVṬ) *vyutpanno deśakālādibhede 'py anupadeśam ity upadeśam antare-*

any human, *regardless of the place and time in which he lives*, can *immediately* (*sakṛt*) distinguish a cow from a horse, and express that distinction. A foreigner, however, *unless he is first instructed in the matter*, cannot *immediately* recognize a Brahmin or a *śūdra* and say: "this man is a Brahmin" or "this man is a *śūdra*."

Dharmakīrti then draws his conclusion: "We do not see any property that is strictly limited (*viniyata*) to those two as is the case for [cows and horses]. And [since] we do not see it, how could we recognize that difference?"[140] We have seen already that many of the VSū's arguments concluded with a comment to the effect that brahmanity is uncertain (*aniścita/aniyata*). Before reaching that conclusion, its author had shown that factors such as the Veda, knowledge (*jñāna*), conduct (*ācāra*) or activity (*karman*) were not the exclusive signs or discriminants of brahmanity since they were shared, for example, by Rāvaṇa the demon, *śūdras*, fishermen and *vaiśyas* respectively.[141] When we follow Śākyabuddhi and Karṇakagomin's presentation,[142] we find that Dharmakīrti's approach was the same. According to them, we must understand by a "property strictly limited to those two," a property that belongs or is constantly present only among the individuals of a same class. For them, moreover, when Dharmakīrti rejects the existence of all properties that would be strictly limited to the individuals instantiating a given class, he means to say that all criteria are fallacious (*vyabhicārin*). And this means that no property alleged to characterize the Brahmins or other similar instances, is not also found among the *śūdras* or other

---

ṇainaṃ jātibhedaṃ lokaḥ pratipadyate / ayaṃ gaur ayam aśva iti / naivaṃ brāhmaṇādibhedam anupadeśaṃ pratipadyate /.

[140] PVSV 157.15–16: *na tadvad anayoḥ kaṃcid api guṇaṃ viniyataṃ paśyāmaḥ / apaṣyantaś ca kathaṃ bhedaṃ pratipadyemahi /.*

[141] See note 76, p. 30, above.

[142] PVṬ P *ñe* 27b3–5 = PVSVṬ 558.14–17: *na... anayor brāhmaṇaśūdrayoḥ kaṃcid api guṇaṃ viniyataṃ samānajātīyāsv eva vyaktiṣu sthitaṃ paśyāmaḥ / guṇagrahaṇam upalakṣaṇam / evam ākṛtibhedaṃ śaktibhedaṃ ca viniyataṃ na paśyāmaḥ / apaśyantaś cākṛtyādibhedaṃ kathaṃ śūdraviprayor jātibhedaṃ pratipadyemahi / naiveti yāvat /.*

dissimilar instances. Dharmakīrti's argument may in fact be reformulated in logical terms: no concomitance (*niyama* or *vyāpti*) is found between the proposed specifying criteria and the instances that they should specify. That approach clearly parallels the one that guided and inspired the VSū, ŚKA and KDAM. For in order to accept, even provisionally, the reality of a class like brahmanity, Dharmakīrti required that a threefold difference of specific form, property and function be observed. Although he did not give any example of what those terms could refer to, this enabled Śākyabuddhi and Karṇakagomin to argue,[143] based on several elements of a discussion found in Patañjali's *Mahābhāṣya*,[144] that neither the recitation of the Veda, nor the daily purificatory rites (*śaucācāra*),[145] which I take to be examples of functions and properties, are present in all Brahmins without ever being present in the *śūdras*. As for the difference of form, the "early" literature had already spoken of specific form, configuration and external physical aspect, and Karṇakagomin had glossed "specific form" by "configuration." In looking for an example of a specific form, both commentators thus assert that there is not, among Brahmins, any shared difference pertaining to their external physical aspect,[146] such as all having

---

143 PVṬ P *ñe* 27b5–6 = PVSVṬ 558.17–19: *tathā hy adhyayanaśaucācārādiviśeṣaḥ sarvo vyabhicārī / yaś ca gaurapiṅgalakeśatvādilakṣaṇa ākārabhedaḥ kalpyate sa brāhmaṇeṣv api keṣucin nāsti / śūdreṣu ca vidyate keṣucit /*.

144 *Mahābhāṣya* on Pāṇini II 2.6 (*nañ*), vol. 1, p. 411: *tapaḥ śrutaṃ ca yoniś cety etad brāhmaṇakārakam / tapaḥśrutābhyāṃ yo hīno jātibrāhmaṇa eva saḥ // tathā gauraḥ śucyācāraḥ piṅgalaḥ kapilakeśa ity etān apy abhyantarān brāhmaṇye guṇān kurvanti /*. On that passage, see the discussion in Halbfass (1976, 281[9]–282[10]).

145 Note that in a different context, Śākyabuddhi and Karṇakagomin define purity (*śauca*) as follows (PVṬ P *ñe* 45b1–2 = PVSVṬ 578.21–22): *śaucaṃ dvividham / bāhyam āntaraṃ ca / bāhyaṃ snānādi / āntaraṃ steyādinivṛttiḥ /*. "Purity is of two kinds, external and internal. External, it consists in the ablutions, etc; internal, it consists in abstaining from theft, etc."

146 Again in a different context, Śākyabuddhi and Karṇakagomin give to the physical aspect (*ākāra*) the Abhidharmic definition of the visible

a clear complexion (*gaura*) and reddish-brown hair (*piṅgalakeśa*). For those physical features can be found in some *śūdras*, while they are absent in some Brahmins.[147]

Let us summarize those four lines from Dharmakīrti in light of Śākyabuddhi's and Karṇakagomin's comments. Dharmakīrti subordinates the acceptation of a difference of class to the observation of a threefold shared difference pertaining to specific form, property and function in the individuals alleged to instantiate each class. That condition, however, is necessary but not sufficient, for according to Dharmakīrti, it entails a corollary condition requiring that this difference be known independently of any instruction. The first necessary condition is not met, however, since no discriminating factor is indeed strictly limited to all individuals of a given class at the exclusion of all those of another class. Each factor is therefore fallacious. Since that condition is not met, Dharmakīrti does not seem to consider it useful, in that context, to criticize the thesis of the direct perceptibility of classes as it is implied by the problem of education. We will see below[148] that this task was taken up mainly by Prajñākaragupta, in the context of a discussion of caste. We will also see[149] that for Dharmakīrti, to negate that the class can be apprehended without instruction is to assert its strict conventionality.

2.3.3 Explanation

After developing his argumentation against a realist ontology of classes and class differences (*jātibheda*), Dharmakīrti needed to describe and explain the empirical social situation that cased

(*rūpa*); PVṬ P *je* 471b1–2 = PVSVṬ 580.20–21: *ākāro varṇasaṃsthānādiḥ /*. "[By] external physical aspect [we mean] the colour, configuration, etc."

[147] The argument is reminiscent of a long modern debate based on contradictory anthropological data, an interesting example of which is found in Bouglé (1993, 106–114).

[148] See section 2.4.3, p. 127, below.

[149] See section 2.4.2, p. 123, below.

disagreement. And on this point, his position is in perfect continuity with the classical Buddhist explanations. For him, as well as for Śākyabuddhi and Karṇakagomin, the question is to be formulated in those terms: once the realist hypothesis has been rejected, how can we explain the fact that the words "Brahmin" and "*śūdra*" give rise to distinct cognitions?[150] Dharmakīrti's answer holds in one sentence: "Although there is no class difference [between the Brahmin and the *śūdra*], the difference in cognitions[151] (*pratītibheda*) that, in society, follows from the difference in denominations ['Brahmin' and '*śūdra*'] may [very well] come from their practising particular occupations (*vyāpāraviśeṣa*) [such as muttering prayers and sacrifices],[152] and from [the fact that they are born in a] family (*anvaya*) [traditionally involved in such occupations],[153] as is the case with denominations like 'healer,'[154] 'merchant,' etc. (*vaidyavaṇigvyapadeśa*)."[155]

According to Dharmakīrti, then, no appeal to ontology is necessary to account for the fact that different denominations give rise to different cognitions. As in the earlier Buddhist literature, from the VāS to the AgS and the VSū to the KDAM, Dharmakīrti holds that social denominations refer to professional activities and to means of livelihood, to the needs of a given social group that have become fixed over several generations, yet without depending on any hereditary determinism, as in the Brahmanic

---

150 PVṬ P *ñe* 27b6–7 ≈ PVSVṬ 558.20–21: *yadi na jātibhedo vipraśūdrayoḥ kathaṃ tarhy ayaṃ brāhmaṇādiśabdaśravaṇād bhinnā pratītir bhavatīti /.*

151 PVSVṬ 558.23 glosses: *buddhibhedo 'yaṃ brāhmaṇo 'yaṃ śūdra iti pratītibhedaḥ.*

152 PVṬ P *ñe* 27b8–28a1 = PVSVṬ 558.24: *vyāpāraviśeṣānuṣṭhānāj japahomādikriyāviśeṣānuṣṭhānāt.*

153 PVṬ P *ñe* 28a1 = PVSVṬ 558.25: *tathābhūtavyāpārānuṣṭhāyinaḥ kulād utpatteḥ.*

154 On healers (*vejja*), see Fick (1972, 237[153–54]); modern Baidyas in Bouglé (1993, 14 and note 5).

155 PVSV 157.16–18: *yo 'py ayaṃ nāmabhedānvayo loke pratītibhedaḥ so 'saty api jātibhede vyāpāraviśeṣānuṣṭhānād anvayāc ca syād vaidyavaṇigvyapadeśādivat /.*

theory of mixed classes. The only determinism of which one may speak is thus a social determinism, not a biological determinism. And it is only due to repetition. Dharmakīrti's examples of the healer and the merchant are here quite significant, for both of them, while considered *śūdras*, are nonetheless included among the mixed. The situation thus leads to an absurdity that is well depicted by Śākyabuddhi and Karṇakagomin: "For example, among the *śūdras* who, [as *śūdras*], belong to the same class (*tulyajātīya*), denominations such as 'healer' are used because [those *śūdras*] practise such and such particular occupations and because of [the fact that they were born in] a family [traditionally involved in those occupations. But] still there is not, [among those *śūdras*], any difference of class. It must be for the Brahmins, [*kṣatriyas*], etc., as it is for the [*śūdras*, who bear different denominations although they are all *śūdras*]."[156]

Dharmakīrti insisted above that the distinctions between Brahmins and *śūdras*, or between healers and merchants, are not due to their intrinsic nature, for example to their birth or other criteria, but to the fact that the world knows a multitude of occupations. The lexicographic conventions that come to be associated with those occupations do not tell us anything, however, about the mode of being of the individual to which they are associated. Accordingly, as Śākyabuddhi and Karṇakagomin insisted in their introduction or commentary to PV I 295,[157] the difference is not one of intrinsic nature, but is due to worldly conventions. It is therefore not ultimately true (*pāramārthika*), but merely conventional (*sāṅketika*), which is to say that it is not apprehended through direct perception, but through learning.

---

[156] PVṬ P *ñe* 28a2–3 = PVSVṬ 558.26–28: *yathā tulyajātīyeṣu śūdreṣu tasya tasya vyāpāraviśeṣasyānuṣṭhānād anvayāc ca vaidyādivyapadeśāḥ pravartante / na tāvatā jātibhedaḥ / tadvad brāhmaṇādiṣv api syāt /.*

[157] See note 122, p. 104, above.

2.3.4 Conclusion

Just as fire remains fire and its consuming power does not increase or decrease whether it is lit by a Brahmin, a *kṣatriya*, a *vaiśya* or a *śūdra*, the contribution of a Brahmin or a *śūdra* as a cooperating cause to the efficiency of Vedic mantras will be exactly the same since the difference between them is not real, but conventional. Dharmakīrti can thereore conclude his argument as follows: "Consequently, [since] they are used by an [ontologically undifferentiated person, Brahmin or *śūdra*], those mantras receive from this [person] an undifferentiated intrinsic nature. It is therefore in an undifferentiated manner that they must yield results."[158] *Quod erat demonstrandum*.

158 PVSV 157.19–20: *tad ime 'viśiṣṭena prayujyamānā mantrās tato 'viśiṣṭam eva svabhāvam āsādayanti / tenāviśeṣeṇaiva phaladāḥ syuḥ //*. PVṬ P *ñe* 28a3–4 = PVSVṬ 559.10–11 gloss *aviśiṣṭena* as *brāhmaṇaśūdrādinā* and *tataḥ* as *brāhmaṇādeḥ*.

2.4 On the perceptibility of class (*jāti*)

2.4.1 Kumārila[159]

---

[159] On the general problem of classes (*jāti*) and specific form (*ākṛti*) in Kumārila, see D'Sa (1980, 151–165). In the section that follows, I present Kumārila's answer to the question formulated by Pārthasārathimiśra in his introduction to ŚV, *vanavāda*, 26–29: *yadi pratyakṣā jātiḥ kim iti tarhi naratvādivad brāhmaṇatvādikam api sahasaiva na gamyate* /. "If, [as you claim], the class is perceptible, why is it then that [un]like [a class] such as humanity, [a class] such as brahmanity is not immediately apprehended?" Similar is TV on MīSū I 2.2/II 5.17–18: *kasmāt punar mātāpitṛsambandhānabhijñāś cakṣuḥsannikṛṣṭeṣu manuṣyeṣv anākhyātaṃ na pratipadyate* /. "Why is it then that when he has visual contact with humans beings, the [person] ignoring the relation [of those humans] to their mothers and fathers does not recognize [a Brahmin] without having [first] been instructed [on the matter]?" Immediately before that question [= II 5.16–17], Kumārila had begun to say that since brahmanity, like treehood (*vṛkṣatva*), is well known in society (*lokaprasiddha*), it is not a scriptural object (*śāstraviṣaya*), but is rather directly perceptible: *nāyaṃ śāstraviṣayo lokaprasiddhatvād vṛkṣatvādivat / kathaṃ punar idaṃ lokasya prasiddham / pratyakṣeṇeti brūmaḥ* /. "This is not a scriptural object since, like treehood, etc., it is well known in society. [Question:] But how is this [brahmanity] well known in society? [Answer:] We hold that it is through direct perception." On those various questions, see Halbfass (1976, 294[22]ff). On the position of the Prābhākara school, see Halbfass (1976, 301[29]ff). The Prābhākaras, and especially Śālikanātha, reject the existence of the class "brahmanity," as well in fact as any ontological differentiation within the universal "humanity" (*puruṣatva*).

Halbfass (1976, 302[30]) comments: "Whereas Kumārila tries to develop an autonomous metaphysical and epistemological justification, the Prābhākaras simply sanction what the tradition admits and no more... Brahmanity, etc., means nothing more than belonging to determined genealogies (*santativiśeṣaprabhavatva*), and those genealogies don't need any metaphysical or epistemological justification, since tradition has made them familiar and common among human beings (*lokata eva prasiddhāḥ*). No hypostasis of the caste(s)' universals is required to warrant the applicability of the words 'Brahmin,' etc., and the feasibility of the Vedic prescriptions specified for the castes."

Several elements of Kumārila's discussion of class (*jāti*), especially in the TV, support the hypothesis that he knew of at least some of the Buddhist arguments and, more importantly, was fully aware of their *relevency*. His task thus first consisted in finding a way to neutralize the Buddhist critique by avoiding the points that were shown to be weak in the Mīmāṃsā position, and then also to *reaffirm the principle of the perceptibility of classes*.

I believe that in order to neutralize the Buddhist critique without himself relying on the points that had been shown to be weak, Kumārila had to make some concession on two important points. (1) First, he had to concede that, with the exception of birth (*yoni*), no criterion (*nimitta*) of class membership is applicable to the Brahmins alone at the exclusion of all *kṣatriyas*, *vaiśyas* and *śūdras*. For example: the Brahmanic sacred thread (*upavīta*), memorizing the Veda (*adhyayana*) or even teaching the Vedic recitation (*adhyāpana*).[160] (2) Kumārila then had to con-

---

160 TV on MīSū I 2.2/II 5.20–23: *api ca / vyutpannaśabdo 'pi nimittāntarād ṛte naiva pratipadyate / na copavītādhyayanādi nimittam / varṇatrayasādhāraṇatvāt / adhyāpanādy api bhinnācārakṣatriyavaiśyapratiyogitvāt sandigdham / sarvaṃ ca dṛṣṭaśūdreṣu sambhāvyamānatvād aniścitam /*. "Moreover, even a [man] to whom the word ['Brahmin'] has [previously] been explained does not in any way recognize [a Brahmin] without another criterion. But neither is the sacred thread, nor the recitation of the Veda, etc., the criterion [of brahmanity] since they are common to the three classes [of the twice-born. As for] the teaching of Vedic recitation, it is also a doubtful [criterion of brahmanity] because it also occurs (*pratiyogin*) among *kṣatriyas* and *vaiśyas* of wrong conduct. All [criteria] are [in fact] indeterminate since they can occur in [people] who are seen to be *śūdras*." This corresponds without a doubt to the Buddhist's position, but Kumārila never criticizes those arguments when developing his own view. See especially TV on MīSū I 3.27/II 217.14–15: *tulyaśiraḥpāṇyādyākāreṣv api saṅkīrṇalokadṛṣṭigrāhyeṣu brāhmaṇādiṣu mātāpitṛsambandhasmaraṇād eva varṇavivekāvadhāraṇaṃ bhavati*. "In the case of [classes] such as the Brahmins, even though ordinary view may grasp them confusedly [as] having physical aspects – the head, the hands, etc. – that are the same [as those of people belonging to other classes], it is through the memory of their relations to their mothers and fathers that a class distinction is

cede that without prior instruction, nobody can distinguish a Brahmin from a *śūdra* upon first seeing them, as we do for example with entities that belong to the class of trees (*vṛkṣatva*).

Those important concessions led Kumārila to develop his own position from three separate angles. (1) First, he raised several issues with direct perception to convince his audience that perception is not free of all mnemonic or conceptual cognitive elements. (2) On several occasions in the TV and in the *vanavāda* and *ākṛtivāda* sections of the ŚV, he also defended the *principle* that all classes are not apprehended in the same way and by the same method (*itikartavyatā*). (3) Finally, Kumārila built his entire defence of class on the notions of birth (*yoni*) and direct kinship. This line of argument required that he examined in detail the only Buddhist argument now likely to present a threat to the system, namely the argument insisting on women's fickleness and their frequent sexual misconduct.[161] Let us look briefly at each of those points, as they appear in the TV on MīSū I 2.2.

In order to establish the perceptibility of a class like brahmanity, Kumārila first has to adopt a wider theory of direct perception than the Buddhist's. More specifically, he must make room for the intervention of concepts or memories in the process of direct perception. In TV on MīSū I 2.2, Kumārila makes three comments that are sufficient to relativize the strict immediateness of perception as conceived by the Buddhists. He first notes that "the cause of a perception (*pratyakṣanimitta*) is not necessarily apprehended by perception itself since it is observed that the eye, for example, even though it is not apprehended [by perception], is [nonetheless] a cause [of perception]."[162] He then reminds his audience that he has already "proved that, even if it is interrupted by an intermediate mnemonic knowl-

---

[to be] determined." See also Halbfass (1976, 294[22]–295[23] and 298[26]).

161 See section 1.3.3, p. 35, and 2.1.1.2, p. 71, above, and section 2.5.4, p. 146, below.

162 TV on MīSū I 2.2/II 6.7–8: *na cāvaśyaṃ pratyakṣāvagatam eva pratyakṣanimittaṃ bhavati / cakṣurāder anavagatasyāpi nimittatvadarśanāt /*.

edge (*āntarālikasmṛti*), perception [still] follows from contact (*sambandha*) of the sense faculties [with the object]."[163] Finally, Kumārila holds that "it is not the case that what is not immediately (*sahasā*) perceptible by all [people] is imperceptible also for those who observe it [more] carefully (*nipuṇataḥ*)."[164] We shall see below that the number and nature of those comments are not innocent.

Kumārila's second line of argument, on the plurality of modes of direct apprehension of class, first appears in ŚV, *vanavāda*, 26–29. In those verses, without abandoning in any way the *principle* of the perceptibility of classes, Kumārila asserts that there are different modes of apprehension for different classes.[165] Thus, while we can tell the difference between gold and copper from their respective colour, and while we know from its configuration that an object is a pot, it is based on his birth that we recognize an individual's brahmanity. When kings govern correctly, adds Kumārila, brahmanity can also be recognized by looking at people's conduct.[166] A passage from the TV offers the same ar-

---

163 TV on MīSū I 2.2/II 6.8–9: *āntarālikasmṛtivyavahitam api cendriyasambandhānusāri pratyakṣam...*

164 TV on MīSū I 2.2/II 6.9–10: *na ca yat sahasā sarvasya pratyakṣaṃ na bhavati tan nipuṇato 'pi paśyatāṃ na pratyakṣam...*

165 On that passage, see also Halbfass (1976, 295[23]–296[24]).

166 ŚV, *vanavāda*, 27–29: *suvarṇaṃ bhidyate rūpāt tāmratvāder asaṃśayam / tailād ghṛtaṃ vilīnaṃ ca gandhena ca rasena ca // bhasmapracchādito vahniḥ sparśanenopalabhyate / aśvatvādau ca dūrasthe niścayo jāyate svanaiḥ // saṃsthānena ghaṭatvādi brāhmaṇatvādi yonitaḥ / kvacid ācārataś cāpi samyag rājānupālitāt /*. "Without hesitation, gold is differentiated from copper, etc., through its colour, while clarified butter is [differentiated] from oil by its smell and flavour. A fire covered with ashes is apprehended by means of touch, while determining [that such an object is] a horse, etc., [even when it is] located at a distance, [is possible] because of the neighs. The fact of being a pot, etc., [is determined] by the configuration [of the object], and the fact of being a Brahmin [is determined] by birth as well as, in some [places], by conduct, because it is correctly preserved by the kings." In TV on MīSū I 2.2/II 6.24–7.11, however, Kumārila is far less ready to accept that conduct may be a pertinent sign of class membership. For him, the pro-

gument.[167] Making an implicit reference to the preceding passage (the reference is explicit in the *Nyāyasudhā* I 26.12 of Someśvara), Kumārila there says that he has already explained how the method can apply to the apprehension of classes. For example, while the visual faculty (*ālokendriya*) or some differences in the physical aspect (*ākāraviśeṣa*) are the cause of apprehension of certain classes, one may directly apprehend the class to which one belongs by remembering the class of one's generators (*utpādakajātismaraṇa*).[168] Kumārila adds, however, and this is important, that only the relation to the mother is perceptible: "The relation between the generated [person] and the generator, which is directly perceptible only in the case of the mother but is known by inference or authoritative testimony in other cases, is the cause [of apprehension of the class]."[169] In his commentary on ŚV, *vanavāda*, 29bd, Pārthasārathimiśra explains that we must understand by "birth" the relation with the father and mother, so that perception of a class such as brahmanity depends on

---

blem is that such a criterion fails to ensure class fixity (*avasthitatva*). It must be noted that his arguments against conduct are similar to those of the VSū and the KDAM. See the English translation by Jhā (1983, 10). See also Halbfass (1976, 299[27]).

167 On the context and meaning of that passage, see Halbfass (1976, 296[24]ff).

168 TV on MīSū I 2.2/II 5.24–6.6: *naiṣa doṣaḥ / kvacid dhi kācij jātigrahaṇa itikartavyatā bhavatīti varṇitam etat / tena yathaivālokendriyānekapiṇḍānusyūt[a]śabdasmaraṇavyaktimahattvasannikarṣākāraviśeṣādayo 'nyajātigrahaṇe kāraṇaṃ tathaivātrotpādakajātismaraṇam /*. "This is not a fault [on our part] since [we have already] explained that the method for [perceptually] apprehending a class is of a [different] type in [each] particular case. Therefore, just as the cause of the apprehension of other classes [consists for example in] the visual faculty, memory of a word regularly associated with many individuals, contact with the size of an individual, difference in the physical aspect, etc., so, in the case of [brahmanity, etc., the cause of the apprehension of the class consists in] the memory of the class of the [two] generators."

169 TV on MīSū I 2.2/II 6.6–7: *ayaṃ cotpādyotpādakasambandho mātur eva pratyakṣo 'nyeṣāṃ tv anumānāptopadeśādyavagataḥ kāraṇaṃ bhavati /*.

whether we know the individual's father and mother (*mātāpitṛjñānāpekṣa*).[170] Perceiving that type of class therefore depends on the previously acquired knowledge of the parents' class, a knowledge in which Kumārila finds the cause of the perception itself.

Considering that the apprehension of a person's class depends exclusively on the knowledge or memory of his parents' class, it is understandable that Kumārila put so much effort to relativize the impact of the argument that the identity of a class can hardly be certified because of women's frequent sexual misconduct.[171]

---

170 NRĀ 440.7–8: *yonito mātāpitṛsambandhāt* (/) *yathā ca mātāpitṛjñānāpekṣaṃ brāhmaṇyādeḥ pratyakṣatvaṃ tathā 'rthavādādhikaraṇe svayam eva vakṣyati* /. "Based on birth, i.e., based on the relation [of a given individual with his] mother and father. And [Kumārila] will state himself, in the section on *arthavāda*, the way in which [a class] such as brahmanity is perceptible depending on the knowledge of the mother and father."

171 TV on MīSū I 2.2/II 6.10–21: *stryaparādhāt tu durjñāno 'yaṃ sambandha iti svayam eva vakṣyati* / *na ca tāvanmātreṇa pratyakṣatā hīyate* / *na hi yad giriśṛṅgam āruhya gṛhyeta tad apratyakṣam* / *na ca strīṇāṃ kvacid vyabhicāradarśanāt sarvatraiva kalpanā yuktā* / *lokaviruddhānumānāsambhavāt* (/) *viśiṣṭena hi prayatnena mahākulīnāḥ parirakṣanty ātmānam* / *anenaiva hetunā rājabhir brāhmaṇaiś ca svapitṛpitāmahāpāramparyāvismaraṇārthaṃ samūhalekhyāni pravarttitāni* / *tathā ca pratikulaṃ guṇadoṣasmaraṇāt tadanurūpāḥ pravṛttinivṛttayo dṛśyante* / *na ca bhartṛvyatirekakṛtena varṇasaṅkaro 'parādhena jāyate* / *dṛśyate hy aparādhinīnām api svabhartṛnimittaḥ prasavaḥ* / *tadaparādhanimittas tu tāsām aśubhaphalopabhogo bhaven na tv apatyānāṃ varṇasaṅkaraḥ* / *na ca viniyogato varṇāntarair eva saha pramādaḥ* (/) *sarveṇa cotpāditasya naiva varṇāntarāpattiḥ* / *saṅkarajātānām api ca punar utkarṣāpakarṣābhyāṃ saptame pañcame vānyataravarṇāpattiḥ smaryate* / *tatra hy etāvanmātram āgāmikaṃ pratyetavyam* / *na hy ayaṃ puruṣeyattāniyamo laukikapramāṇagamyaḥ* /. "But [Śabara] himself will say [below*] that because of women's misconduct, this relation is difficult to know. But the perceptibility [of a class such as brahmanity] is not lost for so much. For what could be apprehended [only] after having climbed a mountain is not imperceptible [just for that reason]. Moreover, it is not justified to conclude (*kalpanā*) from the observation of women's fault in a given case, [that it applies] in

Having shown the weakness of that argument, Kumārila can then conclude and present his position: "That is why, just as the difference between a female and a male cuckoo is known by means of a certain criterion although they are similar, [classes] such as brahmanity are knowable through direct perception supported by teaching, memory and the tradition."[172] The real pur-

---

every case, since one cannot draw an inference that would be contradicted in worldly affairs (*lokaviruddha*). And indeed, those who are well-born (*mahākulīna*) guard themselves with a particular caution [against such practices]. That is the reason why genealogical documents (< Jhā; *samūhalekhya*) are elaborated by kings and Brahmins in order to forget nothing of the succession of their own ancestors. And indeed, one observes that, since each family preserves the memory of [its genealogical] merits and defects, one acts or refrains [from acting] accordingly. Moreover, the commingling of classes does not [necessarily] result from [a woman's] transgression in the absence of her husband. We indeed observe that even in the cases of [women] who misbehave, birth is caused by their own husband. It could happen that those [women] enjoy the unpleasant result of their misconduct, but their offspring will not belong to a mixed class [as a result]. Moreover, it is not necessarily the case that the negligence (*pramāda*) [of those women occurs] only with [men from] other classes. And a new class is not the lot of the [individual] conceived by just any [man]. Besides, even in the case of those who were born in a mixed class, it is taught [in the *Smṛti***] that an entirely new class may occur (*anyataravarṇāpatti*) in the fifth or seventh [generation] after their elevation or decline (*utkarṣāpakarṣa*). Here, however, this is the only scriptural thing that ought to be acknowledged. For indeed, this restriction pertaining to the number of generations is not knowable by the ordinary means of cognition." See also Halbfass (1976, 298[26] note 103) for a reference to an identical problem in the *Prakaraṇapañcikā* of Śālikanātha. According to Halbfass, Śālikanātha sees in this argument nothing but "artificial scepticism." On that question in Śrīdhara and Kumārila, see respectively Halbfass (1976, 293[21]) and (298[26]).

*On MīSū I 2.13: *stryaparādhāt kartuś ca putradarśanam /*.

**See *Nyāyasudhā* I 21.26–27.

172 TV on MīSū I 2.2/II 6.22–23: *tasmāt saty api sārūpye yathā kenacin nimittena strīpuṃskokilādivibhāgajñānaṃ tathaiva darśanasmaraṇapāramparyānugṛhītapratyakṣagamyāni brāhmaṇatvādīni*... On Kumārila's

pose of the discussions that preceded thus becomes clear: the demonstration, on the one hand, that direct perception is not free of non-perceptual components and, on the other hand, that a given entity's belonging to a given class is determined each time on the basis of different criteria, intended to demonstrate that knowledge of a class such as brahmanity does not lose its perceptual character simply because it is based on memory and enquiry. Kumārila concludes: "But here is what was learned from the previous arguments: brahmanity does not consist in the cumulation of [qualities] like the austerities, etc., nor in the disposition (*saṃskāra*) generated by those [qualities]. The class is not revealed by those [cumulation and disposition], but rather, revealed [as it is] by knowledge of the class of the mother and father, it is attainable by perception."[173]

2.4.2 Dharmakīrti

As I have already said, Dharmakīrti does not address the problem of the perceptibility of classes in the context of his discussion of caste. This will be the task of Prajñākaragupta. A few remarks will therefore be enough here to present Dharmakīrti's position.

We have seen Dharmakīrti assert that despite its provisional character, the difference of class prevailing between a horse and a cow is known immediately and does not require any prior instruction. He opposed the differences of intrinsic nature (*svabhāvabheda*), which are real, to nominal and empirico-practical differences (*nāmavyavahārabheda*) that conform to mere human arbitrariness (*puruṣecchānuvidhāyin*).

---

appeal to remembrance with regard to the determination of caste and lineage, see TV on MīSū I 3.2/II 79.12–13.

173 TV on MīSū I 2.2/II 7.11–13: *etābhir upapattibhis tv ayaṃ pratipādyate / na tapaādīnāṃ samudāyo brāhmaṇyam / na tajjanitaḥ saṃskāraḥ / na tadabhivyaṅgyā jātiḥ / kiṃ tarhi mātāpitṛjātijñānābhivyaṅgyā pratyakṣasamadhigamyā /*.

On the one hand, for Dharmakīrti, whatever is conventional is by definition related to human intention and arbitrariness.[174] And whatever is conventional is by definition unreal, i.e., it does not have the status of a real entity. On the other hand, the ultimately real is coextensive with what is, actually or virtually, directly perceptible. The reality of an entity depends on its capacity to produce an effect (*arthakriyāsāmarthya*) and, in our case, to produce a direct sensory perception.

To assert that the alleged differences of class between the Brahmin and the *śūdra* are not differences of intrinsic nature but nominal and institutional differences is therefore to assert that they are not real, but conventional, and as such that they are not directly perceptible. The problem is very clearly formulated in a passage of the PVSV: "Indeed, a difference of intrinsic nature, which is accessible to the sense faculties, does not depend on explanatory rules, etc.,[175] in order to let itself known, like a difference of [colour] such as blue, etc. On the other hand, [things] the cognitions of which depend on such [explanatory rules] do not have the nature of [real] entities[176] but are rather conventional, like royal banners, etc. Now what is conventional cannot [accurately be said to] be fixed by nature since it occurs due to [human] arbitrariness."[177]

---

[174] The near inseparability of the intentional and the conventional is explained in many passages of the PV. For example, PV I 327ab: *vivakṣā niyame hetuḥ saṅketas tatprakāśanaḥ* /. "The speaker's intention is the cause of the [semantic] limitation [of words, and] the convention reveals that [intention]." See also PVSV 172.22–23 *ad loc*: *tasmād vivakṣāprakāśanāyābhiprāyanivedanalakṣaṇaḥ saṅketaḥ kriyate* /. "That is why, in order to reveal the speaker's intention, a convention is established which is defined as the communication of an intention." Dharmakīrti also says in PV IV 116ab: *saṅketasaṃśrayāḥ śabdāḥ sa cecchāmātrasaṃśrayaḥ* /. "Words, [in order to be meaningful], rely on a convention, and the [latter itself] relies only on the [speaker's] arbitrariness."

[175] PVṬ P *ñe* 73b8 = PVSVṬ 607.11: *paribhāṣā saṅketaḥ* /.

[176] PVṬ P *ñe* 73b8 = PVSVṬ 607.14: *na vastu*[*t*]*o nisargasiddhā viśeṣāḥ* /.

[177] PVSV 173.2–5: *na hi svabhāvabheda indriyagamyaḥ svapratītau paribhāṣādikam apekṣate / nīlādibhedavat / tadapekṣapratītayas tu na vas-*

We know that Kumārila, an intransigent advocate of the perceptibility of classes,[178] did concede that the difference between Brahmins and *śūdras*, while real, was only mediately perceptible by the memory of the class of the direct parents. For Dharmakīrti, the mediateness of that knowledge is enough to disqualify it from being a sensory perception. It also presupposes that its object is not a real entity, but rather a conceptual fiction apprehended mediately by a convention. For him, "the knowledge, which is produced by the force of something real (*vastubalāt*), does not depend on a convention."[179] In fact in that verse which inspired Prajñākaragupta to make several remarks on caste, Dharmakīrti goes even further by holding that any apprehension of a class or a universal requires the mediation of a prior conventional knowledge: "[On the other hand], the [fact of not depending on a convention][180] is not present in [our] cognitions of universals."[181]

According to Dharmakīrti, the teaching or testimony of other people (*paropadeśa*) functions in the same way as conventions in that they are verbal in nature and, therefore, refer in the final analysis to the speaker's intention.[182] Their epistemic validity[183]

---

tusvabhāvāḥ / kiṃ tarhi / sāmayikā rājacihnādivat / yaś ca sāmayikaḥ sa svabhāvaniyato 'yuktas tasyecchāvṛtteḥ /.

178 On Kumārila's general position on perception, see Matilal (1986, 321–324), Bhatt (1989, 145–202) and Taber (2005).

179 PV III 45ac1: *yac ca vastubalāj jñānaṃ jāyate tad apekṣate / na saṅketam...* Manorathanandin explains (PVV 129.4): *bālabādhirāder api bhāvāt /.* "Because it occurs equally in children, deaf people, etc., [who don't have access to linguistic conventions]."

180 PVP P *che* 164b5–6 = PVV 129.4: *etat saṅketānapekṣatvam.*

181 PV III 45c2d: *na sāmānyabuddhiṣv etad vibhāvyate //.*

182 For example, PVSV 126.14–15: *tadarthasya puruṣopadeśāpekṣaṇāt / tadupadeśasya tadicchānuvṛtter anirṇaya eva vedavākyārtheṣu /.* "Since the meaning of [unfamiliar words like '*jambhurāṇa*'] depends on the teaching of the person [who explains them, and] since that [man's] teaching obeys his arbitrariness, there is only indetermination as to the meaning of Vedic utterances."

is subjected to the same requirements as those of conventions. Contrary to sensory perception, it is not immediate, pre-conceptual (*nirvikalpaka, kalpanāpoḍha*, etc.) and non-erroneous (*abhrānta*), but mediate and reliant on inferences. All that we learn, from social behaviour to erudition and religion, depends on some testimony. Whatever we refer to as *culture* depends on some testimony, notably most of the knowledge that does not originate in perception, i.e., the conceptual materials that subsist due to beginningless psychic imprints (*anādivāsanā*). While it may seem trivial to say that testimony belongs to the domain of language, it is still useful to note that language refers to conventions that themselves refer to the conceptual materials, classes, genus and universals that Dharmakīrti calls *sāmānyalakṣaṇa*. Those are fictional and unreal, contrary to the particulars (*svalakṣaṇa*), to the real efficient entities from which direct perceptions originate. In other words, classes will be perceptible only if they are particulars. But whatever is a particular, in so far as it is directly perceptible, requires no prior knowledge, no conceptual or linguistic association. So when Dharmakīrti requires of classes that they be known independently of all teaching, he is requiring that their apprehension be independent of all prior knowledge or verbalization, i.e., of all conceptual or conventional knowledge. Their apprehension must be immediate (*sahasā*, etc.). If classes met those conditions, they would be directly perceptible and, as Prajñākaragupta will say, teachings or testimonies would then be of no use whatsoever. Although the context is different, Dharmakīrti is saying nothing else when he asserts: "Another [per-

---

[183] Scripture (*āgama*) and authoritative testimony (*āptopadeśa*) are special cases of verbal testimony (*upadeśa*). Their epistemic validity or reliability (*avisaṃvāda*, etc.) depend on the criteria discussed and elaborated by Dharmakīrti essentially in PV I 213–217 and PVSV *ad loc.* In a different context, note for example PVSVṬ 576.24: *upadeśasyāprāmāṇyāt* /. "Because the testimony [of another person] is not a means of valid cognition." On those issues, which have no incidence on the present argument, see Yaita (1988), Tillemans (1993) and Eltschinger (2007, 70–75).

son]'s testimony is indeed not stronger [than perception] with regard to a directly perceptible object."[184]

2.4.3 Prajñākaragupta

More than any of his predecessors, Prajñākaragupta made an effort to integrate the specific problem of caste into the ontological discussion on universals. Three passages in his work (PVA on PV II 2, III 45–46 and IV 109) illustrate this very well. In the first passage, which is also the most complete, Prajñākaragupta opens the discussion by proposing three alternatives to the origin of caste: "Being a Brahmin, etc. (*dvijādibhāva*), is certainly not the object of a means of valid cognition. It could for instance be defined either by the possession of a class (*jātiyoga*) or by the lineage (*gotra*), or it could consist in the possession of a specific capacity for a given activity (*kriyāsāmarthyātiśaya*)."[185] In this section, we will only consider the first of those alternatives.

From a systematic perspective, one may say that Prajñākaragupta tries to answer two very closely related questions in his argumentation against classes. (1) First, what is a universal? (2) Second, how do we cognize a universal? In answering that a universal is a superimposition that is cognized only by means of arbitrary conventions, Prajñākaragupta is trying to show that a class such as brahmanity is not a real entity, but a conceptual fiction. And in so far as for Dharmakīrti as well as for him, a class

---

184 PVSV 133.11–12: *na hi pratyakṣe 'rthe paropadeśo garīyān /*. Formulated differently, the problem of class is similar to the problem of the meaning of the Veda in PVSV 168.12–13: *aindriyakatve svayaṃ pratipattiprasaṅgāt / rūpādivat /*. "For if [we accepted that the meaning of the Veda] is sensory, the unwelcome consequence would follow that it would be known by itself, [independently of all teaching], like colour, etc."

185 PVA$_{Ono}$ 21.8–9: *na khalu dvijādibhāvaḥ pramāṇagocaracārī. sa hi jātiyogalakṣaṇo gotralakṣaṇaḥ kriyāsāmarthyātiśayayogo* vā bhavet.* *My interpretation differs from the Tibetan of PVA$_{Tib}$ P *te* 10a8–b1: *bya ba'am nus pa byed du 'phags pa dang ldan pa…*

such as brahmanity depends, in order to be grasped, on a testimony or on teaching, it is understandable that in order to capture the nature of that class, Prajñākaragupta will be especially interested in the problem of word meaning.

In their treatment of word meaning, all of Dignāga's successors have argued insistently that words, or lexical conventions, never refer to real entities. Since the number of real entities is infinite, an infinite number of conventions would be required (< Dignāga). And they would have no practical use if they referred to momentary entities (< Dharmakīrti).[186] In his commentary to PV III 45, Prajñākaragupta makes a correlation between that problem and the problem of classes in order to show that lexical conventions refer only to superimpositions, to general conceptual materials that, erroneously superposed on perceptual data, mask the fundamental alterity of real entities. He says: "When one creates a convention, one does not create it with reference to that which is present only. And the knowledge on which that [convention] depends is a mere superimposition, for if conventionalization (*saṅketana*) occurred without superimposition on the successive [phases of the entity], one could not infer a practical activity since [the resultant convention] would not be extensive [enough]. [Objection:] The cognition [of the universal], at the time of the practical activity, only follows from a word, [independently of all superimposition leading to conventionalization]. [Reply:] If there were no [prior] superimposition on the successive [phases of the entity, that] cognition would not occur. And the knowledge of a universal from a word is not observed to occur independently of a convention. [Objection:] It is certainly the case that [this cognition] occurs independently of [all] word, [and this] through observing other individuals. [Reply:] In that case also, that [perception of other individuals] only amounts to a sign (*liṅga*) [allowing one to infer] that there is a corresponding practical activity. [But] an inferential sign also generates nothing more than a prior superimposition. So classes such as

[186] On this point, see Frauwallner (1932, 274–278).

that of the Hūṇas and the Brahmins, [because they] rest on the power of mere conventions, do not depend on [real] entities."[187] Since the particular perishes as soon as it arises, the convention referring to it would have no practical use. And as Dharmakīrti insists, if a lexical convention has no other purpose than practical activity (*vyavahāra*), it will have to refer to a stable and durable correlate that will be a conceptual product having no ontological consistence.[188]

For Prajñākaragupta, therefore, lexical conventions only refer to superimposed conceptual materials, to unreal universals. In his explanation of PV IV 109, he makes explicit the relations between universals, lexical conventions, the speaker's arbitrariness and psychic imprints (*vāsanā*). Those elements co-occur with one another: "The referent of the intended word is indeed a universal defined as the exclusion of others. And this cannot be negated, since it is due to its being restricted to a psychic imprint that a cognition of that kind arises, [i.e., cognition of the universal that is the referent of the word]. And that psychic imprint, [once] it is awakened (*prabodhita*) due to its restriction to a convention fixed by mere [human] arbitrariness, instigates (*avasthāpayati*) the universal that is connected to it."[189] What

---

187 PVA on PV III 45, 209.4–11: *saṅketo hi kriyamāṇaḥ sannihitamātram avalambya na kriyate / tadapekṣyaś ca pratyayaḥ samāropita eva / tathā hi / pūrvetarādhyāropeṇa vinā saṅketanaṃ yadi / avyāpitāyāṃ naivaṃ syād vyavahārānumāyitā // 216 // śabdasāmarthyād eva vyavahārakāle pratītir iti cet / yadi pūrvāparādhyāropo na syān na bhavet pratītiḥ / na ca śabdāt sāmānyabuddhiḥ saṅketam antareṇa dṛṣṭā / vyaktyantaradarśanād bhavaty eva śabdam antareṇeti cet / tatrāpi tad eva liṅgaṃ tadrūpavyavahārabhāve / liṅgam api pūrvādhyāropam eva janayati nādhikam / tathā hūṇādijātir*[1] *dvijādijātiś ca saṅketamātrabalāvalambinī na vastv apekṣate /*. Compare with PVA$_{Tib}$ P *te* 230b5–231a2. 1: PVA$_{Tib}$ reads *dbyangs la sogs pa'i rigs*, which could correspond to *acādijātiḥ*, as below, "a class like that of the vowels."

188 On this point, see PV I 92 and PVSV 45.20–29, which are summarized in Vetter (1964, 59–60) and translated in Vora and Ota (1982, 15–16).

189 PVA on PV IV 109, 529.28–30: *anyāpohalakṣaṇaṃ hi sāmānyaṃ vācyam iṣṭasya dhvaneḥ / tac ca na pratiṣeddh*[u]*ṃ śakyaṃ vāsanāpratiniyamena tathābhūtapratyayodayāt / sā ca vāsanecchāmātrakṛtasaṅke-*

does this mean? For Prajñākaragupta, universals, psychic imprints and lexical conventions are in a relation of regular co-occurrence: one cannot go without the others. Each word, i.e., each acoustic image (Dharmottara on NB I 5 says: *abhidhānākāra*), is associated, arbitrarily and by convention, with a universal. All universals therefore subsist in the mind as imprints that various factors such as hearing a word are capable of actualizing or awaking, i.e., of bringing to consciousness.

A class like brahmanity is therefore a universal, a superimposition that has at best a negative relation to real entities. It is therefore unreal. We will recall that for Dharmakīrti—and the remark applies also to Prajñākaragupta—, causal capacity and perceptibility are the defining characteristics of real entities. The apprehension of real entities therefore does not require the mediation of conventions.[190] In a more detailed fashion than Dharmakīrti had done in this context, Prajñākaragupta will try to demonstrate that brahmanity is instantiated by individuals only through conventions that are in turn exclusively due to human arbitrariness (contrary, but very provisionally as we have seen, to cowhood or equidity). The universal is not apprehended on the basis of a sign or discriminant that would be directly perceived in the individuals alleged to instantiate it, since all those signs are fallacious (PVṬ/PVSVṬ *vyabhicārin*). Prajñākaragupta states this very clearly in his commentary on PV II 2: "To begin with, nobody can determine the class of the [Brahmin] in the same way as he would for a class like cowhood, simply through a particular physical aspect (*ākāraviśeṣa*), since it is observed

---

taniyamena prabodhitā niyataṃ sāmānyam avasthāpayati /. Compare with PVA$_{Tib}$ P *the* 212b1–3.

190 PVA on PV III 45, 209.11–12: *saṅketasahitaṃ pratyakṣaṃ pramāṇaṃ dvijādijātiṣu cet* / *na* / *vastubalena yaj jāyate na tat saṅketam apekṣate* / *saṅketamātrāpekṣaṇe 'ndhaparamparaiva syāt* /. Compare with PVA$_{Tib}$ P *te* 231a1–3. "[Objection:] Perception accompanied by conventions is the means of valid cognition concerning classes such as Brahmins, etc. [Reply:] No, what is produced by the force of something real does not depend on a convention, and if it did depend only on a convention, we would be facing a succession of blind men."

that the specific forms [of the individuals called Brahmins and *śūdras*, for example], get mixed up. Even the specific form [characteristic of Brahmins] is also observed among those who are considered to be *śūdras*, etc. Contrary to the specific forms of [cows] such as the *bāhuleya*, the [Brahmin] individuals, even among those descending from [the seer] Kuṇḍina, etc., are not observed to differ from the individuals considered to belong to a different class (*vijātīya*)."[191] Prajñākaragupta's method is here not different from that of Dharmakīrti and the commentators on PVSV, nor, for that matter, from the method of the VāS, VSū, KDAM or ŚKA. No specific form or external physical aspect is restricted to the individuals alleged to instantiate a given class. The alleged specific features of some individuals (e.g., the Brahmins) are found in all, or at least in some, dissimilar instances (e.g., the *śūdras*).

If no sign or criterion is found in individuals that could support the direct apprehension of the class they are alleged to instantiate,[192] grasping the universal will require the mediation of

---

[191] PVA$_{\text{Ono}}$ 21.10–14, to be compared with 10.23–26: *na tāvad gotvādijātim iva tajjātim ākāraviśeṣād eva kecid avadhārayitum īśate, ākṛtisaṅkarasya darśanāt. śūdrādyabhimatānām api saivākṛtir upalabhyate. na khalu bāhuleyādyākṛtaya iva kauṇḍinyādīnām api vijātīyābhimatavyaktivilakṣaṇā vyaktaya upalabhyante.*

[192] See also on this point PVA on PV III 46, 209.20–26: *athāpi syād / anugatākārā buddhiḥ padārthadvayadarśane saṅketam antareṇa bhavaty eva / yathā gavādibuddhiḥ śābaleyādidarśanād eva / na tatra saṅketo 'pekṣyate / evaṃ tarhi / brāhmaṇatvam ajātiḥ syāt tathā tasyāpratītitaḥ / dvijādijāter na vyaktir gotvavad vyañjikekṣyate // 218 // gotve yady anyathā vākyaṃ kiṃ sandegdhy atra kaścana / brāhmaṇatve tu sandegdhi kiṃ dvijo 'yam iti dhvaneḥ // 219 //*. Compare with PVA$_{\text{Tib}}$ P *te* 231a6–231b1. "Suppose it be urged: when observing two [similar] entities, a cognition whose aspect is common [to both cases] does indeed arise independently of a convention. For example, from the mere observation of *śābaleya* [cows], etc., the cognition of a cow [arises]. In this case, convention is not depended upon. [To this we answer:] But in this way, brahmanity would not be a class since it is not cognized in that manner. [Indeed], the [Brahmin] individual is not regarded as revealing a class such as [the class] of Brahmins in the same way as [*śā*-

an arbitrary convention. This is what Prajñākaragupta is saying in his commentary to PV IV 109: "To be a Brahmin, etc., is not revealed by the individual [himself, but] is arbitrarily restricted, since [brahmanity] is excluded from what differs from it by a word that functions due to convention (*saṅketavṛttiśabda*). Surely, classes like brahmanity cannot be revealed by an individual because his colour and configuration are not restricted. That is why those [classes] can only be revealed by the force of a convention [arbitrarily] restricted to [some] individuals <?characterized (*upalakṣita*) by a conduct restricted to [those] individuals?>."[193]

Now, we have seen that for Kumārila, apprehension of the class is mediated by knowledge or memory of the class of the direct parents. We have seen also that for Dharmakīrti, the fact of being mediated disqualifies the knowledge of class from being a direct perception. That knowledge, in so far as it is a verbal communication, is the result of instruction (*upadeśa*), and that instruction is conventional in nature.[194] Instruction relies upon

---

baleyas, etc., reveal] cowhood. [Moreover], if [someone should tell] a lie concerning [something's] cowhood, will anybody have doubts regarding this [cowhood]? Yet from the words: 'This [one] is not a Brahmin,' one does [certainly] have doubts regarding [his] brahmanity.*" *The Tibetan of PVA III 219cd reads: *bram ze 'di min zhes brjod pa'am // bram ze nyid la the tshom 'gyur //*, where the first part obviously corresponds to the Sanskrit *na dvijo 'yam iti*.

193 PVA on PV IV 109, 530.1–3: *brāhmaṇāditvam avyaktaṃ vyaktyā niyatam icchayā / saṅketavṛttiśabdena tadanyavinivṛttitaḥ // 174 // na khalu dvijatvādijātayo 'niyatavarṇasaṃsthānātmatayā vyaktyā vyaktuṃ śakyāḥ / tatas tā vyaktiniyatācāropalakṣitavyaktiniyatasaṅketabalād evābhivyaktibhājaḥ /*. There are important discrepancies in PVA$_{Tib}$ P *the* 212b3–5.

194 PVA on PV IV 109, 530.4–6: *nanu na kenacid atredānīṃ kṛtaḥ saṅketo 'nādisvabhāvasiddhavācyavācakabhāvasambhavāt / na / upadeśasyaiva saṅketatvāt / api ca / brāhmaṇo na brāhmaṇa iti na*[1] *kāraṇam etat / yat tu tasya dṛṣṭahetutvaṃ*[2] *tad atra sādhyam anyathā caṇḍālādijātīnām āsāñ ca kaḥ parasparo vibhāgaḥ /*. 1: According to PVA$_{Tib}$, *'di ni rgyu ma yin no*; 2: according to PVA$_{Tib}$, *'dir ni de'i rgyu mtshan mthong ba'i rgyu gang yin pa*, where the Tib. *rgyu mtshan* has no Skt. equivalent. "[Objection:] Nobody creates a convention with regard to this

lexical conventions that in turn depend on the speaker's arbitrariness. Any instruction is therefore ultimately based on conceptual fictions. In a passage from his voluminous commentary to PV II 2, Prajñākaragupta reiterates, sometimes with citations, the important points of Dharmakīrti's critique according to which an instruction both raises doubt about the speaker's credibility and is redundant if its object also falls in the domain of direct perception. He says: "[To accept] the epistemic validity of another person's testimony in the case of a perceptible object is not rational since people's testimony also proceeds differently, [i.e., erroneously]. If a class like brahmanity were grasped by perception, the testimony of another person would be useless. For the other person's testimony is no more valuable when it comes to a perceptible object. Moreover, if this were the case, [i.e., if another person's testimony were more valuable than direct perception for a directly perceptible object], no doubt would follow from another person's testimony."[195]

In his commentary to PV III 45, Prajñākaragupta comes back to the uselessness of another person's testimony in the knowledge of directly perceptible classes. But here, he connects this critique to the problem of the verifiability of another person's testimony, a question of central importance to Buddhist epistemologists. We know that for philosophers, authoritative testimony (*āptopadeśa*) and scripture (*āgama*) are frequently treated

[brahmanity] nowadays because there is a relation between the signified and the signifier that is naturally established from beginningless time. [Reply:] That is not so, because of the conventionality of the testimony itself. Moreover, [to say] '[this man] is a Brahmin, [this man] is not a Brahmin,' is no reason [for the cognition of such a class]. However, [you] have to prove here that it has an observable cause, [for] otherwise, what would be the mutual difference between classes such as the *caṇḍāla*'s and the [Brahmin's]?"

195 PVA$_{Ono}$ 21.17–22.3; compare with PVA 10.28–30: *paropadeśaprāmāṇyaṃ pratyakṣārthe na yuktimat / upadeśo hi lokānām anyathāpi pravartate // 62 // yadi khalu brāhmaṇatvādijātiḥ pratyakṣeṇekṣyate, paropadeśasya vyarthatā. na hi pratyakṣe 'rthe paropadeśo garīyān. tathā cet, na paropadeśataḥ sandehaḥ syāt.*

as synonymous, so that the conditions of their respective reliability (*avisaṃvāda*) are identical. The discourse of an authority who would never take a stand on perceptible or "objectively" inferable states of affairs could only be reliable on the (rather weak) ground of its internal consistency. Prajñākaragupta will therefore condition the very possibility of a testimony to its truth-value, and the latter to the perceptibility of the state of affairs that it attempts to describe. He says: "[Objection:] Perception itself works as a cooperating cause (*sahakārin*) [of another person's testimony in the apprehension of that class]. [Reply:] To this we answer that if [a class like brahmanity] is grasped through perception, [another person's] testimony is useless. [But] if [that class] is not grasped through perception, [another person's] testimony is [still] useless. [Indeed], if [that class] is grasped through perception, what use is there of a testimony since it is grasped by this [perception] alone. But if [a class] cannot be known through perception, could a thousand testimonies make it known? In the case of an empirical [thing], indeed, there could be a human testimony such as 'I have seen this'. But in the case of a supersensible [thing like] brahmanity, the testimony is incapable [of making it known, as Śabara himself acknowledges when he says:] 'That which has the human mind for its [sole] source is not a means of valid cognition'."[196] On the one hand, another person's testimony and direct perception are redundant: if brahmanity were directly perceptible, nobody would need, in the presence of a Brahmin, the instruction of a third person in order to know that this is a Brahmin. On the other hand, testi-

---

[196] PVA on PV III 45, 209.13–17 and 20: *pratyakṣam api sahakāri vidyata iti cet / atrocyate / pratyakṣeṇa gṛhītaṃ ced upadeśo nirarthakaḥ / pratyakṣeṇāgṛhītaṃ ced upadeśo nirarthakaḥ* // 217 // *yadi pratyakṣeṇa gṛhītaṃ kim upadeśena tenaiva grahaṇāt / atha pratyakṣeṇa pratyetum aśakyaṃ kim upadeśasahasreṇāpi śakyaṃ pratyāyitum / dṛṣṭe hi puruṣopadeśo mayaitad dṛṣṭam iti syāt / atīndriye tu dvijātitve nopadeśasya sāmarthyāt / ... tat puruṣabuddhiprabhavam apramāṇam eva* [*iti*] /. ŚBh on MīSū I 1.2/ I 17.6–7, translation adapted from Biardeau (1964, 78). Compare with PVA_{Tib} P *the* 231a3–6, which suggests the reading *nopadeśasya sāmarthyam.*

mony is a legitimate verbal knowledge if it pertains to a state of affairs that is "objectively" accessible (i.e., through direct perception and through an "objective" inference),[197] but not directly apprehended by the person to whom the verbal communication is addressed. A class like brahmanity however fails to meet this condition for it is supersensible. The only possible solution for the advocate of classes and castes would be to trace the origin of brahmanity and the other castes to scriptures, i.e., here to the Veda. But the Veda is not a means of valid cognition. Furthermore, as Śāntarakṣita, Kamalaśīla and Prajñākaragupta insisted, the Veda has nothing to say about such and such an individual belonging to such and such a class.[198]

Both Prajñākaragupta and Dharmakīrti reject the claim that direct perception and another person's testimony contribute *together* to knowledge. Direct perception cannot use testimony as a cooperating cause and *vice versa*. Direct perception is no more accompanied by testimony than testimony is accompanied by direct perception. Their epistemological functions are distinct. More importantly, Prajñākaragupta insists that their hypothetical cooperation would make it impossible to validate or invalidate another person's testimony. And this is a fundamental requisite. In the present case, a testimony of the form "the individual x is a Brahmin" would be verifiable or refutable only if it met the following two conditions: (1) brahmanity has to be perceptible and (2) perception and testimony operate distinctly. Prajñākaragupta formulates the principle of those conditions in PVA, verse II 63: "If perception establishes (*prasādhaka*) something independently of [another person's] testimony, then [only] is it capable of establishing the veracity of a testimony, not otherwise."[199] In the passage that follows, Prajñākaragupta elaborates on that problem by means of an example that is frequently

---

197 On those various points, see Tillemans (1986, 1990 and 1993) and Eltschinger (1998, 2007).

198 See sections 2.5.4.1, p. 138, and 2.5.4.2.2, p. 152 below.

199 PVA$_{Ono}$, verse II 63, 22.5–6: *upadeśaṃ vinādhyakṣaṃ yady arthasya prasādhakam / tadopadeśasatyatvaṃ vidhātuṃ nānyathā kṣamam //*.

used in discussing the epistemic validity of scriptures:[200] "When, indeed, one suspects of being false a testimony pertaining to gold, etc., that [testimony] is discarded by an observation through perception. On the contrary, if one suspects of being false a testimony pertaining to a class [like brahmanity], the truth cannot result from a perception whose aspect grasps the intrinsic nature of the class. For indeed, in the case of gold, etc., what is observed causes no harm [to the testimony] because the statement 'Gold is only of such a kind' is corroborated by the real presence of a particular colour. But in our case, the mere stretching out of the feet [in the statement] 'Brahmanity is only of such a kind' is not a [valid] defence [of the reality of a class like brahmanity].... Indeed, in so far as the statement corresponds [to a perception] (*ekavākyatayā*), gold is genuine (*satya*), contrary to brahmanity."[201]

Let us summarize Prajñākaragupta's position. Brahmanity is the arbitrary and conventional referent of a word, and the referent of a word is a superimposition, a universal that subsists in our psyche as a latent impregnation. That description is more than enough to exclude brahmanity from real entities and, consequently, from the set of directly perceptible things. Moreover, the individuals alleged to instantiate that class bear no perceptible and restrictively limited signs that could make that class known. All those signs are fallacious. The knowledge of such a class therefore depends on instruction or testimony, both of which are conventional, so that the criteria used to determine whether an individual belongs to a class are also arbitrary. Now

[200] On this point, see Eltschinger (1998, 78–80).

[201] PVA$_{Ono}$ 22.15–23.6, to compare with PVA 11.3–9: *kāñcanādyupadeśasya hi yadā 'satyatāśaṅkā, tadā pratyakṣadarśanād asau nivartate. naivaṃ jātyupadeśasyāsatyatāśaṅkāyāṃ pratyakṣāt satyatā jātisvarūpagrahaṇākārāt. suvarṇādau hi rūpaviśeṣasadbhāvād evambhūtam eva suvarṇaṃ bhavatīti vyavahārasya parisamāpter dṛṣṭasya na kācit kṣatiḥ. atra tu punar evaṃvidham eva brāhmaṇyam iti na pādaprasāraṇamātraṃ trāṇam... ekavākyatayā hi suvarṇaṃ satyaṃ bhavati, na tu brāhmaṇyam.*

on the one hand, everything that requires a convention or a testimony for its apprehension is *ipso facto* unreal and, therefore, imperceptible. On the other hand, only what is directly perceptible or, more generally, "objectively" apprehensible, can properly be the object of a testimony. Accordingly, the class is either directly perceptible, in which case reliance on testimony proves useless, or it is imperceptible and cannot therefore be the object of a verifiable or refutable testimony. In the first case, Kumārila and the Naiyāyikas commit the fault of subordinating direct perception to the testimony. In the second case, they commit the double fault of asserting the direct perceptibility of class without being able to provide any objective basis for its existence other than blind faith.

2.5 Post-Dharmakīrtian developments of the argumentation

In the section that follows, I wish to report the innovations or modifications brought to the argumentation against class by Dharmakīrti's heirs Śāntarakṣita,[202] Kamalaśīla and Prajñākara-

---

202 In the final chapter of the TS(P) (= XXVI, *atīndriyadarśipuruṣaparīkṣā*), verses 3775–3780, Śāntarakṣita and Kamalaśīla, following Śākyabuddhi (see section 2.5.1.1, p. 138, below), express their indignation with the arrogance of Brahmins. They directly reply to the objections formulated in TS 3224–3227, which are reminiscent of the radically anti-Buddhist arguments presented in Kumārila's TV. There we are told that the *Smṛtis*, the epics and the *Purāṇas* are authoritative for the Mīmāṃsā only because their teachings are rooted in the Veda (see section 2.1.2.2, p. 87, above). The Buddhist teachings, however, in so far as they are not in any way based on the Veda (*avedamūla*), are a sign of bewilderment or must aim at the bewilderment of their auditors (*śiṣyavyāmohanārtham*). If, moreover, the Buddhist dharma were to originate from the Veda, it would have only been passed to the Brahmins specialized in the Veda, and not, as the opponent protests, to stupid *śūdras*. Kamalaśīla introduces Śāntarakṣita's reply with three hypotheses to account for the Brahmins' arrogance (TSP 920.7–12): *bhavataiva mūrkhaśūdrebhya ity atiprakaṭam uccair asadbhūtajātimadoddhatena cetasā bruvatā sphuṭataram ātmana eva prakaṭitam iha vidvajjanasa-*

gupta. It is important to note, however, that I do not intend to analyze the internal logic of the argument of each given author, but instead offer a taxonomy of all the arguments that they had to propose. In so doing, I group the arguments in three categories indicated by the third digit of each section number, and further divide those categories according to their chronology, indicated by the fourth digit of the section number and corresponding to Śākyabuddhi (660–720), Śāntarakṣita (725–788), Kamalaśīla (740–795), Karṇakagomin (around 800) and Prajñākaragupta (around 800). I will assess those developments in the general conclusions.

2.5.1 Biological and genealogical arguments

2.5.1.1 This chapter began with a translation of the last verse of PV I (= PV I 340) where Dharmakīrti listed the pride of caste among the five marks of stupidity[203] (*jāḍyaliṅga*). In their commentary to that verse, Śākyabuddhi and Karṇakagomin develop two hypotheses (*pakṣa*) to account for the Brahmins' pride:[204]

---

dasi mahāmaurkhyam / tathā hi kadācid brāhmaṇatvākhyaṃ sāmānyaṃ nāma vastvantaram astīty evam upakalpayantas tatra bhavanto viprā garvārbudam udvahanti / yad vā jātakarmādibhiḥ saṃskṛtatvam ātmanaḥ samīkṣya / brāhmaṇapitṛkṛtāṃ cātmano brāhmaṇīgarbhaprasūtim ālambya /. "You [Brahmins], when you are saying loudly and very openly, with a mind filled with pride in an unreal caste, that [the teachings of the Buddha were given] to stupid *śūdras*, it is your own immense stupidity that is most clearly displayed in this assembly of learned people! For you Brahmins, bear up [your] immeasurable arrogance (*garvārbuda*) on this point by supposing, sometimes, that a universal called 'brahmanity' really exists as a distinct real entity, or by considering yourself consecrated (*saṃskṛta*) by birth rituals, etc., and by reclaiming for yourself a birth due to a Brahmin father from an embryo [carried] by a Brahmin woman."

203 See the epigraph to chapter II above.

204 The commentary to PV I 340b2 begins with a problem close to that of the "true Brahmin." PVṬ P *ñe* 85a1–2 ≈ PVSVṬ 618.24–25: *śīlādiguṇavaikalye 'pi brāhmaṇo 'ham iti jātivādenāvalepo darpo jāḍyaliṅgam ayuktatvāt /*. "Arrogance, i.e., the pride [that the Brahmins get] on account

(1) a realist ontology of universals meant to explain the real existence of classes like brahmanity, and (2) the fact of being born from an embryo (*garbha*) carried by a Brahmin woman and having a Brahmin father.[205] As he did earlier in his commentary, Śākyabuddhi refuses to elaborate on the ontological hypothesis since, according to him, it falls under the *apoha* critique of real universals (*vastubhūtasāmānya*).[206] And he is hardly saying more about the obstetric or genealogical hypothesis: "The second [hypothesis] also does not [justify the Brahmins' pride] since the bodies of male and female Brahmins, because they are of an impure nature, are not distinct from a body different [from theirs, that of a *śūdra*, for example]."[207]

2.5.1.2 That argument occurs also in the writings of Kamalaśīla, where it is reintroduced in his preamble to Śāntarakṣita's treatment of the genealogical hypothesis (see note 202 above), as well as in his commentary on TS 3575 (see section 2.5.2, below): "The [Brahmins'] pride is also unjustified under the third hypothesis, for it has [already] been said that, since they consist of impure

---

of caste (*jātivādena*) [when they say] 'I am a Brahmin,' though they are devoid of qualities like morality, is a mark of stupidity because it is not founded." On morality (*śīla*) as a characteristic feature of the "true Brahmin," see part I of the conclusion, below.

205 PVṬ P *ñe* 85a2–3: *de ltar na bram ze nyid kyi spyi gzung nas lan gnyis skyes pa dag rigs smras pas dregs par 'gyur ram / pha bram ze dang bram ze mo'i mngal nas skyes pa gang yin pa de la brten nas rigs smra bas dregs par 'gyur grang* [P *drang*] *na* /. "This is how the Brahmins (*dvija*) could either take pride on account of caste by grasping a universal [consisting in] brahmanity, or they could take pride on account of caste by appealing to [their] birth from an embryo [co-produced] by a Brahmin father and a Brahmin mother." PVSVṬ 618.25–26 is partly corrupted: [*tathā hi pra...gṛ*]*hītvā jātivādāvalepaḥ syāt / brāhmaṇena pitrā brāhmaṇyā garbhe ya utpādas taṃ vā samāśritya* /.

206 PVṬ P *ñe* 85a3–4 = PVSVṬ 618.27: *vastubhūtasāmānyaniṣedhān na pūrvaḥ pakṣaḥ* /. "Since real universals were refuted [above], it is not the first hypothesis." See section 2.1.2.1, p. 85, above.

207 PVṬ P *ñe* 85a4 = PVSVṬ 618.27–28: *nāpy uttaro brāhmaṇabrāhmaṇīśarīrayor aśucisvabhāvatvena śarīrāntarād aviśeṣāt* /.

[elements] like semen, blood, etc., there is no difference whatsoever between the bodies of male and female Brahmins and the bodies of *śūdra*s, etc."[208]

2.5.1.3 The argument of later philosophers is therefore an extension and a fusion of the biological and genealogical arguments found in the old literature (see respectively sections 1.2, p. 17, and 1.3.1, p. 26, above). For it is argued that the physiology and organic constitution of the individuals reputed to be Brahmins from birth do not justify a differentiation into castes. This was already convincingly demonstrated in the AsS, the ŚKA and the KDAM, where it was argued that whoever may be the direct parents of Brahmin and *śūdra* children, those children are born under the same conditions, from blood and semen.

2.5.2 The "true Brahmins": substitution of the paradigm of brahmanity

Śāntarakṣita discusses the ontological hypothesis only very briefly in TS 3575–3577, where it is clearly connected to the question of the reality of universals discussed in chapters XIII (= *sāmānyaparīkṣā*) and XVI (= *śabdārthaparīkṣā*) of the TS. He says: "Why [do you still stubbornly take] pride in [your] caste when the class has been refuted hundreds of times? And if an additional property has not been established [among Brahmins compared] to [men who are] different from them, why is this [caste] regarded as superior (*viśiṣṭa*)?"[209] In their *apoha* critique of realist ontologies, it is typical of Buddhist epistemologists to make no distinction between the two meanings of *jāti* as referring to caste or to a class or universal. The result is that the critique of class is also considered to apply *in extenso* to caste (see section

---

[208] TSP 921.5–6: *tṛtīye 'pi pakṣe na yukto madaḥ / na hi brāhmaṇabrāhmaṇīśarīrāṇāṃ śūdrādiśarīrataḥ śukraśoṇitādyaśucimayatvena kaścid viśeṣo 'stīty uktam etat /.*

[209] TS 3575: *śataśaḥ pratiṣiddhāyāṃ jātau jātimadaś ca kim / tadanyātiśayāsiddhau viśiṣṭā sā ca kiṃ matā //.*

2.1.2.1, p. 85, above). But Śāntarakṣita's position is here interesting because he sets the conditions for a reversal of the paradigm of brahmanity. He asserts in TS 3575 that the individual instances of a class will be superior only if they possess an additional property (*atiśaya*). In other words, he introduces a new requirement in the debate on caste superiority according to which the properties of being a Brahmin and being the owner of an additional property (*atiśayavattva*) must be co-extensive. As was the case with all the arguments analyzed so far, Śāntarakṣita will therefore try to demonstrate, as we shall see in the remaining sections of this chapter, that it is impossible to establish that co-extension *as long as brahmanity must meet an innative criterion*. Since such a co-extension remains unestablished, the identity between brahmanity and superiority (*vaiśiṣṭya*) also vanishes and, with it, the justification for the pride that one can take in his caste. But Śāntarakṣita goes further in TS 3575–3577, where he reproduces a series of arguments that is perfectly analogous to the structure of all the canonical discussions against the naturalization of caste. The Brahmanic criteria or discriminants of brahmanity are demolished and replaced by the Buddhist criteria or discriminants of "true brahmanity" that give an ethical flavour to the concept of Brahmin. In TS 3576–3577, Śāntarakṣita thus preserved the normative character of brahmanity (i.e., the co-extension of "being a Brahmin" and "possessing an additional property"), but replaced the innative Brahmanic criterion with the ethical and soteriological criterion advanced by Buddhists from the very beginning. That criterion states that every individual, *independently* of his original social extraction, will be a Brahmin, i.e., will be superior, once he has eradicated his vices and defilements and acquired the qualities (*guṇa*) that really make him superior. Here then is the reversal of the paradigm of brahmanity, in the words of Śāntarakṣita: "Now [if they are] receptacles of [moral] qualities like sovereignty [because they] have eradicated all [their moral] impurities, all [humans], without distinction [relative to the caste to which they belong by birth], could also be Brahmins if they possessed those [qualities]. If the individual instances (*samāśraya*) of the [Brahmin caste] are established as [individually] superior, [then their] superiority [will be justified]. Otherwise, [it will] not [be justified] in any way, no more than a caste of Brahmin hunters, etc.[210]"[211]

Kamalaśīla's commentary makes very clear the distinction between the two elements of the sequence proposed by Śāntarakṣita. Kamalaśīla first develops the properly descriptive pole of the criteria or discriminants according to which we have no empirical knowledge of *any* psychic or physiological property that would *specify* some individuals as Brahmins and exclude all others. He says: "Indeed, we do not perceive any additional property among Brahmins [at birth] compared to *śūdras*, etc., neither with respect to such [psychic features] as discernment or intellectual penetration,[212] nor with respect to such [physiological features] as feces, urine, flesh or blood. How then, when no additional property is established, [can] this class be distinguished as possessing that [additional property], so that, filled with pride on account of [your] caste, you speak thus: '[Masters like the Buddha], following Manu's example, etc., would have im-

---

210 Brahmin hunters are mentioned in the *Dasabrāhmaṇajātaka*, IV 361ff; see Fick (1972, 216–20[140–43] and 246[160]). According to Renou, the "ten types of unworthy Brahmins" are reminiscent of "the pseudo-Brahmins (*brahmabandhu*) of the Veda and more specifically of the ten classes of Atri (373ff)" (English translation of Renou 1981, 57). Such occupations are generally reserved for those who are excluded from the system of the four castes.

211 TS 3576–3577: *vaśitvādiguṇādhārāḥ prakṣīṇāśeṣakalmaṣāḥ / sarve 'py atrāviśeṣeṇa tadyoge ca [d]vijātayaḥ // bhaveyur yadi sidhyanti viśiṣṭās tatsamāśrayāḥ / vaiśiṣṭyam anyathā naiva lubdhakadvijajātivat //.*

212 In the VāS [Sn. 627], the Buddha defines the true Brahmin as one who possesses intellectual penetration and is deep in discernment (*gambhīrapaññaṃ medhāviṃ*). In the SoS, morality is the fourth defining characteristic of brahmanity. To be wise (*paṇḍita*) and possessing intellectual penetration (*medhāvin*) make up the fifth characteristic, which then merges into discernment (*paññā*). See part I of the conclusion, below.

parted this [teaching rooted in the Veda] only to those [Brahmins who are] versed in the Veda'?"[213]

Kamalaśīla can conclude, after integrating the old "egalitarian" theme of the true Brahmin: "If, however, in so far as [you are] the individual instances of the Brahmin caste,[214] you were by nature the [exclusive] receptacles of a multitude of qualities like sovereignty, supremacy, free wil! and compassion, [people from whom] every vice has disappeared without exception, then you would be superior. Otherwise, even if you were connected [by birth] to the Brahmin caste, how could [your] superiority, like that of a Brahmin hunter (*lubdhaka*), fisherman (*kaivarta*) or currier (*carmakāra*), etc.,[215] ever be established?"[216]

2.5.3 Activity (*kriyā*) and sacraments (*saṃskāra*)

2.5.3.1 The hypothesis that pertains to rituals also finds no rest at the hands of Śāntarakṣita: "Moreover, [sacraments] like birth rituals are commonly established [among Brahmins], as they are among [people] other than them [i.e., among those considered to

---

213 TSP 920.22–25: *tathā hi śūdrādibhyo na prajñāmedhādibhir viṇmūtramāṃsaśoṇitādibhiś ca viprāṇām atiśayam upalabhāmahe / tat katham atiśayāsiddhau satyāṃ sā tadādhārā jātir viśiṣyate yena bhavatā jātivādāvalepoddhatenaivam abhidhīyate vedavādibhya eva taṃ prayaccheyur yathā manvādaya* iti /*. *TS 3226; see note 202, p. 137, above.

214 I read *brāhmaṇajātisamāśrayeṇa* as *brāhmaṇajātisamāśrayatveṇa*.

215 On those despised Brahmins, see Law (1937, 24–25), who refers to *Jātaka* I 146. On the *cammakāra*, see Fick (1972, 327[210]). On the modern *camār* or "leather" people, see the comments of Dumont (1972, 92–93[77–78]).

216 TSP 920.25–28: *yadi tu brāhmaṇajātisamāśrayeṇa bhavantaḥ prakṛtyaiva vaśitveśitvaprākāmyakaruṇādiguṇagaṇādhārāḥ prahīṇāśeṣaduritā* bhaveyus tadā bhaved bhavatāṃ vaiśiṣṭyam / anyathā lubdhakakaivartacarmakārādibrāhmaṇasya iva saty api brāhmaṇajātiyoge katham eva** vaiśiṣṭyaṃ sidhyet /*. Compare with TSP$_{\text{Tib}}$ P *ye* 394a2–4. *K reads *prahīṇāśeṣadūrita*; read *prahīṇāśeṣadurita*, as in TSP$_{\text{Tib}}$ P *ye* 394a5: *sdig pa ma lus pa spangs par gyur*. **K reads *katham iva*; read *katham eva*.

be artificial Brahmins].[217] Those habits are factitious, [like the name-giving ceremonies],[218] for they are found also among artificial [Brahmins]."[219] The strategy used in TS 3578 is formally similar to the one that guided the refutation of the previous realist argument. The proving properties that are alleged to characterize only the Brahmin class (in this case, receiving various sacraments) are shown to occur among individuals from other classes, i.e., among certain dissimilar instances of the property to be proved. For we find that individuals belonging to (pseudo-)classes not habilitated to receive the sacraments, according to the Brahmanic norm, nonetheless receive them. The logical reason is therefore inconclusive.

2.5.3.2 We have seen above that Prajñākaragupta's effort to invalidate the reality of class essentially consisted in an attempt to separate direct perception from the testimony of others, from conventions and from speech, both in terms of ontology and epistemology. In so doing, he was developing on Dharmakīrti's argumentation. Prajñākaragupta's de-legitimization of a person's testimony in fact led his opponents, under PV II 2, to formulate an objection that tended to minimize the importance of another person's testimony in the knowledge of a person's class. That objection marks the introduction of the second hypothesis examined by Prajñākaragupta, namely the hypothesis that class could consist in the possession of a specific capacity for a given activity. The nature of that hypothesis and its critique are close to what we saw in Śāntarakṣita: "[Objection:] It is through a particular activity such as the recitation of the Veda that one knows [a class like brahmanity], not through the mere testimony [of another person]."[220]

---

217 TSP 921.4: *tadanyavad iti kṛtrimābhimatabrāhmaṇeṣv iva.*

218 TSP 921.4–5: *sāṃvṛta iti nāmakaraṇādivat sāṃvyavahārikāḥ.*

219 TS 3578: *jātakarmādayo ye ca prasiddhās te tadanyavat / ācārāḥ sāṃvṛtās te hi kṛtrimeṣv api bhāvinaḥ //.*

220 PVA$_{Ono}$ 23.8: *adhyayanādinā kriyāviśeṣeṇa jñāyate, nopadeśamātrāt.*

Prajñākaragupta states the principle of his answer in verse II 65: "An activity [such as the recitation of the Veda] can be established [as specific] if brahmanity [has been established, but] brahmanity [cannot be established] through an activity. [As for] sacraments they cannot also be [used to establish the class] without a [prior] determination of the class."[221] Prajñākaragupta's answer consists in forcing his opponent to admit that one could infer that a given individual practises certain activities on the basis of his brahmanity, i.e., because he is a Brahmin, but not the opposite, as the opponent would have it. But in order even for that inference to be valid, a preliminary condition must be met, namely the proving property "being a Brahmin" must be established. However, the imperceptibility of class and the unacceptability of another person's testimony result in this logical reason being unestablished (*asiddha*).

That hypothesis having been rejected, what remains to be done is to refute the opposite position which posits the co-extension of the two properties "being a Brahmin" and "practising specific activities." We have seen that in his critique of the justification of brahmanity through the sacraments, Śāntarakṣita referred to the existence of artificial Brahmins who nonetheless receive the sacraments. Prajñākaragupta's argument is based on a similar empirical premise, for he argues that those men who were born Brahmins are not the only ones to receive the sacraments and to memorize and recite the Veda. Since the proving property is found also among individuals belonging to the class of dissimilar instances, the opponent's argument is inconclusive, and the latter is left with no other choice but to admit that all men who share that property are Brahmins... This is exactly Prajñākaragupta's conclusion: "Indeed, neither the memorization or recitation of the Veda, nor the sacraments make a [person] excluded from a class [like brahmanity] a Brahmin, etc., since [if

---

221 PVA$_{Ono}$, verse II 65, 23.10–11: *dvijātitve kriyā sādhyā na kriyāto dvijātitā / saṃskārā api naiva syur jātiniścayavarjitāḥ //*.

this were the case], the unacceptable conclusion [would follow that] all [men] could be a Brahmin."[222]

2.5.4 Lineage (*gotra*) and genealogy

2.5.4.1 According to Kamalaśīla, the third hypothesis that could possibly legitimize pride in one's caste was genealogical. The arguments put forward by Śāntarakṣita to counter that hypothesis try to show that the property advanced by Brahmins as a logical reason, namely "being born from a Brahmin father and mother," is inconclusive because it is doubtful[223] (*sandigdha*). Partially modelled on CŚ IV 22,[224] Śāntarakṣita's reply goes as follows: "[Because] a great amount of time has passed and [because of] women's extreme fickleness, [your] brahmanity, even if it existed, cannot be ascertained. Indeed, according to you, no one is [capable of] knowing supersensible entities, and the permanent Veda has said nothing of the purity of your lineage."[225]

For Śāntarakṣita, therefore, two facts threaten the purity of the Brahmanic lineage and, consequently, the genealogical argument. On the one hand, since time passes, a person who now belongs to the Brahmin class may come from a lineage that was originally not Brahmanic.[226] On the other hand, a lineage that

---

222 PVA$_{Ono}$ 23.12–13: *jātivarjitasya hi na svādhyāyādhyayanasaṃskārādayo dvijātitvādikam ādadhati, sarvasya tathā dvijatvaprasaṅgāt.* On the antecedents to those arguments, see note 76 (3), p. 30, above.

223 According to TSP 921.7–8: *api ca sandigdham eva bhavato brāhmaṇapitṛkatvam ity ato na yukto mada ity ādarśayann āha.*

224 See section 2.1.1.2, p. 71, above.

225 TS 3579–3580: *atītaś ca mahān kālo yoṣitāṃ cāticāpalam / tad bhavaty api niścetuṃ brāhmaṇatvaṃ na śakyate // atīndriyapadārthajño na hi kaścit samasti vaḥ / tvadanvayaviśuddhiṃ ca nityo vedo 'pi noktavān //.* On women's fickleness, see also TSP 856.25–857.1.

226 Kamalaśīla states the problem very clearly in TSP 921.13–14: *kālāntareṇa kadācid abrāhmaṇagotrako 'pi san bhavān brāhmaṇaḥ sāṃvṛta ity api sambhāvyate.* "It is also possible that after some time, even if one day you were from a non-Brahmanic lineage, you [have become] a Brahmin, [in reality] a factitious [Brahmin]."

was originally Brahmanic may degenerate because of women's venality. He says: "[Moreover], even if you were preceded by Brahmin [ancestors in the lineage], it is also possible that you are a bastard (*jārajāta*) due to your mother's misconduct. We find indeed as a general rule that women, lovesick and having an unstable mind, transgress even the limit of their own family vow."[227] In both cases, Śāntarakṣita's and Kamalaśīla's arguments borrow from the non-philosophical literature (AmbS, VSū, ŚKA and KDAM, as well as AsS and VSū), and from Āryadeva and Candrakīrti.

Śāntarakṣita and Kamalaśīla add to those two factual arguments a principled argument based on Mīmāṃsā epistemology, as it faced the following question: how can the purity of the lineage (*anvayaviśuddhi*) of a Brahmin be certified? More precisely: how can a Mīmāṃsaka be sure of it? For it is well known that the Mīmāṃsā rejects all perception of supersensible things. But in rejecting a type of perception that can be quite useful in such contexts, the Mīmāṃsā *ipso facto* deprives itself of all justification for pride in one's caste. Moreover, the Veda that the Mīmāṃsā holds as the unique epistemic authority on supersensible matters does not teach anything about the purity of the various lineages.[228] In so far as the principles of his epistemology

---

[227] TSP 921.14–16: *saty api brāhmaṇapūrvatve bhavato mātṛcāritradoṣeṇa jārajātatvam api sambhāvyata eva / tathā hi prāyeṇa yoṣito manmathāturāś capalacetasaḥ svakulavratasīmānam atipatyāpi vartamānāḥ samupalabhyante /*. On the structure of a gerundive + *vṛt*, see Bronkhorst (1990, 302–303). On that motif, see sections 1.3.3, p. 35, 2.1.1.2, p. 71, and 2.4.1, p. 116, above.

[228] Śāntarakṣita's and Kamalaśīla's arguments against the naturalization of class appear to be modelled on the arguments developed by Dharmakīrti, in PVSV, against the possibility of establishing the meaning of Vedic words in the context of his critique of the authorlessness (*apauruṣeyatā*) of the Veda. On many occasions, the Mīmāṃsaka refers to the uninterrupted character of the lineage of explanation of the Veda as a guarantee of the accuracy of the meaning of Vedic words (see for example PVSV 168.15–16: *vedavat tadvyākhyānam apy apauruṣeyaṃ sampradāyāvicchedād āgatam / tato 'rthasiddhir iti cet /*). But against this position, Dharmakīrti argues (see PVSV 168.4–26) that during all that

are those of the Mīmāṃsā, a Brahmin therefore cannot guarantee the purity of his Brahmanic lineage. We will see more clearly below, with Prajñākaragupta, that the permanence of the Veda has unwelcome consequences in the discussion of lineage.

2.5.4.2.1 We have already mentioned that Prajñākaragupta identified three hypotheses to account for an individual's brahmanity after showing how the fact of being a Brahmin, etc., is not accessible to any means of valid cognition. The fact of being a Brahmin could (1) be defined by the possession of a class, (2) be defined in terms of lineage or (3) consist in the possession of a specific capacity for a given activity. Now as we have noted many times already, while the essential part of Prajñākaragupta's critique focuses on the perceptibility of classes and pays marginal attention to the third hypothesis, his treatment of the genealogical hypothesis connected to lineage is more elaborate than Śāntarakṣita's and Kamalaśīla's.

Here, the formal structure of the argument is similar to that of the argument against brahmanity being defined in terms of an activity. To establish brahmanity using lineage as a logical sign supposes that lineage can be established independently of brahmanity as an element of the proof. But as his conclusion clearly indicates, that is impossible according to Prajñākaragupta: "Being of the [Brahmin] lineage is possible [only] if brahmanity has

---

time, unscrupulous teachers may have wished for the corruption of the tradition (as it occurred with Mādhava in the casẹ of the Sāṅkhya, according to Śākyabuddhi and Karṇakagomin, as well as with some compilers of Buddhist Mahāyāna sutras; see PVSVṬ 595.21–23). The recensions (*śākhā*) of the Veda, moreover (see PVSV 169.4–13), are notoriously unstable. Still, the Mīmāṃsakas reject the authority of any person who sees supersensible things for determining the meaning of a Vedic word (see PV I 319bd: *tatra ko 'tīndriyārthadṛk / anekārtheṣu śabdeṣu yenārtho 'yaṃ vivecitaḥ //*). And the Veda does not teach the meaning of each of its words to Brahmins (see PV I 312ab: *artho 'yaṃ nāyam artho na iti śabdā vadanti na /*; PVSV 165.6–8 *ad loc.*; see also PV I 317cd: *na vedayati vedo 'pi vedārthasya kuto gatiḥ //*; PVSV 167.5–6 *ad loc.*). There is therefore no determination of the meaning of Vedic words.

first been established (*sthita*). [But] since it has not been established, how [can we speak of] lineage? This is [indeed] a row of blind men[229]."[230] As was the case with the use of activity as a logical sign, the proving property and the property to be proved serve as the foundation of one another. The argument is begging the question (*anyonyāśraya*, Yamāri)[231] and the proof is therefore unacceptable. Let us now examine the different steps of Prajñākaragupta's reasoning.

The opponent states his position as follows: "The class is defined by lineage, and that is how we call 'Brahmin' the descendant (*apatya*) of Brahma."[232] Here as in many of the texts already discussed (see section 1.3.3–4, p. 35–49, above), the Brahmanic lineage goes back to Brahma rather than the Vedic seers. Prajñākaragupta's initial answer is an extension of some "old" Buddhist critiques of the Brahmins' anthropogonic claims (see section 1.3.4, p. 42, above). He writes: "If brahmanity is simply the result of being the descendant of Brahma, an absurd consequence follows (*atiprasajyate*) [since] nobody anywhere is ac-

---

229 On that expression, see Ono (1993, 53 note 372). In its own context, the *Caṅkī Sutta* makes an interesting use of the string of blind men, which it explains as follows (M.N. II 170): *evam eva kho, Bhāradvāja, andhaveṇupamaṃ maññe brāhmaṇānaṃ bhāsitaṃ sampajjati; — purimo pi na passati majjhimo pi na passati pacchimo pi na passati. taṃ kiṃ maññasi, Bhāradvāja? nanu evaṃ sante brāhmaṇānaṃ amūlikā saddhā sampajjatīti?* "Even so, methinks, Bhāradvāja, do the words of the brahmans turn out to resemble a string of blind men: neither does the foremost one see nor does the middle one see nor does the hindmost one see. What do you think about this, Bhāradvāja? This being so, does not the faith of the brahmans turn out to be groundless?" Translation by Horner (1970, 360).

230 PVA$_{\text{Ono}}$, verses II 73cd–74ab, 25.6–7: *brāhmaṇatve sthite pūrvaṃ tadgotratvasya sambhavaḥ / tadasthiteḥ kathaṃ gotraṃ seyam andhaparamparā //.*

231 See Ono (1993, 53 note 371).

232 PVA$_{\text{Ono}}$ 24.10–11: *gotralakṣaṇā jātiḥ. tathā ca brahmaṇo 'patyaṃ brāhmaṇa iti hi vyapadiśanti.*

cepted not to be born from Brahma's body."[233] To define lineage as the fact of being a descendant of Brahma is equivalent to saying that every human is a Brahmin. Prajñākaragupta continues: "If [we suppose that] the distinction into classes [has developed] in the meantime, [i.e., between the time of birth from Brahma and today], how could [this distinction] be causeless? [And if we suppose that this distinction has developed][234] during that interval (*antarāle*) through a distinction of activities, nobody finds any interest (*artha*) in lineage."[235] To argue that differentiation is due to the various activities performed over time by Brahma's descendants is equivalent to saying that being of Brahma's descent (i.e., the lineage itself) has no incidence on the process and plays no function in the proof. Moreover, "if we admit that the distinction of the Brahmin lineages, etc., has no beginning [in time], how then can we know [that distinction] since the means of valid cognition do not apply [to it]?"[236]

Prajñākaragupta's argumentation then borrows from themes with which many of the texts already examined have made us familiar. "Moreover, he says, the non-interruption of a lineage cannot be known and for anyone belonging to a lineage (*gotrabhāvin*), the non-interruption [of his lineage] is not guaranteed. Otherwise, how could [mixed castes like] the *sūta*, the *māgadha* and the *caṇḍāla*[237] be possible?"[238] More than Śāntarakṣita and

233 PVA$_{Ono}$, verse II 67, 24.12–13: *brahmaṇo 'patyatāmātrād brāhmaṇye 'tiprasajyate / na kaścid abrahmatanor utpannaḥ kvacid iṣyate //*.

234 According to Ono (1993, 51).

235 PVA$_{Ono}$, verse II 68, 24.14–15: *antarā jātibhedaś cen nirnimittaḥ katham bhavet / antarāle kriyābhedād gotreṇārtho na kasyacit //*.

236 PVA$_{Ono}$, verse II 69, 24.16–17: *atha dvijādigotrāṇām anādir bheda iṣyate / jñāyatāṃ sa kathaṃ nāma pramāṇasyāpravṛttitaḥ //*. I omit PVA$_{Ono}$, verse II 70ab, 24.18, on which see Ono (1993, 51 and note 362).

237 The genealogical identity of the *caṇḍāla* is constant (Brahmin woman and *śūdra* man). But the genealogical identity of the *sūtas* and the *māgadhas* varies. Prajñākaragupta's argument requires, however, that the three women here involved be Brahmins, as was said also by Yamāri (see Ono 1993, 52 note 366). The *Kauṭilīya Arthaśāstra* meets that condition: Brahmin woman + *kṣatriya* man = *sūta*; Brahmin woman + *vai-*

Kamalaśīla, Prajñākaragupta's argument echoes many strategies initiated in the "old" literature against lineage (see section 1.3.3, p. 35, above). In the classical Brahmanic theory on the mixture of castes, social differentiation is to be understood neither in occupational terms, nor in ethical terms, but rather in terms of transgression of the endogamy of a class and caste. Each individual falling under a denomination other than the four castes thus originates from the union of two individuals belonging to heterogeneous denominations distinct from his own. The virtually infinite differentiation into castes, i.e., into mixed classes, can therefore ultimately be traced back to the possible combinations of the four castes. And Prajñākaragupta's argument can be reformulated as follows: the non-interruption of lineage is very unlikely since, in order to explain the appearance of denominations such as those mentioned in the passage quoted above, the theory on mixed castes itself postulates that some Brahmin men and women (here, women) must *necessarily* have transgressed the rules of the class. To belong to a lineage is therefore not equivalent to being the representative of a continued lineage in a close circuit. In fact, the representative of a lineage may be the offspring of a Brahmin woman and a non-Brahmin man, or the descendant of someone who is not "really" a Brahmin.

The last argument used by Prajñākaragupta to show that lineage is not established as a sign of brahmanity also echoes some

---

śya man = *māgadha*; Brahmin woman + *śūdra* man = *caṇḍāla*. *Kauṭilīya Arthaśāstra* III 7.26–28 (Kangle 1969, I. 107.1–2): *śūdrād āyogavakṣattacaṇḍālāḥ / vaiśyān māgadhavaidehakau / kṣatriyāt sūtaḥ /*. "26. From a *śūdra* (are born of a *vaiśya*, a *kṣatriya* and a Brahmin woman respectively) the *āyogava*, the *kṣatta* and the *caṇḍāla*. 27. From a *vaiśya* (are born) the *māgadha* and the *vaidehaka* (of a *kṣatriya* and a Brahmin wife respectively). 28. From a *kṣatriya* (is born) the *sūta* (of a Brahmin wife)." Translation by Kangle (1972, II. 215). On the professions attributed to those mixed classes by the Brahmanic theory, see Fick (1972, 5–8[4–6]).

238 PVA$_{\text{Ono}}$, verses II 70cd–71, 24.19–25.2: *avicchedaś ca gotrasya pratyetuṃ śakyate na hi // avicchedo na niyataḥ kasyacid gotrabhāvinaḥ / sūtamāgadhacaṇḍālāḥ kathaṃ sambhavino 'nyathā //*.

familiar themes: "How do we know that, in the beginningless course of the lineage, a woman has not erred? Women, indeed, are always lovesick (*kāmārta*)."[239] What was only supposed by the previous arguments is here made explicit. A Brahmin woman may therefore have had intercourse with one or many non-Brahmin individuals and have given birth to children who, according to the Brahmanic theory, are necessarily non-Brahmins.

2.5.4.2.2 We saw above that for Śāntarakṣita and Kamalaśīla, the Mīmāṃsā could not justify the purity of ancestry of the Brahmanic lineages by appealing to the authority of a person who has knowledge of the super-sensuous. And neither could it be done by appealing to the Veda, since it is silent on this point. Prajñākaragupta makes an important philosophical contribution to that argument. The principle of his contribution may have been inspired by Dharmakīrti as well as by certain difficulties inherent to the Mīmāṃsā position on the permanence of words and the Veda. He says: "There is moreover no Vedic statement that could establish the brahmanity, etc., of a given individual. As for the statement of a universal [like brahmanity], it is equally not formulated (*anuktasama*) [there]."[240] In his commentary, Prajñākaragupta is able to pinpoint the internal contradiction in his opponent's argument: "The Veda indeed does not teach that [individuals] like Devadatta, etc., are Brahmins because [individuals like Devadatta] have not always existed, whereas the Veda has always existed [according to you, Mīmāṃsakas]. How [then could] the teaching of the Veda have an object when [that] object does not exist [yet]?"[241] Not only does the Veda remain silent on the class to which individuals may belong; it could not

---

239 See above, notes 223ff., pp. 146ff., above. PVA$_{Ono}$, verses II 72cd–73ab, 24.4–5: *anādigotrapaddhatyām asyāṃ na skhalanaṃ striyā / iti jñātaṃ kathaṃ nāma kāmārtā hi sadā striyaḥ //.*

240 PVA$_{Ono}$, verse II 77, 25.14–15: *na ca vedavacaḥ kiṃcid dvijatvādiprasādhakam / vyakteḥ sāmānyavacanam anuktasamam eva tat //.*

241 PVA$_{Ono}$ 25.16–18: *na hi vedo devadattādīnāṃ brāhmaṇatvam upadiśati, sarvadā 'vidyamānatvāt, vedasya ca sarvadā bhāvāt. arthasyābhāvakāle vedopadeśaḥ kathaṃ sārthakaḥ.*

say anything of that nature without *ipso facto* compromising its permanence. For it is indeed a contradiction to say that a permanent, i.e., ahistorical, Veda may deliver a teaching on historical facts or individuals. Around 800 CE, the argument already had a long history involving proponents like Jaimini, Śabara and Kumārila themselves.[242] Dharmakīrti had stigmatized at length the absurdities that resulted from a doctrine of permanence applied to the Veda and to the relation between word and object.[243] To have used that argument in the critique of caste was an innovation of Prajñākaragupta, who could conclude: "How can a Veda that lacks an object be associated later on with [that] object? How can a [permanent Veda] whose nature is indifferent (*udāsīnasvarūpa*) be engaged with that [object that appeared later on][244]?"[245]

2.5.5 Superior capacities of Brahmins

Prajñākaragupta finally attacks one last possible sign of brahmanity, namely the hypothetical superior capacities of Brahmins.

---

242 Jaimini, MīSū I 1.27–28, where a correlation is made between the problems regarding the authors of the parts of the Veda and the mention of impermanent, i.e., produced, entities. MīSū I 1.27: *vedāṃś caike sannikarṣāt puruṣākhyāḥ* /. "Some people say that the Vedas are similarly composed (*sannikarṣa*) because they are named after persons." Translation by Clooney (1990, 166). MīSū I 1.28: *anityadarśanāc ca* /. "Also, because we find ephemeral things (mentioned in the Veda)." Translation by Clooney (1990, 166). Examples are found also in the ŚBh on MīSū I 1.28/I. 121.7–10. See also ŚV, *vedanityatādhikaraṇa*, 13cd–14ab, and the interesting NRĀ *ad loc.* See also TV on MīSū I 1.39, 49 and 50.

243 The clearest statement of Dharmakīrti's critique appears in PV I 232 and PVSV *ad loc.* One of the arguments used by Dharmakīrti to refute the reality and permanence of the relation between the word and the object consists in denying the possibility that the relation be permanent if the correlata of which it is necessarily made are impermanent. See PV I 231ab: *sambandhinām anityatvān na sambandhe 'sti nityatā* /.

244 According to Yamāri, quoted in Ono (1993, 54 note 377).

245 PVA$_{\text{Ono}}$, verse II 78, 26.1–2: *anarthakaḥ kathaṃ vedaḥ paścād arthena saṅgataḥ / udāsīnasvarūpasya tatra vyāpṛtatā katham* //.

"If it is admitted that brahmanity consists in the possession of a particular capacity, [we will reply that] no superior capacity is observed in any [Brahmin][246] today."[247] Prajñākaragupta's answer typically seems to be directed at the Mīmāṃsaka, who accepts the permanence of the world from the perspective of classes or universals. A Mīmāṃsaka should therefore agree that the *actual* non-observation of a specific property is sufficient to establish its absence *throughout eternity*. As for the rest of the argument, it is formally limpid: the scriptures of all traditions attest that in the distant past, there were Brahmin *and* non-Brahmin men (yogins) who possessed superior capacities. If we take the possession of superior capacities as a sign or criterion of brahmanity, it follows that all of them, Brahmins as well as non-Brahmins, were Brahmins: "[Objection:] We hear that, [although] in the past, [such a superiority has nonetheless existed]. [Reply:] Vain words, since [that superior capacity is understood] of all [men, Brahmins and non-Brahmins alike]![248] [Indeed], the yogins' highly superior capacity, perfected in the past [and] attested in all scriptures, is celebrated unanimously [today]."[249]

2.5.6 Conclusions

Let us note that on two points, Śākyabuddhi, Śāntarakṣita, Kamalaśīla, Prajñākaragupta and Karṇakagomin remain faithful to Dharmakīrti. Firstly, the critique of the naturalization of caste is considered as virtually superfluous in so far as the theory of exclusion is sufficient to reject the reality of classes. Secondly, the specific argumentation against the naturalization of caste borrows as much as possible from "canonical" sources. Every argu-

---

[246] According to Yamāri; see Ono (1993, 53 note 373).

[247] PVA$_{Ono}$, verses II 74cd–75ab, 25.8–9: *atha śaktiviśeṣaṇayogo brāhmaṇyam iṣyate / idānīṃ dṛśyate naiva śakter atiśayaḥ kvacit //*.

[248] According to Yamāri; see Ono (1993, 53 note 374).

[249] PVA$_{Ono}$, verses II 75cd–76, 25.10–12: *śrūyate pūrvakālaś cet sarvatreti vṛthāvacaḥ / sarvāgamaprasiddhānāṃ śakter atiśayo mahān / yogināṃ gīyate pūrvasiddhānām avigānataḥ /*.

ment used by those philosophers (and all attempts to explain the phenomenon) can be traced, at least in its principle, to the biological or genealogical arguments found in the older literature.

Let us note also that those authors, after Dharmakīrti, take the Mīmāṃsaka Brahmins as their target. In Dharmakīrti and Prajñākaragupta, that reorganization leads to a radical critique of the direct perceptibility of classes defended by Kumārila and the Naiyāyikas. In Śāntarakṣita, Kamalaśīla and Prajñākaragupta, it further leads to a notable reformulation of old genealogical arguments. For those authors show the disastrous consequences, on the certification of genealogical identity, of a rejection of the authoritative teacher and yogic perception in supersensible matters.

Let us finally note that contrary to Dharmakīrti (and therefore also contrary to Śākyabuddhi and Karṇakagomin), Śāntarakṣita, Kamalaśīla and Prajñākaragupta do not offer any explanation of social divisions. While Dharmakīrti accepted the occupational principle, those authors do not even mention it (which obviously does not mean that they do not accept it). Moreover, and here they follow Dharmakīrti, none of them appeal to an explanation derived from the AgS. The reason for this occultation, in my opinion, is that the aetiology of the AgS belongs to the domain of the imperceptible and therefore to the domain of scriptures, with all the epistemic fragility that an appeal to scriptural authority implies for those philosophers. Dharmakīrti and his successors must obviously have sought to develop an argumentation that was free of any scriptural element.

Chapter 3

Conclusions

I.

When we look at Indian Buddhism's polemical texts, we find that the tradition never was abolitionist. As Fick has already noted, the Buddhist social reflection is done within the context of the four classes and accepts the empirical reality of social groups designated by names that essentially refer to professions. To say that Indian Buddhism was not abolitionist is to say that it never sought to question the factual existence of those groups, and that it obviously never was reformative nor, *a fortiori*, revolutionary. But here as elsewhere, Buddhism mostly rejected realism. Each social denomination is considered to refer only to an inconstant number of human individuals, perhaps to none, instead of corresponding to a permanent class that would be instantiated by those individuals and would participate to their ontological determinations. Statutory denominations thus only exist conventionally. But while an individual, due to his life circumstances, only belongs by convention to a given denomination instead of another, those denominations are nonetheless part of our daily practices and are the determinants, in the world, of an empirical classification. To say that Indian Buddhism never was abolitionist moreover immediately requires an important nuance. For while it does not deny, nor hopes to abolish, the presence of statutory designations in the world, Indian Buddhism is, in theory and perhaps also in fact, uniformly abolitionist in its soteriology. Indeed, it never intends to reproduce within its own order a principle of differentiation and hierarchical organization. Such principle is considered irrelevant and illegitimate. The only legitimate classification principle that it does accept is based on the degree of development of knowledge, practice and, correlatively, morality.

Let us take one step back. What is, almost uniformly, the target of the Buddhist arguments? Those arguments first attack the Brahmins' pride in caste (*avalepa, mada, māna, darpa,* etc.), the pride and arrogance that they take in their birth and condition as Brahmins (AmbS, etc., ŚKA, KDAM, KM, PV, etc., TS, TSP). We have seen, however, that that critique is extensible to other social groups, since Āryadeva and Candrakīrti attack the pride of kings and, indirectly, of *kṣatriyas* (CŚ, CŚV). To criticize the Brahmins' self-conceit is mainly to discuss and neutralize the *justifications* that they advance for their pride. The Brahmanic legitimizations, here, are numerous, but they all aim at establishing something like a naturality to caste. For to justify pride in caste always comes down, for the Brahmins personified in the Buddhist texts, to including caste in an immutable order of things, in a dharma where the natural and the cultural, the cosmic and the social, never cease to interpenetrate each other. To justify his haughtiness, the Brahmin must therefore in some way naturalize the privilege that he takes for himself. And in order to naturalize that privilege, he will use several strategies. He will sometimes seek criteria, signs or discriminants (*liṅga, nimitta, viśeṣaṇa*) that point to some alleged real essence of caste (VāS, etc., VSū, ŚKA, KDAM, PVṬ, PVSVṬ, TS, TSP, PVA). Sometimes, the legitimization is genealogical and may be integrated or not to the lists of criteria. When the justification is genealogical, it ranges from direct filiation by the family (*kula*; AsS, etc., VSū, ŚKA, KDAM, PVṬ, PVSVṬ, TSP) to filiation by lineage (*gotra*), a lineage whose origin may go back to the Vedic seers (AmbS, etc., VSū, ŚKA, KDAM, CŚ, CŚV, TS, TSP, PVA) as well as to some events connected with the origin of humanity (AsS, etc., VSū, ŚKA, KDAM, PVA). To attempt to naturalize caste is to make of every individual belonging to a given social denomination the instantiation of a class in the ontological sense of the word.

The Buddhist arguments therefore uniformly try to neutralize the various Brahmanic attempts to naturalize caste, especially brahmanity, and to legitimize pride in caste. I will not return here to the Buddhist arguments themselves. Let it be noted, however, that in order to neutralize the hypotheses (*pakṣa*) that Brahmins formulated on the basis of various discriminants, Buddhist texts regularly follow an inductive method. Explicitly or implicitly, all proceed by positive and negative concomitance: none of the discriminants advanced by the Brahmins are found to apply only to Brahmin individuals (similar instances, *sapakṣa*) at the exclusion of all individuals alleged to instantiate a heterogeneous class (dissimilar instances, *vipakṣa*). To infer the real existence of brahmanity is thus in every case fallacious (*vyabhicārin*, PVṬ/PVSVṬ) since no invariable concomitance (*vyāpti*), positive or negative, can ever be established between brahmanity (the property to be proved, *sādhyadharma*) and the retained criterion or discriminant (proof, logical reason, *sādhanadharma*). None of the criteria or discriminants alleged to reveal the essence of brahmanity therefore accounts for a real brahmanity that would be hermetically closed upon itself.

The texts do not deny the empirical existence of Brahmins as a group, but criticize the pretension to reality of a brahmanity that serves to crystallize the Brahmin's pride. That is to say that Buddhist texts totally disapprove of the *explanation* provided by Brahmins to account for their status and the partition of society. Yet, it is important to note that Buddhist texts do not appear to directly criticize as such the theory of mixture of classes (*varṇasaṅkara*). No direct critique of that theory is ever formulated. Instead, its foundations and presuppositions are undermined, the first of which being the idea that biological birth exhaustively determines the status. It must be insisted, moreover, that Buddhists and Brahmins are faced with the same problem, i.e., how to explain the empirically observable differentiation of Indian society. In answering that question, Buddhists are trying to replace a theory on the innateness of status that provides a complicated and absurd explanation of the phenomenon, by a theory that accounts for the acquisition of a status through the professional occupation and means of livelihood of each social group (VāS, etc., AgS, etc., VSū, KDAM, CŚ, CŚV, PV, PVṬ, PVSVṬ). In neutralizing the Brahmanic justifications, Buddhists are substituting an occupationalist theory to an innative theory, an occupationalist theory that is heuristically simpler. For social denomination here does not refer to the result of a genealogical combination, but to the means of livelihood typical of those to whom it is applied. The Buddhist strategy is fairly clear: through a systematic critique of every naturalist or innative justification, it is possible to present a new theory that is both simpler in terms of its principles and more thorough in terms of the *facts* that it proposes to integrate and explain.

The occupationalist theory, moreover, is all the more satisfying because of its clearly processual character. For the Buddhists are not just replacing the innative perspective by one of their own. To a static conception of society, they substitute a *dynamic* conception. In so doing, Buddhist texts express the attitude that shines through their analyses of consciousness and knowledge, as well as their ontology.

It is therefore not sufficient, in the Buddhist texts that we have examined, to show the occupational character of status and denomination. It is also important to explain the origin of a professional occupation and means of livelihood. In that respect, Buddhism and Brahmanism are distinct from one another in the same way that "difference" conceptually differs from "differentiation." For Buddhist texts argue that statutory differences are not only due to the means of livelihood, but are also the fleeting *result* of a process. Those texts, therefore, have no more difficulty explaining the origin of a means of livelihood than its eventual disappearance.

It will be useful to remember here that in the beginning, Buddhism was established and perhaps grew directly in the first urban centres of the Ganges basin. And it is quite probably in the cities that the process of social differentiation was more easily observable as it grew in intensity. It is therefore not absurd at all to think that the Buddhist position has kept a faithful memory of its first urban home and of the required attention to social differentiation. Whether the AgS was or was not originally filled with polemical irony, I find it significant that the explanatory model that it proposes was perpetuated, in the discussion of caste, all the way to Candrakīrti. Animated or not with polemical intentions, its general explanation is present from the LP to the MVastu, including the AKBh. The CŚ IV 21–CŚV sequence is also an excellent illustration of the complementarity between occupationality and processuality. Where Āryadeva asserts that caste consists only in the means of livelihood, Candrakīrti comments on an aetiological and processual explanation of the appearance of the statuses and denominations of the Brahmins, king/*kṣatriyas*, *vaiśyas*, *śūdras* and *karmakāras*.

With or without the support of the Brahmanic normative literature, Buddhist texts are also very attentive to *changes of status*. They frequently cite MS X 92 (VSū, ŚKA, KDAM, CŚV), which shows that even according to Brahmanic authorities, some activities lead to the fall of caste, but which also includes various expiation procedures designed to reintegrate the caste. One can therefore become again a Brahmin, just as one can stop being a Brahmin. And this in itself looks like a rejection of the attempts to naturalize caste and brahmanity on the part of the most orthodox Brahmanic authorities. But for Buddhists, the fall and rehabilitation admitted by the normative texts do not explain all changes of status. In order to account for those changes, it will not be enough to cite the legal Brahmanic texts according to which a Brahmin will become a *śūdra* within three months if he sells milk. Buddhists will also insist on the fact that any given individual who adopts such and such a means of livelihood will, in due time, belong to the caste indicated by that means of livelihood and verbally designated by the name of the latter (CŚ, CŚV). In the Buddhist explanation, therefore, observation of statutory changes contributes, in the same way as the aetiological explanations, to complement the occupationalist perspective with a processual and dynamic conception of society. Any given portrayal of a society, when it is based on observations made at any given moment, can be explained in terms of a process of differentiation leading to the appearance of different statuses and denominations.

The processual aspect corollary to the occupationalist position has, moreover, an important consequence not entirely devoid of "deconstructive" motivations. When the *Puruṣasūkta* (VSū, ŚKA, KDAM) tells the story of the origins of humanity, it carefully gives the priority to Brahmins. That priority is due as much to the sequence itself as to the prestige connected with the place of birth of Brahmins, i.e., the mouth of the primeval man. In the aetiology proposed by Buddhist sources, however, the first differentiation leads to the appearance of the king (Mahāsammata; i.e., he who was elected by the people, *mahāsammata*) and the *kṣatriyas*. And if one wants to justify some form of pre-eminence, it is the pre-eminence of the *kṣatriyas* alluded to in the AmbS that is confirmed, although justifying a pre-eminence is clearly not that text's intention. But more importantly, the very notion of a process of differentiation neutralizes at least partially any claim to hierarchy. For it is difficult, not to say abusive, to grant some *hierarchical* pre-eminence to any of the statuses that appeared successively, notably to Brahmins, when the various interests and functions derive from a group that was *initially undifferentiated* (socially, sexually, etc.). One will therefore suspect that the Brahmin's self-arrogated pre-eminence was nothing less than an usurpation.[1]

From that perspective, I cannot resist making a connection between two passages examined earlier. We saw that in the AgS and some of its variants, the Brahmins who are not meditators are reciters of the Veda. Upon returning to society, they compose Vedic mantras. We also saw that Dharmapāla accused the Brahmins of having confiscated the symbolic power, at some immemorial time that may go back to the AgS's first cosmic pe-

[1] Based on other arguments, and for the period of the Nikāyas, Masefield has also developed the thesis of an usurpation. "From the foregoing it will be clear that by the period covered by the Nikāyas a group of individuals, from the Buddhist point of view of dubious ancestry, had arrogated themselves into a position of religious power and wealth on the basis that they alone embodied the sacred power of Brahman." (Masefield 1986, 160). On Masefield's position, see below.

riod (*kalpa*), by creating out of nothing a Veda that they claimed to be uncreated. That reputation of being uncreated can easily be interpreted as an attempt, once again, to naturalize the foundations of a dominant idea. According to Dharmapāla, Vedic mantras and rituals are the main instruments of the Brahmanic usurpation. This may explain why Buddhists also sought to develop an explanation of the social and symbolic pre-eminence of Brahmins; a pre-eminence (1) that is not warranted by the aetiology of the AgS and its derivatives, and (2) that proves to be especially illegitimate since the "actual" Brahmins are regularly presented as degenerate in Buddhist texts (see below).

With their occupational and processual approach, and by means of meticulous arguments, Buddhists succeeded in exposing the double weakness of the Brahmanic position: the ontological weakness pertaining to caste and brahmanity, and the rhetorical weakness of the Brahmanic claims. The ontological weakness of caste and brahmanity moreover leads to a third aspect of the Buddhist position according to which the different statuses are conventional and relative. Brahmanity is thus indeterminate (*aniścita, aniyata*, VSū) and not established ([*svataḥ*] *asiddha*, CŚV). It is known only in worldly usage (*saṃvyavahāramātra-prasiddha*, PVA). The castes are unreal (*asadbhūta*, TSP). The different statuses are mere designations (*samaññā, sañjñā*[*mātra*], VāS, ŚKA, KDAM, PVṬ, PVSVṬ) that depend on human arbitrariness and only differ nominally (*nāmabheda, puruṣānuvidhāyin*, PV, PVṬ, PVSVṬ). They are but a noise in the world (*ghosa*, MaS) and pertain to conventional practice (*vyavahārabheda*, PV, PVṬ, PVSVṬ). Since they are a teaching (*upadeśa*, PV, PVṬ, PVSVṬ, PVA) and since their knowledge depends on conventions (*saṅketamātra*, PVA), brahmanity and the castes are conventional.

Buddhist texts converge in affirming that, as entities of pure designation devoid of any substantial basis, social statuses are in the end nothing more than superimpositions of divisions, through words and conventions, on a humanity that is ontologically unique and undifferentiated. In so far as they systematically neutralize the Brahmanic arguments supporting an ontological distinction, all Buddhist texts could adopt the refrain of the ŚKA: "That is why I say to you, oh Brahmin, [that what is heard] in the world, namely 'Brahmin,' '*kṣatriya*,' '*vaiśya*' or '*śūdra*,' this is only a designation. [In reality], this is one, all of this is one." In that context, it is easy to understand that, inspired by a conviction supported by numerous arguments, Buddhists refused to bring into the monastic order a classifying and hierarchical structure for which they found no reasoned legitimacy. The order is, in theory if not in fact, egalitarian (at least among men) *with respect to the original social extraction of its members*, and that is what allows the Buddha to say: "And even, monks, as those great rivers, that is to say the Ganges, the Jumna, the Aciravatī, the Sarabhū, the Mahī which, on reaching the ocean, loose their former names and identities and are reckoned simply as the great ocean, even so, monks, (members of) these four castes: noble, brahmin, merchant and low, having gone forth from home into homelessness in this dharma and discipline proclaimed by the Truth-finder, loose their former names and clans and are reckoned simply as recluses, sons of Sakyans."[2]

It is here that the theme of the "true Brahmin" occurs. For the egalitarian orientation does not exclude the principle of a hierarchical gradation within the Buddhist order. That principle, however, no longer depends on social extraction, but rather on the degree of progress on the Path. The true Brahmin—by which we should often understand the accomplished Buddhist, i.e., the Arhat, or even the Buddha—is distinguished by his knowledge and morality. That theme, which is omnipresent in the earlier literature, has not retained our attention here. It would itself require more than a book. Let us note, however, that while its

---

2 Vin. II 239: *seyyathāpi bhikkhave yā kāci mahānadiyo seyyath' īdaṃ / Gaṅgā Yamunā Aciravatī Sarabhū Mahī tā mahāsamuddaṃ pattā jahanti purimāni nāmagottāni mahāsamuddo tv eva saṅkhaṃ gacchanti, evam eva kho bhikkhave cattāro 'me vaṇṇā khattiyā brāhmaṇā vessā suddā te tathāgatappavedite dhammavinaye agārasmā anagāriyaṃ pabbajitvā jahanti purimāni nāmagottāni samaṇā Sakyaputtiyā tv eva saṅkhaṃ gacchanti /*. Translation by Horner (1988, 334).

classical formulations may be found in the DhP and the SoS, it is also very present at least in the majority of the non-philosophical texts that we have examined. In the SoS as elsewhere, the recurring characteristic marks of the "true Brahmin" consist in discernment (*paññā*) and morality (*sīla*), where discernment is further divided into possessing intellectual penetration (*medhāvin*) and being wise (*paṇḍita*). Morality is omnipresent from the VāS to the PVSVṬ (except for TS and TSP), and discernment from the VāS to the TSP (except for PV). In addition to morality, the VSū and the KDAM mention, as characteristics of the (true) Brahmin (*brāhmaṇalakṣaṇa*), truth or truthfulness (*satya*), austerities (*tapas*), universal compassion (*sarvabhūtadayā*) and control of the senses (*indriyasaṃyama*). The characteristic of the (true) *caṇḍāla* (*caṇḍālalakṣaṇa*) is to be completely deprived of those qualities. Regarding the conditions of a possible superiority, Śāntarakṣita mentions sovereignty, etc. (*vaśitvādiguṇa*), and the complete eradication of moral impurities (< *prakṣīṇāśeṣakalmaṣa*). Finally, to discernment and sovereignty, Kamalaśīla adds intellectual penetration (*medhā*), supremacy (*īśitva*), freedom of will (*prākāmya*) and compassion (*karuṇā*).[3] As for Āryadeva, Candrakīrti, Dharmakīrti and Prajñākaragupta, they do not directly discuss, in the passages examined above, the problem of the "true Brahmin."

Masefield (1986) has demonstrated quite well the continuity between the dominant themes of the "degeneration of Brahmins" and the "true Brahmin."[4] For him, the Buddhists "also saw in the Brahmin of their day a degeneration of the former ideals of Vedic society which they cherished and it was these the Buddhists claimed they were preserving. The Buddhists' criticism of the Brahmin was a spiritual rather than a social criticism and in

---

3 Śāntarakṣita and Kamalaśīla also reintroduce the old etymology of the word "Brahmin" (notably from the AgS and DhP); TS 3589ab: *ye ca bāhitapāpatvād brāhmaṇāḥ pāramārthikāḥ* /. TSP 923.5: *bāhitapāpadharmatvād brāhmaṇā iti niruktiḥ* /. See note 17, p. 8, above.

4 On those themes and their interconnection, see Masson (1975, 97ff) and Masefield (1986, 150ff).

claiming that the arahant was the true brahmin, on a par with the *ṛṣi*'s of olden times, they were advocating a reform, a return to the conservatism of the past, rather than an innovation."[5] For Masefield, the Buddhist critique is a *reaction* to the moral and spiritual breaches of Brahmins who no longer embody their old ideals, i.e., a reaction against unnoble (*anārya*) Brahmins. The Buddhists "did not reject the institution of the *varṇa* but rather restored to Aryan society the earlier conservatism it was in danger of losing."[6] When we relate Masefield's conclusions[7] to my

---

5 Masefield (1986, 160).

6 Masefield (1986, 161).

7 Some further remarks must be made on Masefield's view (1986, 160) that the Buddhist critique was motivated "by no egalitarian ethic on behalf of the despised clans" and that, "indeed, it was rather the other way round for the evidence of the Nikāyas suggest that it was the altogether more conservative cause of the kṣatriyans that the Buddhists favoured." If, by "egalitarian ethics," we understand the modern normative notion of an ethics that tends to favour equality of rights and opportunities, then it is true that Buddhism did not develop its critique of the naturalization of social statuses on the basis of an "egalitarian ethics" on behalf of the despised (with the important nuance that the despised can access—and appear to have accessed—the monastic Buddhist order). An egalitarian ethics of that kind would in fact contradict a *certain* retributivism of the social statuses accepted by Buddhism (cf. below), since the mechanicalism of the law of karma ensures a retributive justice. I believe, however, that Masefield is jumping to conclusions when he says that it was "the other way round" and that the Buddhists favoured the cause of the *kṣatriyas*. For to say, as in the AmbS, that "the *kṣatriya* is the best *of those among this folk who put their trust in lineage*" (translation by Horner 1970, 122; my emphasis), is not equivalent to saying that the Buddha or the Buddhists wanted to substitute a superiority of the *kṣatriya* to that of the Brahmin. A claim of that sort would, on the one hand, fall under the same criticisms as those that were directed against the Brahmins (as was the case when they became the target of Āryadeva's and Candrakīrti's arguments). That claim is even harder to support when we consider that, according to B.G. Gokhale's estimation, 134 of the 328 descriptions of religious men and women found in the *Theragāthā* and *Therīgāthā* seem to have been Brahmins, 75 *kṣatriyas*, 98 *vaiśyas* and 11 *śūdras* (Gombrich 1988, 55–56). Considering, moreover, that the Buddha *was not a kṣa-*

own problematic, it becomes obvious that the Buddhists criticized pseudo-Brahmins, Brahmins whose decadence begged for a substitution of self-legitimacy based on the excellence of one's birth by a self-legitimacy based on spiritual excellence. In other words, the Brahmin's pride will only find a legitimate justification (if we suppose that pride can be legitimate!) in knowledge and practice, and not through caste and birth (*jāti*). The Buddhist arguments therefore serve to neutralize the erroneous justifications that degenerate Brahmins advance for their superiority. It is then clear that once true brahmanity will be "restored," no co-extensiveness should be expected between the true Brahmins (i.e., the Arhats) and those who are Brahmins by birth (i.e., the Brahmin caste; *brāhmaṇavarṇa*).

II.

I hope to have succeeded in showing that on a majority of points (formal structure of the arguments against the discriminants or criteria, genealogical arguments, position and general explanation of the phenomenon), there is a remarkable continuity, from the Sn to Prajñākaragupta, in the Buddhist argumentation against the naturalization of caste and the Brahmin's pride. This should not, however, lead us to overlook some important *ruptures*. First, as one would expect, none of the Buddhist texts shows all the features of the general picture that we described. That general picture is rather a systematization, a partially arbitrary reconstruction based on Buddhist literature. Each text remains silent on one argument or another, or even on a large number of arguments or explanations that we have examined. They moreover present many variants when we analyse them in details. But this can probably all be explained by the variety of their objectives and the diversity of traditions and/or transmissions. It should

triya (Gombrich 1988, 49–50), one may wonder how the ex-members of the non-*kṣatriya* classes would have come to support the cause of the *kṣatriyas*.

be noted also that the emergence of new arguments and positions within the philosophical tradition, starting with Āryadeva, marks the appearance of personal preoccupations and makes it possible to distinguish more clearly the interests and preferences of each philosopher. In that respect, it seems clear that in this intellectual tradition, no substantial modification and no new element were brought to the debate, except of course for Dharmapāla's biting diatribe reported above. It also seems clear that those authors (Āryadeva, Dharmapāla, Candrakīrti) take the Brahmins and *kṣatriyas in general* as their target, as was the case in the non-philosophical literature examined in the first chapter. If their opponents still have no definite names, however, and if they do not attack any text or position in particular, it is certainly mostly because until the sixth century, Brahmanic philosophical literature paid very little attention to the "social" aspect of class (*jāti*). The problem of caste is simply absent from their realist ontologies.

The situation changed radically with Kumārila, who seemed to be aware of at least some of the Buddhist arguments. Kumārila developed a radical interpretation of the principle that dharma is rooted in the Veda, and gave an apologetic vocation to his work, marked by a clear anti-Buddhist colouration. His restorative enterprise required arguments to establish the reality of class and, for Kumārila as much as for the later Naiyāyikas, to establish the reality of class meant to establish its *perceptibility*. After Kumārila, addressing the problem of caste therefore requires an ontological and epistemological approach. This is in my opinion the reason why, from Dharmakīrti to Prajñākaragupta, all the Buddhist arguments against the naturalization of caste attack the Mīmāṃsā position. From then on, the Brahmins of the earlier literature appear, according to the descriptions of those authors, to have all embraced the Mīmāṃsaka positions. And this constitutes a first rupture with the preceding tradition. The systematic reorganization of old canonical arguments on genealogical identity is in fact the illustration *par excellence* of the fact that Buddhist epistemologists now depict Mīmāṃsaka Brahmins. Here, the Mīmāṃsā's own premises will play against it. For denying the existence of a person who knows the supersensible makes impossible any certification of the purity of a Brahmanic lineage. As for the Veda, the only means of valid cognition accepted by the Mīmāṃsā in invisible matters, it remains silent on individual genealogies. The Mīmāṃsā itself therefore makes impossible the pride of Brahmins.

Contrary to the situation that prevailed before Dharmakīrti, the problem of caste is no longer distinguished, in Dharmakīrti and his successors, from the general problem of universals. Often explicitly, those authors do not separate their treatment of caste from the theory of exclusion. The latter would suffice to disqualify a realist social version of class. To various degrees, those authors nonetheless feel the need to offer an *ad hoc* solution to that problem, and that is why Śāntarakṣita, Kamalaśīla and Prajñākaragupta massively reintroduce the arguments fixed by the tradition.

The picture is here contrasted. Firstly, *only* Dharmakīrti (and therefore, of course, Śākyabuddhi and Karṇakagomin) reproduces the occupationalist Buddhist position. Secondly, *none* of those authors refer to the processual aspect of the Buddhist position, so that we find in their work no etymology or explanation derived from the AgS. That silence could be explained by the fact that they are very careful about integrating doctrinal points that very clearly belong to the domain of utterly imperceptible things and, therefore, to what is only scripturally knowable. Finally, however, in comparison to Āryadeva, Dharmapāla and Candrakīrti, we find in the later philosophers a timid (although more important in Kamalaśīla) reappearance of the old theme of the "true Brahmin." Now this all leads to a first important discovery: two important characteristics of a "Buddhist position" have vanished in the treatment offered by Buddhist epistemologists. Second: those philosophers have developed a powerful theoretical tool that gives a solid basis to Buddhist "nominalism." The theory of exclusion shows the ontological weakness of classes, while the philosophy of language that follows from it (or is inherent to it) shows the arbitrary as well as conventional character of social denominations. For classes have no extra-linguistic correlata since they are pure intellectual products. They do not have the status of real entities and, as such, remain imperceptible. Since they are imperceptible, their cognition depends on teaching, which is itself verbal and therefore arbitrary. Whoever has not received some prior teaching will therefore not *recognise* a Brahmin. Dharmakīrti's introduction, and Prajñākaragupta's systematic development, of the question of teaching in the context of caste are a direct answer to Kumārila. What was lost in terms of occupationality and processuality is therefore regained with conventionality. Those philosophers readjust the Buddhist argumentation to meet Kumārila's challenge. Dharmakīrti's efforts, and especially those of Prajñākaragupta, are an echo and even a product of the reorientation of the debate operated by Kumārila. In Prajñākaragupta finally, there is a perfectly harmonious coexistence of the "new" epistemology with the traditional arguments.

III.

This study, finally, will have tossed aside the "karmic" aspect of the question. But no matter how closely related they may be or may have been thought to be, the correlation between the questions of status and retribution of actions is very marginal in the texts here examined. Nonetheless, it seems appropriate, at the end of this study, to say a few words about it. Hopefully, the reader will forgive the terseness and rather *speculative* character of what follows.

Let me begin by formulating the problem along those lines: Buddhism must elaborate a position that does not create a contradiction between (1) the *conventionality* of caste that is almost unanimously professed and (2) the retributive character of social statuses. All the Buddhist arguments indeed converge in affirming that caste is not an ontological determination of the human being. It does not condition, nor does it affect, his mode of being or psychophysical constitution. In theory at least and contrary to the realms of existence (*dhātu*), levels (*bhūmi*), destinies (*gati*) and other modes of birth (*yoni*), this appears to mean that caste cannot be included among the real conditioning factors of a psycho(-physical) complex's future existence. For the Buddhists, statutory denomination is only the result of occupation, which is variable by definition. While an individual's social status may change in a given human existence, a living being's destiny or mode of birth cannot vary in a given existential sequence. The only (provisionally) acceptable class thus appears to consist in *humanity*, a class that incidentally coincides, in a significant way, with one of the five (or six) destinies. We know, moreover, as Buddhist texts have clearly demonstrated, that humanity cannot be divided into sub-classes. This means that actions can only determine the generic membership to a "human" class, but not to a hypothetical sub-class of Brahmins, *kṣatriyas*, *vaiśyas* or *śūdras*. The hypothesis is confirmed by a passage of the ŚKA already cited: "For it is indeed as a result of their own actions that creatures are determined to have the same marrow, nails, skin, ribs, stomach and mouth/face. Under such circumstances, oh Brahmin, there is no difference [between them]. What difference due to caste could there be?"[8] The fact that we are reborn as humans and not as *caṇḍālas* or Brahmins in fact seems to be the conclusion of the *Vasala* and *Vāseṭṭha Sutta* of the Sn.[9]

The reality of the situation, even in that context, is however far more complex. That only one class of humans coincides with one destiny obviously does not exclude the possibility for innumerable internal variations within that class; variations that can in turn be explained in terms of retribution of actions. The *Karmavibhaṅga* literature is very instructive in this regard. Let us first note the refrain of the *Cūḷakammavibhaṅgasutta* (CKVS): "Deeds are one's own, brahman youth, beings are heirs to their deeds, deeds are matrix, deeds are kin, deeds are arbiters. Deed

---

8 See section 1.2, p. 17, note 61, p. 24, above.

9 See Sn. 136, 142 and 650.

divides beings, that is to say by lowness and excellence."[10] This is the Buddha's answer to Subha (CKVS)/Śuka (KV) the Māṇava, son of Todeyya/Taudeya, who questions the Buddha on the distribution of beings into lower and superior beings in terms of their life duration, health, beauty, reputation, wealth and wisdom.[11] The Buddha then offers a detailed presentation of the categories of action leading to each inequality.

Buddhist literature does not avoid the question of low (*nīca°*) and superior (*ucca°*) social extractions. But importantly, it addresses the question not in terms of caste or class (*jāti, varṇa*), but in terms of the family (*kula*), which is not free of ambiguity. Depending on certain actions,[12] beings may therefore be born alternatively in a low or superior extraction[13] (Pali *nīcākulīna/uccākulīna*,[14] Skt. *nīcakulīna/uccakulīna*). But *nothing* is said to the

---

[10] M.N. III 203, which is identical to *Milindapañha* 65.27–30: *kammassakā, māṇavu, sattā kammadāyādā kammayonī kammabandhū kammapaṭisaraṇā. kammaṃ satte vibhajati yadidaṃ hīnappaṇītatāyāti*. Translation by Horner (1967, III. 249). Compare with KV 30.3–5: *karmasvakān ahaṃ māṇava sattvān vadāmi karmadāyādān karmayonīn karmapratiśaraṇān / karma māṇava sattvān vibhajati / yad idaṃ hīnotkṛṣṭamadhyatāyām /*. See the translation by Lévi (1932, 111).

[11] Compare M.N. III 202–203, KV 40.9–19 and *Milindapañha* 65.11–16.

[12] Described in M.N. III 205 and KV 40.9–19. For the lower extraction (*nīcakula*) we have: *stabdhatā* (stiffness), *abhimānitā* (having a high opinion of oneself), *amātāpitṛjñatā* (not recognizing one's mother and father), *aśrāmaṇyatā* (failing to live as a recluse), *abrāhmaṇyatā* (failing to live as a Brahmin), *kulajyeṣṭhāpacāyitā* (showing a lack of respect for family elders), *mātāpitror apratyupasthānam* (failing to serve one's parents), *āryāṇāṃ śīlavatām apratyupasthānam* (failing to serve virtuous saints), *anyeṣāṃ gurusthānīyānām ācāryopādhyāyānām apratyupasthānam* (failing to serve other people like the guru's substitutes, preceptors and teachers), *nīcakulānāṃ sattvānāṃ paribhavaḥ* (humiliating people of a low extraction). The opposite of each of those actions leads to a superior social extraction (*uccakula*).

[13] Compare with the passage of the ŚKA cited in section 1.3.4.1 and note 110, p. 46, above.

[14] *Milindapañha* 65.15–16 reads: *nīcākulīna* and *mahākulīna*.

effect that they may be born as Brahmins, *kṣatriyas*, *vaiśyas* or *śūdras*.

We must not ignore, at this stage, the partially mythological theme of the being to be reborn (*gandhabba/gandharva*), i.e., the intermediate being (*antarābhava*, not recognized unanimously) who is transmigrating from one existence or destiny to another as a result of his past actions. Let it be recalled that the being to be reborn is supposed to have the form (*ākṛti*) of the existence to come and toward which he is moving. In that respect, already in the pre-uterine state, he possesses his ontological determinations. Now for one thing, Buddhist texts unanimously deny the possibility of making a correlation between social status and specific form (*ākṛti*). Moreover, the AsS clearly states that the being to be reborn is neither a Brahmin, nor a *kṣatriya*, nor a *vaiśya*, nor a *śūdra*.[15] In so far as we admit (1) that the being to be reborn possesses both the form and the determinations of the existence to come and (2) that he is neither a Brahmin, nor a *kṣatriya*, nor a *vaiśya*, nor a *śūdra*, we must admit that caste is not part of the karmic determinations of the existence to come, at least not directly or ontologically. The only "social" determinism in which the being to be reborn is engaged is again related to family. For his actions, the divine eye and sometimes desire contribute to push him in the place where his future parents are having intercourse, and where rebirth (*pratisandhi*) will occur.

In practice, however, every family clearly belongs to a caste and falls under a statutory denomination. Every child therefore undeniably belongs to his family's caste, at least before he chooses, as he may, a means of livelihood different (though generally inherited) from that of his father. In that case, according to the Buddhist perspective, he will receive in due time a new statutory denomination. One must never forget, however, that according to Buddhist texts, those denominations are pure conventions based on professional activity. The caste seems to be only one of the conventional, accidental, and possibly fleeting

---

15 AsS, M.N. II 156–57.

determinations of the family and, therefore, of the child who is born therein. From that perspective, actions do not lead to being reborn into a caste that would ontologically determine the individual or his future existence, but in a family by which he is socially determined, i.e., a family that determines his chances, if I may say. Upon closer analysis, this is probably one meaning of the Sautrāntika critique of the homogeneous character (*sabhāgatā/nikāyasabhāga*) professed by the Sarvāstivādin-Vaibhāṣikas.

As tenuous as its textual basis may be, that hypothesis has the advantage of preserving a great coherence to the Buddhist position, a coherence that is lost as soon as we accept a class like the homogeneous character. It depicts a tradition that is *both* concerned with denying any ontological consistence to caste, *and* with keeping a certain retributivism to social statuses. It would indeed have been vain to develop such an argumentation and, in the end, to neglect, or worse, to deny its conclusion upon addressing the question of karma.

IV.

This book only covered what an arbitrarily fixed category of texts had to say of the question of caste. And while they advance many arguments and propose something of a Buddhist position on caste, the texts that we have examined will one day have to be re-read in light of historical and epigraphic facts. For this is the condition of a true history of ideas. The texts have nothing to propose, for example, on an eventual politico-economical explanation of the non-abolitionism professed by Buddhism. Would a real abolitionist engagement have presented the risk of alienating the monastic order from princely liberalities?[16] Would it

[16] But note that at least during the early medieval period (500–1200), the Saiddhāntika and Śākta Śaivas were the major recipients of royal patronage in spite (1) of their strong anti-caste rhetoric and sometimes even practice, and in spite (2) of the kings' self-celebrated commitment

have been a threat to its very survival? Invoking the oft-repeated notion of a prostrated Buddhism that remained foreign to worldly affairs clearly does not do away with those questions. Furthermore, while the texts seem to agree in professing an abolitionist position when it comes to soteriology, certain canonical passages seem to attest the perpetuation, within the monastic order, of tensions and demands related to the original social extraction of some of its members.[17] While they may be rich in arguments, the texts fail to describe how the Buddhist order accommodated itself of those tensions and demands.[18]

The arguments represent of course only one aspect, maybe minor, of a study on "Buddhism and the question of caste." Future research will undoubtedly expose the arguments, the position and the norm in a better way than I have done here. I doubt even less that a good understanding of the subject requires a study of epigraphic and annalist documents since the situation may have been, and indeed must have been far more complex than the picture depicted in polemical literature. Then only will we be in a position to avoid the rumours and the biases to which this work inevitably fell. The Buddhist treatment of caste nonetheless remains impressively relevant. For we have not in the least refrained, even outside the race question, from naturalizing social statuses, so that the vast majority of points raised in the Buddhist argumentation remain a burning question, even today.

---

to the protection of the *varṇāśramadharma*. On this, see Sanderson (2009, 41–44).

17 This is the case, e.g., of the legends pertaining to the Arhat Pilindavatsa, who used to despise his fellow monks because he had been reborn as a Brahmin during 500 lifetimes. On this legend, see Eltschinger (2005, 420–421).

18 Modern avatars of that phenomenon are described in Abeysekara (1999).

Bibliography and abbreviations

Abeysekara 1999 — Ananda Abeysekara: Politics of Higher Ordination, Buddhist Monastic Identity, and Leadership in Sri Lanka. *Journal of the International Association of Buddhist Studies* 22/2 (1999): 255–280.

AbhD — *Abhidharmadīpa* (Vimalamitra). Padmanabh S. Jaini (ed.): *Abhidharmadīpa with Vibhāṣāprabhāvṛtti*. Patna 1977: Kashi Prasad Jayaswal Research Institute (Tibetan Sanskrit Works Series 4).

AgS — *Aggañña Sutta* (= D.N. III 80–98).

AK(Bh) — Prahlad Pradhan (ed.): *Abhidharmakośabhāṣya by Vasubandhu*. Patna 1967: Kashi Prasad Jayaswal Research Institute (Tibetan Sanskrit Works Series 8).

AKVy — Unrai Wogihara (ed.): *Sphuṭārthā Abhidharmakośavyākhyā: The Work of Yaśomitra*. Tokyo 1989 (1936[1]): Sankibo Buddhist Book Store (The Publishing Association of Abhidharmakośavyākhyā).

Alper 1989 — Harvey P. Alper (ed.): *Mantra*. Albany 1989: State University of New York Press (Suny Series in Religious Studies).

Alsdorf 1977 — Ludwig Alsdorf: Das Bhūridatta-Jātaka. Ein anti-brahmanischer Nāga-Roman. *Wiener Zeitschrift für die Kunde Südasiens* 21 (1977): 25–55.

AmbS — *Ambaṭṭha Sutta* (= D.N. I 87–110).

AsS — *Assalāyana Sutta* (= M.N. II 147–157).

Balbir 1991 — Nalini Balbir: Le discours étymologique dans l'hétérodoxie indienne. Pp. 121–134 in Jean-Pierre Chambon and Georges Lüdi (eds.): *Discours étymologiques. Actes du Colloque international organisé à l'occasion du centenaire de la naissance de Walther von Wartburg*. Tübingen 1991: Max Niemeyer.

Barua 1959 — P.L. Barua: The Doctrine of Caste in Early Buddhism. *Journal of Asiatic Society of Pakistan* 4 (1959): 134–156.

Bhatt 1989 — Govardhan P. Bhatt: *The Basic Ways of Knowing: An In-Depth Study of Kumārila's Contribution to Indian Epistemology*. Delhi 1989: Motilal Banarsidass.

BHSD — Franklin Edgerton: *Buddhist Hybrid Sanskrit Dictionary*. Delhi 1993 (New Haven 1953[1]): Motilal Banarsidass.

Bhūridattajātaka — See Alsdorf 1977.

Biardeau 1964 — Madeleine Biardeau: *Théorie de la connaissance et philosophie de la parole dans le brahmanisme classique*. Paris and La Haye 1964: Mouton & CO (Le monde d'outre-mer passé et présent, première série, études 23).

Bouglé 1993 — Célestin Bouglé: *Essais sur le régime des castes*. Paris 1993 (1900[1]): Presses Universitaires de France.

Brinkhaus 1978 — Horst Brinkhaus: *Die altindischen Mischkastensysteme*. Wiesbaden 1978: Franz Steiner Verlag (Alt-und Neu- Indische Studien herausgegeben vom Seminar für Kultur und Geschichte Indiens an der Universität Hamburg 19).

van den Broeck 1977 — José van den Broeck: *La Saveur de l'immortel (A-p'i-t'an Kan Lu Wei Lun). La version chinoise de l'Amṛtarasa de Ghoṣaka (T. 1553)*. Louvain-La-Neuve 1977: Université catholique de Louvain, Institut Orientaliste (Publications de l'Institut Orientaliste de Louvain 15).

Bronkhorst 1985 — Johannes Bronkhorst: The Origin of an Indian Dietary Rule: Evidence for a Lost Mānava Work on Dharma. *Aligarh Journal of Oriental Studies* 2/1–2 (1985) [= U. C. Sharma (ed.): *Professor Ram Suresh Tripathi Commemoration Volume*]: 123–132.

Bronkhorst 1990 — Johannes Bronkhorst: Pāṇini and the Nominal Sentence. *Annals of the Bhandarkar Oriental Research Institute* 71 (1990[1991]): 301–304.

Clooney 1990 — Francis X. Clooney: *Thinking Ritually. Rediscovering the Pūrva Mīmāṃsā of Jaimini*. Vienna 1990 (Publications of the De Nobili Research Library 17).

CN — Cowell and Neil. See Cowell and Neil 1970.

Collins 1993 — Steven Collins: The Discourse on What is Primary (Aggañña Sutta): An Annotated Translation. *Journal of Indian Philosophy* 21 (1993): 301–393.

Cowell and Neil 1970 — Edward B. Cowell and Robert A. Neil (eds.): *The Divyāvadāna. A Collection of Early Buddhist Legends.* Amsterdam 1970 (Cambridge 1886[1]): Oriental Press NV / Philo Press.

Cox 1995 — Collett Cox: *Disputed Dharmas. Early Buddhist Theories of Existence. An Annotated Translation of the Section on Factors Dissociated from Thought from Saṅghabhadra's Nyāyānusāra.* Tokyo 1995: The International Institute for Buddhist Studies (Studia Philologica Buddhica, Monograph Series 9).

CŚV$_{Tib}$ — Tibetan version of CŚV. P no. 5266, *ya* 33b4–273b6.

CŚ(V) — *Catuḥśataka* (Āryadeva), and *Catuḥśatakavṛtti* (Candrakīrti). See CŚV$_{Tib}$, Suzuki 1994, and Tillemans 1990.

Davidson 2002 — Ronald M. Davidson: *Indian Esoteric Buddhism. A Social History of the Tantric Movement.* New York 2002: Columbia University Press.

DhP — *Dhammapada.* V. Fausbøll (ed.): *Dhammapadam. Ex tribus codicibus hauniensibus palice edidit, latine vertit, excerptis ex commentario palico notisque illustravit...* Osnabrück 1974[R] (Hafnia, Lipsia and Londinum 1855): Biblio Verlag.

Divyāvadāna — See Cowell and Neil 1970.

D.N. I — Thomas William Rhys Davids and Joseph Estlin Carpenter (eds.): *The Dīgha Nikāya.* Vol. I. London 1967 (1890[1]): Pali Text Society.

D.N. III — Joseph Estlin Carpenter (ed.): *The Dīgha Nikāya.* Vol. III. London 1960 (1911[1]): Pali Text Society.

Doniger and Smith 1991 — Wendy Doniger and Brian K. Smith: *The Laws of Manu.* London 1991: Penguin Books.

D'Sa 1980 — Francis X. D'Sa: *Śabdaprāmāṇyam in Śabara and Kumārila: Towards a Study of the Mīmāṃsā Experience of Language.* Vienna 1980 (Publications of the De Nobili Research Library 7).

Dumont 1972 — Louis Dumont: *Homo Hierarchicus: The Caste System and its Implications.* London 1972[R] (1970: Weidenfeld and Nicolson): Paladin. Originally published in French as *Homo Hierarchicus: Le système des castes et ses implications* (Paris 1966: Gallimard). Page references are to the 1972 translation, with references to the original edition appearing in brackets.

Dunne 2004 — John D. Dunne: *Foundations of Dharmakīrti's Philosophy*. Boston 2004: Wisdom Publications.

Dvivedī 1985 — Rāmāyaṇ Prasād Dvivedī (ed.): *Vajrasūcī of Aśvaghoṣa: A Small Tract of Buddhist Philosophy*. Varanasi 1984: Caukhambā Amarabhāratī Prakāśan (Harjīvandās Prācyavidyā Granthamālā 3).

Eltschinger 1997 — Vincent Eltschinger: Bhāvaviveka et Dharmakīrti sur *āgama* et contre la Mīmāṃsā (2). *Études Asiatiques / Asiatische Studien* 50/4 (1997): 1095–1104.

Eltschinger 1998 — Vincent Eltschinger: Bhāvaviveka et Dharmakīrti sur *āgama* et contre la Mīmāṃsā (1). *Études Asiatiques / Asiatische Studien* 51/1 (1998): 57–84.

Eltschinger 2000 — Vincent Eltschinger: *Caste et philosophie bouddhique. Continuité de quelques arguments bouddhiques contre le traitement réaliste des dénominations sociales*. Vienna 2000: Arbeitskreis für Tibetische und Buddhistische Studien Universität Wien (Wiener Studien zur Tibetologie und Buddhismuskunde 47).

Eltschinger 2001 — Vincent Eltschinger: *Dharmakīrti sur les mantra et la perception du suprasensible*. Vienna 2001: Arbeitskreis für Tibetische und Buddhistische Studien Universität Wien (Wiener Studien zur Tibetologie und Buddhismuskunde 51).

Eltschinger 2005 — Vincent Eltschinger: Études sur la philosophie religieuse de Dharmakīrti (1): Le Bouddha comme Śāstṛ et Sugata. *Études Asiatiques / Asiatische Studien* 59/2 (2005): 395–442.

Eltschinger 2007 — Vincent Eltschinger: *Penser l'autorité des Écritures: la polémique de Dharmakīrti contre la notion brahmanique orthodoxe d'un Veda sans auteur*. Vienna 2007: Austrian Academy of Sciences Press (Beiträge zur Kultur- und Geistesgeschichte Asiens 56)..

Eltschinger 2008 — Vincent Eltschinger: Dharmakīrti on Mantras and their Efficiency. Pp. 273–289 in: *Esoteric Buddhist Studies: Identity in Diversity. Proceedings of the International Conference on Esoteric Buddhist Studies, Koyasan University, 5 Sept.– 8 Sept. 2006*. Koyasan 2008: Koyasan University.

Eltschinger 2010 — Vincent Eltschinger: Apocalypticism, Heresy and Philosophy. Towards a Sociohistorically Grounded Account of Sixth Century

Indian Philosophy. Pp. 425–480 in Goshin Shaku *et al.* (eds.): *Investigation of religious pluralism and the concept of tolerance in India*. Tokyo 2010 (march): The Eastern Institute.

Eltschinger (forthcoming) — Vincent Eltschinger: Buddhist Esoterism and Epistemology. To be published in Eli Franco (ed.): *Proceedings of the Panel on the Periodization and Historiography of Indian Philosophy (XIV*[th] *World Sanskrit Conference, Kyoto, September 1–5, 2009).*

Fick 1972 — Richard Fick: *The Social Organisation in North-East India in Buddha's Time*. Translated by Shishirkumar Maitra. Varanasi 1972: Indological Book House. Originally published in German as *Die sociale Gliederung im nordöstlichen Indien zu Buddhas Zeit, mit besonderer Berücksichtigung der Kastenfrage*. Graz 1974[R] (Kiel 1897: C.F. Haeseler): Akademische Druck- und Verlagsanstalt. Page references are to the 1972 translation, with references to the original edition appearing in brackets.

Franco 1997 — Eli Franco: *Dharmakirti on Compassion and Rebirth*. Vienna 1997: Arbeitskreis für Tibetische und Buddhistische Studien Universität Wien (Wiener Studien zur Tibetologie und Buddhismuskunde 38).

Frauwallner 1932 — Erich Frauwallner: Beiträge zur Apohalehre. 1. Dharmakīrti. Übersetzung. *Wiener Zeitschrift für die Kunde des Morgenlandes* 39 (1932): 247–285.

Frauwallner 1933 — Erich Frauwallner: Beiträge zur Apohalehre. 2. Dharmakīrti. Übersetzung (Fortsetzung). *Wiener Zeitschrift für die Kunde des Morgenlandes* 40 (1933): 51–94.

Frauwallner 1935 — Erich Frauwallner: Beiträge zur Apohalehre. 3. Dharmakīrti. Zusammenfassung. *Wiener Zeitschrift für die Kunde des Morgenlandes* 42 (1935): 93–102.

Frauwallner 1954 — Erich Frauwallner: Die Reihenfolge und Entstehung der Werke Dharmakīrtis. Pp. 142–154 in Johannes Schubert and Ulrich Schneider (eds.): *Asiatica. Festschrift Friedrich Weller*. Leipzig 1954: Otto Harrassowitz.

Gautama — L. Srinivasacharya (ed.): *Gautamadharmasūtram, maskari bhāṣyopetam/Goutama - Dharmasutra with Maskari Bhashya*. Mysore 1917: Government Branch Press (Government Oriental Library Series, Bibliotheca Sanskrita 50).

Gethin 1997 — Rupert Gethin: Cosmology and Meditation: From the Aggañña-Sutta to the Mahāyāna. *History of Religions* 36/3 (1997): 183–217.

Gokhale 1958 — V. V. Gokhale: The Vedānta-Philosophy described by Bhavya in his Madhyamakahṛdaya. *Indo-Iranian Journal* 2 (1958): 165–180.

Gombrich 1988 — Richard Gombrich: *Theravāda Buddhism: A Social History from Ancient Benares to Modern Colombo.* London and New York 1988: Routledge.

Gombrich 1992 — Richard Gombrich: The Buddha's Book of Genesis? *Indo-Iranian Journal* 35 (1992): 159–178.

Gonda 1975 — Jan Gonda: The Indian Mantra. Pp. 248–301 in: *Jan Gonda: Selected Studies.* Vol. IV, *History of Ancient Indian Religion.* Leiden 1975: E.J. Brill.

Halbfass 1976 — Wilhelm Halbfass: Zur Theorie der Kastenordnung in der indischen Philosophie. Pp. 272[3]–316[44] in: *Nachrichten der Akademie der Wissenschaften in Göttingen, 1. philologisch-historische Klasse, Jahrgang 1975.* Göttingen 1976: Vandenhoeck & Ruprecht.

Halbfass 1983 — Wilhelm Halbfass: *Studies in Kumārila and Śaṅkara.* Reinbek 1983: Dr. Inge Wezler, Verlag für orientalistische Fachpublikationen (Studien zur Indologie und Iranistik, Monographie 9).

Halbfass 1990 — Wilhelm Halbfass: *India and Europe: An Essay in Philosophical Understanding.* Delhi 1990: Motilal Banarsidass. Originally published in German as *Indien und Europa. Perspektiven ihrer geistigen Begegnung* (Basel 1981: Schwabe & CO).

Halbfass 1992 — Wilhelm Halbfass: *On Being and What There Is: Classical Vaiśeṣika and the History of Indian Ontology.* Albany 1992: State University of New York Press.

Harvey 1995 — Peter Harvey: *The Selfless Mind: Personality, Consciousness and Nirvana in Early Buddhism.* Richmond 1995: Curzon Press.

Hattori 1994 — Masaaki Hattori: The Vaiśeṣikasūtras as referred to by Bhāvaviveka in his Tarkajvālā. *Études Asiatiques / Asiatische Studien* 47/2 (1994) [= Johannes Bronkhorst (ed.): *Proceedings of the Panel on Early Vaiśeṣika, Hong Kong, August 1993*]: 699–706.

Hayes 1984 — Richard Hayes: The Question of Doctrinalism in the Buddhist Epistemologists. *Journal of the American Academy of Religion* 52 (1984): 645–670.

Hayes 1988 — Richard Hayes: *Dignāga on the Interpretation of Signs.* Dordrecht, Boston and London 1988: Kluwer Academic Publisher (Studies of Classical India 9).

von Hinüber 1991 — Oskar von Hinuber: Linguistic Considerations on the Date of the Buddha. Pp. 183–193 in Heinz Bechert (ed.): *The Dating of the Historical Buddha / Die Datierung des historischen Buddha.* Part I. Göttingen 1991: Vandenhoeck & Ruprecht (Abhandlungen der Akademie der Wissenschaften in Göttingen, philologisch-historische Klasse 189).

Honda 1967 — Megumu Honda: Sāṃkhya Philosophy described by its Opponent Bhavya. *Journal of Indian and Buddhist Studies* 31 (1967): 436–442.

Horner 1970 — Iseline Blew Horner: *The Collection of the Middle Length Sayings (Majjhimanikāya).* Vol. II. London 1970 (1957[1]): Pali Text Society.

Horner 1988 — Iseline Blew Horner: *The Book of the Discipline (Vinaya-Piṭaka).* Vol. V, Cullavagga. London 1988 (1952[1]): Pali text Society.

Huber 1908 — Édouard Huber: *Aśvaghosa: Sūtrâlaṃkâra.* Traduit en français sur la version chinoise de Kumārajīva. Paris 1908: Ernest Leroux.

Jhā 1983 — Gaṅgānātha Jhā: *Kumārila Bhaṭṭa. Tantravārttika: A Commentary on Śabara's Bhāṣya on the Pūrvamīmāṃsā Sūtras of Jaimini.* Vol. I. Delhi 1983 (Calcutta 1924[1]): Śrī Satguru Publications.

Johansson 1979 — Rune E. A. Johansson: *The Dynamic Psychology of Early Buddhism.* London and Malmö 1979: Curzon Press (Scandinavian Institute of Asian Studies, Monograph Series 37).

de Jong 1988 —Jan Willem de Jong: Buddhism and the Equality of the Four Castes. Pp. 423–431 in J. Duchesne-Guillemin, W. Sundermann and F. Vahman (eds.): *A Green Leaf: Papers in Honour of Professor Jes P. Rasmussen.* Leiden 1988: E. J. Brill (*Acta Iranica* [Second Series] 28, *Hommages et Opera* 12).

Joshi 1967 — Lalmani Joshi: *Studies in the Buddhistic Culture of India: During the Seventh and Eighth Centuries A.D.* Delhi 1967: Motilal Banarsidass.

Kane 1974 — Pandurang Vaman Kane: *History of Dharmaśāstra (Ancient and Mediæval Religious and Civil Law).* Vol. II, part I. Poona 1974 (1941[1]):

Bhandarkar Oriental Research Institute (Government Oriental Series Class B, 6).

Kangle 1992 — R. P. Kangle: *The Kauṭilīya Arthaśāstra*. 3 vols. Delhi 1992[R] (Bombay 1965–1972): Motilal Banarsidass.

Kapani 1992 — Lakshmi Kapani: *La Notion de saṃskāra*. Vol. I. Paris 1992: Collège de France (Publications de l'Institut de Civilisation Indienne 59/1).

Katsura 1991 — Shoryu Katsura: Dignāga and Dharmakīrti on *apoha*. Pp. 129–146 in Ernst Steinkellner (ed.): *Studies in the Buddhist Epistemological Tradition: Proceedings of the Second International Dharmakīrti Conference*. Vienna 1991: Austrian Academy of Sciences Press (Beiträge zur Kultur- und Geistesgeschichte Asiens 8).

Kawasaki 1976 — Shinjo Kawasaki: The Mīmāṃsā Chapter of Bhavya's *Madhyamaka-hṛdaya-kārikā*. Text and Translation. (1) Pūrvapaksa. *Studies 1976. Institute of Philosophy, the University of Tsukuba*: 1–16.

Kawasaki 1992a — Shinjo Kawasaki: *Issaichi Shisō no Kenkyū* 一切智思想の研究 *[A Study of the Omniscient Being (sarvajña) in Buddhism]*. Tokyo 1992: Shunjusha.

Kawasaki 1992b — Shinjo Kawasaki: Discrepancies in the Sanskrit and Tibetan Texts of Bhavya's *Madhyamaka-hṛdaya-Tarkajvālā* (the 9th and 10th Chapters). Pp. 131–143 in Zuiho Yamaguchi and Shoren Ihara (eds.): *Tibetan Studies: Proceedings of the 5th Seminar of the International Association of Tibetan Studies*. Vol. I. Narita 1992: Naritasan Shinshoji.

KDAM — *Kalpadrumāvadānamālā*. Pp. xxx–xci in Speyer 1902–1909, vol. II.

Keith 1978 — Arthur Berriedale Keith: *The Karma-Mīmāṃsā*. Delhi 1978[R] (Calcutta 1921): Oriental Books Reprint Corporation.

Klimkeit 1981 — Hans-Joachim Klimkeit: *Der politische Hinduismus. Indische Denker zwischen religiöser Reform und politischem Erwachen*. Wiesbaden 1981: Otto Harrassowitz.

KM — *Kalpanāmaṇḍitikā* (Kumāralāta). See Huber 1908 and Lüders 1926.

Kośa — See LVP 1980.

Krasser 2011 — Helmut Krasser: Bhāviveka, Dharmakīrti and Kumārila. Pp. 193–242 in Toru Funayama: *Chūgoku-Indo syūkyō-shi tokuni bukkyō-shi ni okeru syomotsu no ryūtsū-denpa to jinbutsu-idō no chiiki-tokusei* 中国印度宗教史とくに仏教史における書物の流通伝播と人物移動の地域特性 *[Regional characteristics of text dissemination and relocation of people in the history of Chinese and Indian religions, with special reference to Buddhism]*. (A Report of Grant-in-Aid for Scientific Research (B): Project Number 19320010. March, 2011.)

Krishan 1986 — Y. Krishan: Buddhism and the Caste System. *The Journal of the International Association of Buddhist Studies* 9/1 (1986): 71–83.

KV — *Karmavibhaṅga*. Pp. 21–105 in Lévi 1932.

KVU — *Karmavibhaṅgopadeśa*. Pp. 153–167 in Lévi 1932.

Lamotte 1976 — Étienne Lamotte: *Histoire du bouddhisme indien: des origines à l'ère Śaka*. Louvain-la-Neuve 1976[R] (1958): Institut Orientaliste de l'Université de Louvain (Publications de l'Institut Orientaliste de Louvain 14).

Lang 1992 — Karen C. Lang: Āryadeva and Candrakīrti on the *dharma* of Kings. *Études Asiatiques / Asiatische Studien* 46/1 (1992) [= Johannes Bronkhorst, Katsumi Mimaki and Tom J.F. Tillemans (eds.): *Études bouddhiques offertes à Jacques May à l'occasion de son soixante-cinquième anniversaire*]: 232–43.

Lang 2003 — Karen C. Lang: *Four Illusions. Candrakīrti's Advice for Travelers on the Bodhisattva Path.* New York 2003: Oxford University Press.

Law 1937 — Bimal Church Law: *Concepts of Buddhism*. Leiden 1937: The Kern Institute.

Law 1980 — Bimal Church Law: *India as Described in Early Texts of Buddhism and Jainism*. Delhi 1980 (London 1941[1]): Bharatiya Publishing House.

Lévi 1932 — Sylvain Lévi: *Mahākarmavibhaṅga (La grande classification des actes) et Mahākarmavibhaṅgopadeśa (discussion sur le Mahā Karmavibhaṅga)*. Paris 1932: Librairie Ernest Leroux.

Lindtner 1997 — Christian Lindtner: Bhavya on Mīmāṃsā. Pp. 91–123 in Agata Bareja-Starzyńska and Marek Mejor (eds.): *Aspects of Buddhism: Proceedings of the International Seminar on Buddhist Studies, Liw, 25 June 1994*. Warsaw 1997: Oriental Institute of Warsaw University (Studia Indologiczne 4).

Lorenzen 1991 — David N. Lorenzen: *The Kāpālikas and the Kālāmukhas: Two Lost Śaivite Sects*. Delhi 1991: Motilal Banarsidass.

LP — Eugène Denis (ed.): *La Lokapaññatti et les idées cosmologiques du bouddhisme ancien*. 2 vols. Lille and Paris 1976.

Lüders 1926 — Heinrich Lüders: *Bruchstücke der Kalpanāmaṇḍitikā des Kumāralāta*. Leipzig 1926: Deutsche Morgenländische Gesellschaft (Kleinere Sanskrit-Texte 2). Reprinted in *Monographien zur indischen Archäologie, Kunst und Philologie*. Band 1. Wiesbaden 1979: Franz Steiner Verlag, 113–375.

LVP 1928–1929 — Louis de La Vallée Poussin: *Vijñaptimātratāsiddhi: La Siddhi de Hiuan-Tsang*. 2 vols. Paris 1928–1929: Librairie Orientaliste Paul Geuthner (Buddhica, documents et travaux pour l'étude du bouddhisme 1 and 5).

LVP 1980 — Louis de La Vallée Poussin: *L'Abhidharmakośa de Vasubandhu*. Bruxelles 1980[R] (Paris 1923–1931: P. Geuthner / J.B. Istas): Institut Belge des Hautes Études Chinoises (Mélanges Chinois et Bouddhiques 15).

M — Mukhopādhyāya. See Mukhopādhyāya 1954.

Malalasekera 1958 — G. P. Malalasekera and K. N. Jayatilleke: *Le Bouddhisme et la question raciale*. Paris 1958: Unesco (La question raciale et la pensée moderne).

Malalasekera 1971 — G. P. Malalasekera (ed.): *Encyclopaedia of Buddhism*. Vol. III/1. Colombo 1971: The Government of Ceylon, Government Press.

Masefield 1986 — Peter Masefield: *Divine Revelation in Pali Buddhism*. Colombo and London 1986: The Sri Lanka Institute of Traditional Studies / George Allen & Unwin.

MaS — *Madhura Sutta* (= M.N. II 83–90).

Masson 1975 — Joseph Masson: *Le Bouddhisme: chemin de libération. Approches et recherches*. Paris 1975: Desclée de Brouwer (Museum Lessianum, Section missiologique 59).

Matilal 1986 — Bimal Krishna Matilal: *Perception: An Essay in Classical Indian Theories of Knowledge*. Oxford 1986: Clarendon Press.

Mehta 1939 — Ratilal N. Mehta: *Pre-Buddhist India. A Political, Administrative, Economic, Social and Geographical Survey of Ancient India Based Mainly on the Jātaka Stories*. Bombay 1939: Examiner Press.

MHK — *Madhyamakahṛdayakārikā* (Bhāviveka/Bhavya). For MHK IX (*Mīmāṃsātattvanirṇayāvatāra*) and X (*Sarvajñasiddhinirdeśa*), see Kawasaki 1992a: 407–471.

Milindapañha — V. Trenckner (ed.): *The Milindapañho, being dialogues between King Milinda and the Buddhist sage Nāgasena*. London 1962 (1880[1]): Pali Text Society.

MīSū — *Mīmāṃsāsūtra* (Jaimini). See ŚBh.

Miyasaka — See PV III/IV.

MMVR —Serge d'Oldenbourg (ed.): Mahāmāyūrī vidyārājñī. *Zapiski Vostočnago Otdeleniya Imp. Russk. Arkheol. Obstchestva* 9 (1897–1898): 218–261.

MMW — Monier Monier-Williams: *A Sanskrit-English Dictionary*. Delhi 1993[R] (Oxford 1899): Motilal Banarsidass.

M.N. II —Robert Chalmers (ed.): *The Majjhima-Nikāya*. Vol. II. London 1960 (1898[1]): Pali Text Society.

MS — *Manusmṛti*. Vishvanāth Nārāyan Mandlik (ed.): *Mānava-Dharma Śāstra [Institutes of Manu] with the Commentaries of Medhātithi, Sarvajñanārāyaṇa, Kullūka, Rāghavānanda, Nandana, and Rāmachandra*. Delhi 1992 (Bombay 1886): Munshiram Manoharlal Publishers Pvt Ltd.

Mukhopādhyāya 1954 — Sujitkumar Mukhopādhyāya: *Śārdūlakarṇāvadāna*. Santiniketan 1954: Viśvabharati.

MVastu —Émile Senart (ed.): *Le Mahāvastu*. 3 vols. Tokyo 1977[R] (Paris 1882): Meicho-Fukyukai.

Nakamura 1958 — Hajime Nakamura: The Tibetan Text of the Madhyamakahṛdayavṛttitarkajvālā (dBu ma'i sñiṅ po'i 'grel ba rtog ge 'bar ba) corresponding to Prof. Gokhale's Translation. *Indo-Iranian Journal* 2 (1958): 181–90.

NAS — *Nyāyānusāra* (Saṅghabhadra). See Cox 1995.

Norman 1995 — K. R. Norman: *The Group of Discourses (Sutta-Nipāta)*. Vol. I. London 1995: Pali Text Society.

NRĀ — *Nyāyaratnākara* (Pārthasārathimiśra). See ŚV.

Nyāyasudhā — *Nyāyasudhā* (Someśvara). See TV (2).

PTS — (The) Pali Text Society.

Oberhammer 1991 — Gerhard Oberhammer (in collaboration with Ernst Prets and Joachim Prandstetter): *Terminologie der frühen philosophischen Scholastik in Indien*. Vol. I. Vienna 1991: Austrian Academy of Sciences Press (Beiträge zur Kultur- und Geistesgeschichte Asiens 9).

Oldenberg 1903 — Hermann Oldenberg: *Le Bouddha, sa vie, sa doctrine, sa communauté*. Paris 1903: F. Alcan. Originally published as *Buddha: sein Leben, seine Lehre, seine Gemeinde* (Berlin 1881: W. Hertz). Translated in English as *Buddha: His Life, his Doctrine, his Order* (various publishers).

Omae 1989 — Futoshi Omae: Dharmakīrti no seitenkan, Pramāṇavārttika dai 1 shō oyobi jishū no wayaku (3). ダルマキールティの聖典観 — 『プラマーナ・ヴァールティカ』第一章および自註の和訳（3）[Dharmakīrti on Scriptures: A Translation of the Pramāṇavārttika, Chapter I and Svavṛtti (3)]. *Tetsugaku Nenpō* 哲学年報 [*Annals of Philosophy*] 48 (1989): 53–74.

Ono 1993 — Motoi Ono: *Prajñākaraguptas Erklärung der Definition gültiger Erkenntnis (Pramāṇvārttikālaṃkāra zu Pramāṇavārttika II 1–7)*. Part II (annotated German translation). Unpublished PhD thesis. Vienna 1993.

Ono 2000 — See PVA$_{Ono}$.

P — Daisetz T. Suzuki: *The Tibetan Tripiṭaka: Peking edition*. Tokyo and Kyoto 1957: Tibetan Tripitaka Research Institute.

Padoux 1989 — André Padoux: Mantras—What are they? Pp. 295–318 in Alper 1989.

PED — T. W. Rhys Davids and William Stede: *Pali-English Dictionary*. Delhi 1993 (London 1921–1925[1]): Motilal Banarsidass.

Perry 1997 — Bruce M. Perry: Early Nyāya and Hindu Orthodoxy: *ānvīkṣī* and *adhikāra*. Pp. 449–470 in Eli Franco and Karin Preisendanz (eds.): *Beyond Orientalism: The Work of Wilhelm Halbfass and its Impact on Cross-Cultural Studies*. Amsterdam and Atlanta GA 1997: Rodopi (Poznań Studies in the Philosophy of the Sciences and the Humanities 59).

Pind (2009) — Ole Holten Pind: *Dignāga's Philosophy of Language. Dignāga on anyāpoha. Pramāṇasamuccaya V, texts, translation, and annotation*. Unpublished PhD thesis. Vienna 2009: Vienna University.

Praśastapādabhāṣya — Johannes Bronkhorst and Yves Ramseier (eds.): *Word Index to the Praśastapādabhāṣya*. Delhi 1994: Motilal Banarsidass.

PV I — Raniero Gnoli (ed.): *The Pramāṇavārttika of Dharmakīrti: The First Chapter with the Autocommentary*. Rome 1960: Istituto Italiano per il Medio ed Estremo Oriente (Serie Orientale Roma 23).

PV III/IV — *Pramāṇavārttika* (Dharmakīrti), chapters 3 (*pratyakṣapariccheda*) and 4 (*parārthānumānapariccheda*). Yusho Miyasaka (ed.): Pramāṇa-vārttika-kārikā (Sanskrit and Tibetan). *Acta Indologica* 2 (1971–1972): 1–206.

PVA — *Pramāṇavārttikālaṅkāra* (Prajñākaragupta). Rāhula Sāṅkṛtyāyana (ed.): *Pramāṇavārtikabhāṣyam or Vārtikālaṅkāra of Prajñākaragupta (Being a commentary on Dharmakīrti's Pramāṇavārtikam)*. Patna 1953: Kashi Prasad Jayaswal Research Institute (Tibetan Sanskrit Works Series 1).

PVA_{Ono} — Motoi Ono (ed.): *Prajñākaraguptas Erklärung der Definition gültiger Erkenntnis (Pramāṇavārttikālaṃkāra zu Pramāṇavārttika II 1–7)*. Vienna 2000: Austrian Academy of Sciences Press (Beiträge zur Kultur- und Geistesgeschichte Asiens 34).

PVA_{Tib} — Tibetan version of PVA. P no. 5719, *te* 1–*the* 344a6.

PVP — *Pramāṇavārttikapañjikā* (Devendrabuddhi). P no. 5717, *che* 1–390a8.

PVSV — *Pramāṇavārttikasvavṛtti* (Dharmakīrti). See PV I.

PVSVṬ — *Pramāṇavārttikasvavṛttiṭīkā* (Karṇakagomin). Rāhula Sāṅkṛtyāyana (ed.): *Ācārya Dharmakīrteḥ Pramāṇavārttikaṃ (Svārthānumāna Paricchedaḥ) Svopajñavṛttyā Karṇakagomiviracitayā taṭṭīkayā ca sahitam*. Kyoto 1982[R] (Allahabad 1943: Kitab Mahal): Rinsen Books.

PVṬ — *Pramāṇavārttikaṭīkā* (Śākyabuddhi). P no. 5718, *je* 1–*ñe* 348a8.

PVV — *Pramāṇavārttikavṛtti* (Manorathanandin). Rāhula Sāṅkṛtyāyana: *Dharmakīrti's Pramāṇavārttika with commentary by Manorathanandin*. Published as an appendix to the *Journal of the Bhandarkar Oriental Research Institute* 24–26 (1938–1940).

Qvarnström 1989 — Olle Qvarnström: *Hindu Philosophy in Buddhist Perspective: The Vedāntatattvaviniścaya Chapter of Bhavya's Madhyamakahṛdayakārikā*. Lund 1989: Plus Ultra (Lund Studies in African and Asian Religions 4).

Qvarnström 1990 — Olle Qvarnström: The *Vedāntatattvaviniścaya* Chapter of Bhavya's *Madhyamakahṛdayakārikā*. *Wiener Zeitschrift für die Kunde Südasiens* 34 (1990): 181–98.

Renou 1950 — Louis Renou: *Sanskrit et culture: L'apport de l'Inde à la civilisation humaine*. Paris 1950: Payot (Bibliothèque historique).

Renou 1981 — Louis Renou: *La Civilisation de l'Inde ancienne*. Paris 1981 (1950[1]): Flammarion. Translated into English as *The Civilization of Ancient India* (Calcutta 1959: Susil Gupta Private).

Renou and Filliozat 1985 — Louis Renou and Jean Filliozat: *L'Inde classique: Manuel des études indiennes*. Vol. I. Paris 1985[R] (1947): Librairie d'Amérique et d'Orient, Adrien Maisonneuve.

Rhys Davids 1969 — Thomas William Rhys Davids: *Dialogues of the Buddha*. Part I. London 1969 (1899[1]): Luzac & Company.

Rocher 1983 — Ludo Rocher: Karma and Rebirth in the Dharmaśāstras. Pp. 61–89 in Wendy Doniger O'Flaherty (ed.): *Karma and Rebirth in Classical Indian Traditions*. Delhi 1983: Motilal Banarsidass.

S — Rāhula Sāṅkṛtyāyana. See PVA.

s.v. — *sub voce*.

Sanderson 2009 — Alexis Sanderson: The Śaiva Age. Pp. 41–349 in Shingo Einoo (ed.): *Genesis and Development of Tantrism*. Tokyo: Institute of Oriental Culture, University of Tokyo.

ŚBh — *Śābarabhāṣya* (Śabara). K. V. Abhyankar and G. A. Jośī (eds.): *Mīmāṃsādarśanam*. 7 vols. Poona 1970–1976: Ānandāśrama (Ānandāśramasaṃskṛtagranthāvaliḥ 97).

Schmithausen 2005 — Lambert Schmithausen: Man and the World: On the Myth of Origin of the *Aggaññasutta*. *Supplement to the Bulletin of the Research Institute of Bukkyo University* (March 2005): 165–182.

Schneider 1954 — Ulrich Schneider: Acht Etymologien aus dem Aggañña-Sutta. Pp. 575–583 in Johannes Schubert and Ulrich Schneider (eds.): *Asiatica. Festschrift Friedrich Weller*. Leipzig 1954: Otto Harrassowitz.

Senart 1882 — See MVastu.

Senart 1896 — Émile Senart: *Les Castes dans l'Inde: Les faits et le système*. Paris 1896: Annales du Musée Guimet (Bibliothèque de vulgarisation).

Sharma 1958 — Ram Sharan Sharma: *Śūdras in Ancient India: A survey of the position of the lower orders down to circa A.D. 500*. Delhi 1958: Motilal Banarsidass.

Sharma 1985 — Sharmishta Sharma: *Buddhist Avadānas (Socio-Political, Economic and Cultural Study)*. Delhi 1985: Eastern Book Linkers.

Siddhi — *Vijñaptimātratāsiddhi* (Xuanzang). See LVP 1928–1929.

ŚKA — *Śārdūlakarṇāvadāna*. See Mukhopādhyāya 1954 and pp. 611–655 in Cowell and Neil 1970.

Sn. — Dines Andersen and Helmer Smith (eds.): *Suttanipāta*. London 1965 (1913[1]): Pali Text Society.

SoS — *Soṇadaṇḍa Sutta* (= D.N. I 111–126).

Speyer 1902–1909 — Jacob Samuel Speyer: *Avadānaśataka: A Century of Edifying Tales Belonging to the Hīnayana*. Saint Petersburg 1902–1909 (Bibliotheca Buddhica 3).

ŚrBh II — Śrāvakabhūmi Study Group: *Śrāvakabhūmi: The Second Chapter with Asamāhitā bhūmiḥ, Śrutamayī bhūmiḥ, Cintāmayī bhūmiḥ*. Vol. II. Tokyo 2007: The Institute for Comprehensive Studies of Buddhism, Taishō University, The Sankibo Press (Taishō Daigaku Sōgōbukkyō Kenkyūjo Sōsho 18).

Steinkellner and Much 1995 — Ernst Steinkellner and Michael Torsten Much: *Texte der erkenntnistheoretischen Schule des Buddhismus (Systematische Übersicht über die buddhistische Sanskrit-Literatur 2)*. Göttingen 1995: Vandenhoeck & Ruprecht (Abhandlungen der Akademie der Wissenschaften in Göttingen 214).

Suzuki 1994 — Koshin Suzuki: *Sanskrit Fragments and Tibetan Translation of Candrakīrti's Bodhisattvayogacaryācatuḥśatakaṭīkā*. Tokyo 1994: The Sankibo Press.

ŚV — Ganga Sagar Rai (ed.): *Ślokavārttika of Śrī Kumārila Bhaṭṭa with the Commentary Nyāyaratnākara of Śrī Pārthasārathimiśra*. Varanasi 1993: Ratna Publications (Ratnābhāratīgranthamālā 4).

Taber 1989 — John Taber: Are Mantras Speech Acts? The Mīmāṃsā Point of View. Pp. 144–164 in Alper 1989.

Taber 2005 — John Taber: *A Hindu Critique of Buddhist Epistemology: Kumārila on Perception. The "Determination of Perception" Chapter of Kumārila Bhaṭṭa's Ślokavārttika. Translation and Commentary.* London 2005: Routledge Curzon.

Tib. — Tibetan.

Tillemans 1986 — Tom J. F. Tillemans: Āryadeva, Dharmapāla and Dharmakīrti on Scriptural Authority. *Tetsugaku* 哲學 [*The Journal of Hiroshima Philosophical Society*] 38 (1986): 31–47.

Tillemans 1990 — Tom J. F. Tillemans: *Materials for the Study of Āryadeva, Dharmapāla and Candrakīrti.* 2 vols. Vienna 1990: Arbeitskreis für Tibetische und Buddhistische Studien Universität Wien (Wiener Studien zur Tibetologie und Buddhismuskunde 24.1/2).

Tillemans 1993 — Tom J. F. Tillemans: *Persons of Authority: The sTon pa tshad ma'i skyes bur sgrub pa'i gtam of A lag sha Ngag dbang bstan dar. A Tibetan Work on the Central Religious Questions in Buddhist Epistemology.* Stuttgart 1993: Franz Steiner Verlag (Tibetan and Indo-Tibetan Studies 5).

TJ — *Tarkajvālā*, commentary (*Vṛtti*) on MHK. P no. 5256, *dza* 43b7–380a7.

TS(P) — *Tattvasaṅgraha* (Śāntarakṣita) and *Tattvasaṅgrahapañjikā* (Kamalaśīla). Embar Krishnamacharya (ed.): *Tattvasaṅgraha of Śāntarakṣita With the Commentary of Kamalaśīla.* 2 vols. Baroda 1984 and 1988 (1926[1]): Oriental Institute.

TV — *Tantravārttika* (Kumārila). (1) See ŚBh. (2) Mahāprabhulāla Gosvāmī (ed.): *The Mīmāṃsā Darśana of Maharṣi Jaimini, with Śābarabhāṣya of Śabaramuni with the commentaries of Tantravārtika of Kumārila Bhaṭṭa and its commentary Nyāyasudhā of Someśvara Bhaṭṭa...* 4 vols. Varanasi 1984: Tara Printing works.

VāS — *Vāseṭṭha Sutta* (= Sn. pp. 115–123).

Vasiṣṭha — Alois Anton Führer (ed.): *Śrīvāsiṣṭhadharmaśāstram, Aphorisms on the sacred law of the Âryas, as taught in the school of Vasishṭha.* Bombay 1883: The Department of Public Instruction, Bombay.

Verpoorten 1987 — Jean-Marie Verpoorten: Le droit à l'*adhyayana* selon la Mīmāṃsā. *Indo-Iranian Journal* 30 (1987): 23–30.

Vetter 1964 — Tilmann Vetter: *Erkenntnisprobleme bei Dharmakīrti*. Vienna 1964: Hermann Böhlaus Nachf./Kommissionsverlag der Österreichischen Akademie der Wissenschaften (Veröffentlichungen der Kommission für Sprachen und Kulturen Süd- und Ostasiens 1).

Vin. — Hermann Oldenberg (ed.): *The Vinaya Piṭakam: One of the Principal Buddhist Holy Scriptures in the Pali Language*. Vol. II, the Cullavagga. London 1964 (1880[1]): Pali Text Society.

Vora and Ota 1982 — Pradyumna R. Vora and Shinkai Ota: A Translation of Pramāṇavārttika I and Svavṛtti (3). *Saga Ryūkoku Tanki Daigaku Kiyō* 佐賀龍谷短期大学紀要 *[Bulletin of Saga Ryukoku Junior College]* 28 (1982): 1–22.

VSū — *Vajrasūcī*. Pp. 1–43 in Dvivedī 1985 and pp. 218–227 in Weber 1860.

Wakahara 1988 — Yusho Wakahara: Mantora no kōka to zenchisha, Pramāṇavārttikasvavṛtti kenkyū (1) (vv. 292–311) マントラの効果と全知者Pramāṇavārttikasvavṛtti 研究 (1) (vv. 292–311) [Effect of mantras and the omniscient]. *Bukkyō Shigaku Kenkyū* 仏教史学研究 [*The Journal of the History of Buddhism*] 31 (1988): 1–27.

Watters 1961 — Thomas Watters: *On Yuan Chwang's Travels in India (A. D. 629–645)*. Delhi 1961 (London 1904–1905[1]): Munshiram Manoharlal Oriental Publishers and Booksellers.

Weber 1860 — Albrecht Weber: Über die *Vajrasūcī* (Demantnadel) des Açvaghosha. *Philologische und historische Abhandlungen der Königlichen Akademie der Wissenschaften zu Berlin aus dem Jahre 1859* (Berlin 1860): 205–264.

Willemen, Dessein and Cox 1998 — Charles Willemen, Bart Dessein and Collett Cox: *Sarvāstivāda Buddhist Scholasticism*. Leiden, New York and Köln 1998: Brill (Handbuch der Orientalistik, zweite Abteilung, Indien 11).

Williams 1980 — Paul M. Williams: Some Aspects of Language and Construction in the Madhyamaka. *Journal of Indian Philosophy* 8 (1980): 1–45.

Yaita 1987 — Hideomi Yaita: Dharmakīrti on the Authority of Buddhist Scriptures (*āgama*): An Annotated Translation of the Pramāṇavārttikasvavṛttiḥ ad v. 213–217. *Nanto Bukkyō* 南都佛教 [*Journal of the Nanto Society for Buddhist Studies*] 58 (1987): 1–17.

YS — M.B. Shastri (ed.): *Yâjnavalkyasmṛiti or the institutes of Yajnavalkya with the commentary Mitâksharâ of Vijnâneshvara.* Bombay 1892: Janârdan Mahâdev Gurjar, Ramwadi.

Indices

Indian authors

Chinese authors

Modern authors

Gods, prophets, literary characters, etc.

Geographical names

Schools, groups, sects, etc.

Index locorum (Pali)

Index locorum (Sanskrit)

Pali words

Sanskrit words

Tibetan words

Literary genres, works and corpora

BUDDHIST TRADITION SERIES

Gen. Ed. *ERNST STEINKELLNER,*
Joint Gen. Ed. *ALEXANDER VON ROSPATT,*
Founder Ed. Late *ALEX WAYMAN* [ISBN: 978-81-208-0287-2]

1 **Indian Buddhism**—*Hajime Nakamura*
2 **Nagarjuniana**—*Chr. Lindtner*
3 **Chinese Monks in India**—*Latika Lahiri*
4 **Buddhism in Central Asia**—*B.N. Puri*
5 **Dharmakirti's Theory of Hetu- Centricity of Anumāna**—*Mangala R. Chinchore*
6 **The Legend of King Aśoka**—*John S. Strong*
7 **Buddhist Insight**—*George R. Elder*
8 **Buddhism Transformed**—*Richard Gombrich* and *Gananath Obeyesekere*
9 **The Buddhist Tantras**—*Alex Wayman*
10 **The Lion's Roar of Queen Śrīmālā**—*Alex Wayman* and *Hideko Wayman*
11 **The Buddha Nature**—*Brian E. Brown*
12 **Evolution of Stupas in Burma**—*Sujata Soni*
13 **Buddhist Parables**—*Eugene Watson Burlingame*
14 **The Debate of King Milinda**— *Bhikku Pesala*
15 **The Chinese Madhyama Āgama and the Pāli Majjhima Nikāya**—*Bhiksu Thich Minh Chau*
16 **Sudden and Gradual**—*Peter N. Gregory*
17 **Yoga of the Guhyasamājatantra**—*Alex Wayman*
18 **The Enlightenment of Vairocana**—*Alex Wayman* and *R. Tajima*
19 **A History of Indian Buddhism**—Tr. *Hirakawa Akira*, Ed. *Paul Groner*
20 **Introduction to the Buddhist Tantric Systems**—*F.D. Lessing* and *Alex Wayman*
21 **Anāgatavaṃsa Desanā**—Tr. *Udaya Meddegama*, Ed. *John C. Holt*
22 **Chinnamasta**—*Elisabeth Anne Benard*
23 **On Voidness** —*Fernando Tola* and *Carmen Dragonetti*
24 **Nāgārjuna's Refutation of Logic (Nyāya) Vaidalyaprakaraṇa**—*Fernando Tola* and *Carmen Dragonetti*
25 **The Buddhist Art of Nagarjunakonda**—*Elizabeth Rosen Stone*
26 **Discipline**—*J.C. Holt*
27 **Philosophy and its Development in the Nikāyas and Abhidhamma**—*Fumimaro Watanabe*
28 **Untying the Knots in Buddhism**—*Alex Wayman*
29 **Early Buddhist Theory of Knowledge**—*K.N. Jayatilleke*
30 **Calming the Mind and Discerning the Real**—Tr. *Alex Wayman*
31 **A Comparative Study of the Pratimoksha**—*W. Pachow*
32 **Rise of the Esoteric Buddhism in the Tibet**—*Eva M. Dargyay*
33-35 **Saṃyuktābhidharmahṛdaya (3 Parts)**—*Bart Dessein*
36 **A Millennium of Buddhist Logic (Pt. I)**—*Alex Wayman*
37 **The Buddhist Pilgrimage**—*Duncan Forbes*
38 **Chanting the Name of Mañjuśrī**—*Alex Wayman*
39 **The Literature of the Personalists of Early Buddhism**—*Bhikshu Thich Thien Chau*
40 **The Laṅkāvatāra Sūtra** —*D.T. Suzuki*
41 **Studies in the Laṅkāvatāra Sūtra**—*D.T. Suzuki*
42 **The Vimalakīrti Sūtra**—*Burton Watson*
43 **The Gāndhārī Dharmapada**—*John Brough*
44 **Imaging Wisdom**—*Jacob N. Kinnard*
45 **Pain and Its Ending**—*Carol S. Anderson*
46 **Apparitions of the Self**—*Janet Gyatso*
47-49 **Rules for Nuns according to the Dharmaguptakavinya (3 Parts)**—*Ann Heirmann*
50 **The Chinese Hevajraṛantra**—*Ch. Willemen*
51 **The Historical Buddha**—*H.W. Schumann*, Tr. from the German *M.O'c Walshe*
52 **Dana:** Giving and Getting in Pali Buddhism—*Ellison Banks Findly*
53 **Hermeneutics and Tradition in the Sanadhinirmocana Sutra**—*John Powers*
54 **Skillful Means**—*John W. Wehroeder.*
55 **The Two Truths in Chinese Buddhism**—*Chang-Qing Shih.*
56 **The Bodhisattva Path**—*Jan Nattier*
57 **Becoming the Buddha**—*Donald K. Swearer*
58 **Approaching the Land of Bliss**— Eds. *Richard K.Payne* & *Kenneth K. Tanaka*
59 **Indian Monastic Buddhism**—*Gregory Schopen*
60 **Caste and Buddhist Philosophy**—*Vincent Eltschinger*